BEING HUM
A Christian Anthropology

Liberation and Theology Series

Editorial Committee
Leonardo Boff, Sergio Torres, Gustavo Gutiérrez,
José Comblin, Ronaldo Muñoz, Enrique Dussel,
José Oscar Beozzo, Pedro Trigo, Ivone Gebara,
Jon Sobrino, Virgil Elizondo, Juan Luis Segundo

Ecumenical Consultant
Julio de Santa Ana

Titles in the series
(latter volumes in preparation)

Introducing Liberation Theology
by Leonardo and Clodovis Boff (Vol. 1)
The Trinity and Society by Leonardo Boff (Vol. 2)
Ethics and Community by Enrique Dussel (Vol. 3)
The Holy Spirit and Liberation by José Comblin (Vol. 4)
The Memory of the Christian People
by Eduardo Hoornaert (Vol. 5)
The Bible, the Church and the Poor
by Jorge Pixley and Clodovis Boff (Vol. 6)
Mary, Mother of God, Mother of the Poor
by Ivone Gebara and Maria Clara Bingemer (Vol. 7)
Being Human: A Christian Anthropology
by José Comblin (Vol. 8)
Moral Theology: Dead Ends and Ways Forward
by Antônio Moser and Bernardino Leers (Vol. 9)
Creation and History by Pedro Trigo (Vol. 10)
The God of Christians by Ronaldo Muñoz (Vol. 11)

. . . "this is going to be a series which both illuminates Latin
American realities and provokes thought about the relevance to
the rest of the world of a theology which springs very powerfully
out of these realities - out of the people's suffering and out of a
still vibrant faith."—David L. Edwards, *The Church Times*

José Comblin

BEING
HUMAN

A Christian Anthropology

*Translated from the Portuguese by
Robert R. Barr*

BURNS & OATES

First published in Great Britain in 1990 by
Burns & Oates Ltd., Wellwood, North Farm Road,
Tunbridge Wells, Kent TN2 3DR
and in the United States of America by Orbis Books,
Maryknoll, NY 10545

Originally published in Brazil under the title
Antropologia Cristã by Editora Vozes Ltda,
Petrópolis

Original edition © CESEP – São Paulo 1987

English translation © 1990 Orbis Books

ISBN 0 86012 168 2

Typeset in the U.S.A

Printed in Great Britain by BPCC Wheatons Ltd, Exeter

Liberation and Theology Series

In the years since its emergence in Latin America, liberation theology has challenged the church to a renewal of faith lived in solidarity with the poor and oppressed. The effects of this theology have spread throughout the world, inspiring in many Christians a deeper life of faith and commitment, but for others arousing fears and concerns.

Its proponents have insisted that liberation theology is not a sub-topic of theology but really a new way of doing theology. The Liberation and Theology Series is an effort to test that claim by addressing the full spectrum of Christian faith from the perspective of the poor.

Thus, volumes in the Series are devoted to such topics as God, Christ, the Church, Revelation, Mary, the Sacraments, and so forth. But the Series will also explore topics seldom addressed by traditional theology, though vital to Christian life – aspects of politics, culture, the role of women, the status of ethnic minorities. All these are examined in the light of faith lived in a context of oppression and liberation.

The work of over a hundred theologians, pastoral agents, and social scientists from Latin America, and supported by some one hundred and forty bishops, the Liberation and Theology Series is the most ambitious and creative theological project in the history of the Americas.

Addressed to the universal church, these volumes will be essential reading for all those interested in the challenge of faith in the modern world. They will be especially welcomed by all who are committed to the cause of the poor, by those engaged in the struggle for a new society, by all those seeking to establish a more solid link between faith and politics, prayer and action.

"This is a most enterprising series which should enable those of us who live in the West to listen to what the liberation theologians themselves have to say. It may well open the eyes of Western Christians to the need for liberation in the First World as well." – *The Expository Times*

Contents

Abbreviations and Short Forms

DH	*Dignitatis Humanae.* Vatican II, Declaration on Religious Freedom
DS	Denzinger-Schönmetzer, *Enchiridion Symbolorum*
EN	*Evangelii Nuntiandi.* Exhortation of Paul VI
GS	*Gaudium et Spes.* Vatican II, Pastoral Constitution on the Church in the Modern World
LE	*Laborem Exercens.* Encyclical of John Paul II
Medellín	Final document of the Second General Conference of Latin American Bishops, held at Medellín, Colombia, in 1968
OA	*Octogesima Adveniens.* Apostolic Letter of Paul VI
PP	*Populorum Progressio.* Encyclical of Pope Paul VI
PT	*Pacem in Terris.* Encyclical of John XXIII
Puebla	Final document of the Third General Conference of Latin American Bishops, held at Puebla, Mexico, in 1979. For an English translation, see *Puebla and Beyond* (Maryknoll, N.Y.: Orbis Books, 1979)
RH	*Redemptor Hominis.* Encyclical of John Paul II

Introduction

"All the Church's ways lead to man," said Pope John Paul II in his first encyclical, *Redemptor Hominis.* Consequently, all the paths of theology lead to that destination. Humanity is more than just another object of theology. It is the very center of theology. All other theological objects revolve around humanity, since the purpose of investigating any of them is only to shed light on the lot and destiny of humankind.

When theology assumed the role of our society's dominant ideology, it had to claim to present a total view of human beings and their place in the world. As the sciences of the human began to appear, with their new discoveries, and new concepts, theology sought to integrate them all into its synthesis. Unless it could manage to synthesize all cognitions, all knowledge, it would be unable to continue to direct society. Even after having de facto lost control of Western society, theologians continued for several generations to maintain an idealistic, totalizing vision of human beings—one that could offer at least the equivalent of the great ideologies whose ambition was the intellectual conquest of the world.

The moment theology makes its option for the poor, however, it must abandon its ambition of supplying society with an ideology calculated to furnish the dominant class in that society with all guidance and direction. There will always be ideologies—comprehensive views of the world and of the people in it—to provide political societies, cultures, and civilizations with their comprehensive orientation. Christian theology, for its part, is abandoning this role. In Latin America it exercised it during the era of the colonial empires. Then it retained a nostalgia for it over a number of generations after the collapse of the empires.

1

But since Medellín and Puebla, it has renounced it, at least officially.

Nor does theology any longer claim the role of synthesis or encyclopedia of the human sciences. It would be fatuous for theology to attempt such a task, which it could never accomplish since the very attempt would entail the utterly pointless abandonment precisely of the theological mission.

Nor does theology claim to furnish the equivalent of a philosophy of the human being. Philosophy in our times has gradually emancipated itself from theology and gone about its own task in its own way. Philosophy has even renounced the role of guide and guardian of the city, which Plato had assigned it at the beginning of its history in Greco-Roman civilization.

Nor can theology assume the role of general theory of the liberation of humanity. In the first place, there can be no such theory, as it would of its very nature contain the seeds of future domination and thereby involve an intrinsic contradiction. Second, neither Christianity, nor the church, nor theology has received any such mission as the construction of a blueprint for the liberation of humanity. Christianity, church, and theology have a mission within the liberation of humanity, and in the service of that liberation, but God has entrusted them with no mission of planning, leading, or guiding liberation as if the latter were a single, synthetic process. This, say the critics, has been the peculiar temptation of the church of the West, and the church's failure to resist that temptation is what motivated the protests of Eastern Christians and sixteenth-century Protestant Reformers alike, along with the medieval forerunners and modern successors of the latter.

Then what does Christianity have to offer the liberation of humanity? Not, primarily, a doctrine, a conceptualization of life, or a world plan; but actual men and women gathered in communities. Christianity's contribution to liberation is its Christian communities scattered across the face of the earth.

After all, these communities are Jesus Christ. If Jesus were a mere figure of the past, he would have set an example for humanity, surely, and perhaps even offered it a few concepts after the fashion of some of the founders of the other great religions. But he would not have contributed a great deal besides. In actuality, however, Jesus Christ is present, and manifoldly so, all over the world, in the presence of the Christian communities. Those communities bring something new, something specific to that world: their activity. The activity of the Christian communities in the midst of the world is the Christian contribution to liberation. Teachings, ideas, the Christian themes as such—all these contribute to the world only to the extent that they represent, animate, and stimulate the activity of the communities. Christian teachings on the subject of human beings can help further the liberation of humanity only to the extent that the actual activity of the communities endows them with concrete content. The primary reference of all Christian anthropological concepts, then, is the living experience of the Christian communities. The Bible itself has actual, concrete content only in "coming alive" in the activity of concrete communities.

The activity of these communities is called evangelization. This new anthropological datum represents the part played by Christianity in the liberation of humanity.

Evangelization brings women and men a truth about themselves. In Puebla's terms, it is the mission of the Christian communities to be the vehicle of a truth about human beings. Truth is not a doctrine, a teaching, a series of concepts. Truth is a force that denounces and destroys the lie. Truth is the birth of new reality. By their activity, the communities give birth to a new reality—the reality of humanity.

Chapter 1 will examine the basic theological datum constituted by the new person, the new humanity, which, concretely, is the Christian community throughout history and today.

Evangelization is word at work. As word, it is addressed to a particular audience for a particular purpose. The addressee it selects is a people of the poor, whom it contemplates as the vehicles of humanity's deliverance. The movement of evangelization includes a particular viewpoint on humanity itself. But here as well, actions come before words. It is not on the strength of a doctrine that Christians make an option for the poor. Christians have a particular doctrine on the strength of their option for the poor.

In almost all the major civilizations, what is called or could be called humanism has always been the lifestyle, the mode of being, of a privileged elite, or even of certain selected elements among the elite. Humanisms have nearly always been elitism. Christian truth denounces these humanisms; then, with the poor as its point of departure, it goes in quest of another, different humanism.

But a humanism with its starting point among the poor necessarily comports a realistic option that will exclude all idealism. The history of theological anthropology is nearly always confused with the history of the debates between idealism and realism. Despite the resistance of the greatest doctors, especially St. Thomas Aquinas, idealism has nearly always triumphed, especially in the practice of established regional churches, as well as in universities and other instruments of schooling. These have sought human perfection in a flight to ideal, "spiritual" aims, and have lost sight of humanity's corporeal reality. The privileged forget their bodies. Bodies remind us that they exist when they suffer. This is when we are forced to remember them. No one who has never been truly hungry will fully understand that a human being is first and foremost a being who needs to eat. No one who has never been sick will know what health is. For the poor, the liberation of humanity is the liberation of suffering, crushed, humiliated bodies.

In chapters 3, 4, 5, and 6 I shall examine the various relationships maintained by the body with all that makes it exist as such, as a body. I shall consider the body successively in its relationship with the world, with nature, with other human bodies, and finally, in its distance from other bodies and from matter.

Spirit is not something apart from or parallel with body. On the contrary, spirit is present in every relationship the body maintains. In order to afford a clearer grasp of human spirituality as such, however, chapter 7 will offer a recapitulation of the various aspects of that spirituality.

Christians did not invent human beings. Nor do they construct the history of human beings. They share that history along with everyone else. They cannot foresee the coming stages of the liberation process. They do not know humanity better than others do. On the other hand, what differentiates Christians from non-Christians is more than a different ideology, and indeed, more than a different symbolical system. Christian anthropology is not simply a different manner of expressing what others would state more scientifically. Men and women of the modern age have always demonstrated their readiness to accept Christianity on condition that it limit itself to an attempt to state symbolically what they, the moderns, are able to state in scientific fashion.

But no, the areas of the human sciences on the one hand, and of theology on the other, do not coincide. Theology and science say different things about their object, however much that object — here, human beings — be one and the same for each. There is no science of humanity. The utterance of the human sciences is very precisely limited to the respective aspects from which they examine their object, the human being. Liberation must be the object of discernment, and the Christian person has something special to offer in terms of discernment.

What do Christians have to say to today's human beings about the liberation of humanity? Nothing more and nothing less than what Christians are and do. In them is Christ, created anew in the world of today by the Holy Spirit. The inquiry we undertake in this book, then, is: What sort of humanity, what human value, what genuine human meaning or content is present in our Christian communities? Where and how is Jesus Christ, the new person, present and acting in our day? Who is he? What does he bring to this world of ours?

CHAPTER I

The New Person

The Christian message regarding humanity may be presented under the heading of the Pauline expression, the "new person." With Jesus Christ, a new human being has appeared in the history of the human race. The Reign of God proclaimed by Jesus is precisely that new human being. Not that this new person simply supplants the old one. The new human being does not exist in a pure state. Old and new coexist for the time being, intimately conjoined, and Christians must live their humanness in the form of an ongoing struggle between the new and the old. Their new person must struggle if it is to exist, resisting the pressures of the old, striving to overcome the weight of the old, and creating a new reality with the materials left behind by the old.

Where is this Pauline new person concretely to be found? In the new Christian communities. The struggle against the old person is the struggle of the Christian communities to rescue their mission and destiny—to cast into the history of humanity the new leaven they have received.

In the first section of this chapter I shall attempt to identify precisely what is new in these Christian communities. In the second section I shall examine the connection of this novelty with the battle being waged against the old person, that is, against the world bequeathed to us by the past.

1. THE NEW ELEMENT IN THE CHRISTIAN COMMUNITIES

The novelty of the Christian communities can be seen from three different points of view: first, there is the community itself as the model of the Pauline new person; second, the concrete model of the missionary, who is indispensable if the Christian community is to be genuinely new and genuinely Christian; finally, the practice of the missionaries and their communities: evangelization. The missionaries and their communities are concrete correlatives, and need each other. The missionary works to arouse the communities, and the communities could not exist without the missionary's encouragement and inspiration. Together, missionary and community constitute the basic structure of the new person, new human beings.

(a) Concrete Model of Community

(i). Historical Circumstances. The concrete model of the new Christian community is found mainly in the Third World. We are still far from being able to say that the actual institutions called local or regional Christian churches to be found in the Third World are built entirely on the basis of community. But in the midst of these churches have sprung up living, developing Christian communities, in Latin America, Asia, and Africa. The boundaries of these Christian communities do not coincide with the boundaries of the institutional church. It is for the ecclesiologists to determine these boundaries. Here it is necessary to point out only that the new person proclaimed by Jesus and the New Testament already has a concrete basis and does not belong to the world of ideas alone. Without these Christian communities, the church would not be in a position to proclaim the Pauline new human being. It would be speaking of a fictitious thing, irreality rather than historical reality. After all, historical reality, and the real, concrete meaning of Christian discourse, including that of the texts of the New Testament, are constituted by the Christian communities.

The communities have been born, and subsist, amidst the

poor. By this very fact they fail to receive official or juridical recognition as Christian communities. Their place is so modest, so lowly, that they fail to hold the attention of the heads of the great institutional networks. But in the world of the poor they are meaningful, and they transmit a message.

What is the content of the new communities in terms of human value? In what sense can they be called the basis of the new human being? They have no economic power. They have no political power. They have access neither to natural resources nor to humanity's cultural heritage. They know no systematic religious philosophies or theologies, have no fine arts or any literature, and are utterly ignorant of the refinements of the lifestyles of the elite. Then how can they take on the mission of creating the new person?

First of all, it must be emphasized that the Christian communities of today are not a totally new reality in the history of Christianity. If they were, they could not be called Christian. What they actually do is recover, in our present historical context, an inspiration that lay at the basis of primitive Christianity and that has been reborn ever and again throughout history.

The source of this inspiration is the old solidarity of the people of Israel, with its structures of clan and tribe, locked in constant combat with the domination of the monarchy, the temple hierarchies, or the Law. With Jesus, a community is born that has emancipated itself from family ties, to form new families. The New Testament shows the utter historical reality of Christ and Christianity in the communities and in the apostles. The twin dynamic of community and missionary completely filled the space in which primitive Christianity moved. They constituted the concrete human reality of Christianity. Through the first centuries, the community continued on the same course. When it began to slip into decadence, notably by virtue of its permeation by the structures of the Greco-Roman world, it reappeared, at the same time, in new experiments, conducted out on the margins of the established "communities."

For centuries the principal Christian communities were composed of monks and nuns. We must not forget, however, the countless peasant communities, especially in the East, but also in the West, which maintained the bonds of simple community but which history has ignored. Nothing of the life of these communities will be found inscribed on historical monuments. The memory of their life was erased, just as their hovels were wiped from the geography of their lands. The reason for focussing upon the monks and nuns is that they left more written memorials.

In the Middle Ages, the mendicants made a number of important discoveries concerning the manner of leading a community life. Among these discoveries are many of the roots of contemporary democracy. Of course, these same roots are found in the free medieval cities, with their corporations, brotherhoods, and confraternities. How often mendicants and their cities were bound together in a common lot! Both religious and the laity had gone in quest of a democratic, communitarian way of life.

Such medieval experiments with community were at the origin of the enterprises embarked on in the age of the conquest of the Americas. In the "reductions," the communities established especially by the Jesuits, but also by religious associations of lay people that had sprung up in certain more urbanized regions, the quest for community struck root in the South American continent. After the violent suppression of the Jesuit reductions and the decline of the lay associations, it was the rural missionaries of the nineteenth century, the new associations, and the Catholic Action movements of the twentieth century—all concrete phenomena in the history of the Latin American peoples—that testified to a Christian community in search of its identity. Today's communities seek to reconstruct, in a new historical situation, the same social model. The same "new person" is at work today, striving to be born and to live in a world of opposition, and frequently, of hostility and danger.

(ii). Freedom in Mutual, Voluntary Service. Today's Christian community repeats the basic message of the New Testament: the new person is not the individual, or even the whole of humanity conceptualized as a great machine in which individuals would be mere cogs. Today's Christian community rejects individualism as it rejects collectivism. Christians are keenly aware that, since the dawn of the modern age, a great debate has been raging between two antagonistic, irreconcilable social structures: liberal individualism, and socialistic collectivism (or at least a certain "real socialism").

Many biblical commentators understand St. Paul's new person in an individualistic sense. That product of modernity, the "individual," has exerted an unconscious influence on biblical exegesis. Recent exegesis, however, has criticized this ideological adulteration. For St. Paul, as for all primitive Christianity, the new person is a visible, palpable, concrete social reality: the Christian community. "Put on the new man," and enter into Christian community. Adopt its ways of life.

For that matter, we must not forget that individualism in the modern church has arisen largely as a protest against ecclesiastical "collectivism." Thus the local and regional Christian churches oscillate between two extremes of which they are not always very conscious. They demand total submission to the ecclesiastical "system"; at the same time they preach an individual salvation. It may even happen that both the ecclesiastical system and the local churches are associated in a paradoxical, but viable, historical combination: church government does not promote community structures, but addresses each individual as such. Strangely, each individual is called to work out his or her salvation through total submission to the system dictated by church government.

But the new Christian community represents the new person, as opposed to all social individualism and totalitarianism, be it ecclesiastical, civil, or military.

The new Christian community therefore represents an authentic victory over relationships of domination and subjugation. Here there is no domination of the strong over the weak, of the slave-owner over the slave. Instead of subjugation there is freedom. All take the initiative. No one is obliged to do the will of another. Consent supersedes constraint (Philem. 14). Not that freedom in the community means that all simply do their own will. This would be individualism, if not anarchy. On the contrary, each individual voluntarily serves the good of the community. All serve all. All voluntarily take up the tasks necessary for the good of all.

Freedom without mutual service leads to the individualism characterizing today's liberal societies, and ultimately to the domination of proprietors over those who are accorded no right of ownership. Service without freedom leads to totalitarianism.

St. Paul reflected deeply on community, and furnishes us with its most profound literary expression. For example:

> Remember that you have been called to live in freedom — but not a freedom that gives free reign to the flesh. Out of love, place yourselves at one another's service [Gal. 5:13].

"Love," here, is *agapē*. *Agapē* is the soul of community. A recent bourgeois tradition has begun to translate *agapē* as "love." But "love" denotes an individual, and subjective, disposition. Furthermore, it connotes an emotional or sentimental state. But *agapē* denotes a social phenomenon. *Agapē* is a relationship of mutual commitment among persons joined by ties of blood or adoption. Members of the Christian communities contract mutual relations and obligations — ties and commitments like those of clan or family. A common good, a common heritage, appears among them. All share in this common good. A better translation of *agapē* would be "solidarity," then, in the sense of a bond uniting a whole community. What constitutes a community is not its organization, or its rules, or its submission to a single authority, or particular goals pursued by common accord. A community exists in virtue of its *agapē,* in virtue of the reciprocal commitments held sacred by each of its members. *Agapē* creates a *koinōnia*, a common life, a sharing of all in the same goods. The Letter to Philemon admirably sets forth the combination of all these concepts, which define the bonds of community.

Agapē, then, is the highest good, the gift above all gifts. It is identified with the new person, and it abides forever (1 Cor. 13).

In the strength of *agapē*, St. Paul can say: "I made myself slave of all so as to win over as many as possible" (1 Cor. 9:19). Paul is simply portraying the new person. It is not that the new person is dependent on anything or anyone, either interiorily or exteriorily. He or she only makes use of the gift of freedom to adapt and submit to all. This subjection does not enslave. Freedom is not abdicated; it is simply used, concretely. It becomes a permanent disposition of quest for the good of all. The new person lives and experiences community.

It took centuries of dedication on the part of Christian champions of liberty before the Roman Catholic Church finally recognized, in the Second Vatican Council, the basis of the Christian freedom proclaimed by the New Testament and maintained at times against the will of authorities by the Christian communities of all times. The conciliar Declaration on Religious Freedom (*Dignitatis Humanae*) recognized the right to be wrong. No longer were all rights invested in those who defended (official) truth. "The right to this immunity continues to exist even in those who do not live up to their obligation of seeking the truth and adhering to it" (DH 2). The conciliar declaration as a whole defines and recognizes the foundations of a community freedom, thus avoiding the deviations of modern laissez-faire liberalism. This declaration is the Second Vatican Council's specific contribution to a Christian anthropology. Not without reason has it met with more opposition, both during the Council and since, than any other document of the Council.

(iii). Complementarity of Differences. The biblical images of body, vineyard, or construction are inadequate to represent what transpires in Christian community. They do bring out the notion of the participation of everyone in everything, together with the need each individual member has for the rest of the community. However, one might be tempted to draw more from those images than they actually contain, and think of a unity to be attained merely by the integration of each individual into a whole that would transcend all of its members. A mere absorption of all members into the oneness of the whole would leave those members without freedom. We should find ourselves awash in the modern conflict, the second great battle of the ideologies and societies: the conflict between equality and freedom. We should be expected to believe that Paul chose equality at the expense of freedom.

By no means. No one could have been less inclined to sacrifice the gift of freedom than Paul. We must balance his images of body against his proclamations of freedom. In the first place, there was the doctrine and exemplary practice of the coexistence of Jews and Gentiles in the first Christian communities. Jews need not abandon Judaism, any more than Gentiles need embrace it. The Jewish Christian is still circumcised, and still the heir of Jewish tradition. Jews retain all they have acquired. Pagans need not accept this legacy. Thus, Gentiles and Jews are both absorbed into a higher incorporation. Each group abides in its difference. They are different (corporate) members of the same community.

Paul laid hold of this case and extended his proclamation of equality in freedom to other groups: "There does not exist among you Jew or Greek, slave or freeman, male or female. All are one in Christ Jesus" (Gal. 3:28).

The problem is one of differences. One solution might lie simply along lines of the unity of a living organism. A hand is a hand, and no more than a hand. And so on, with all the other members of the human body. But in this one-sided solution, each member loses its freedom vis-à-vis the entire organism. Equality is present, because no member subjugates another, and none is independent of the others. Each subsists in its particular difference. Another solution would consist in ignoring the differences, and conferring equality in terms of uniformity.

Just so, in the Christian community there is no totality capable of absorbing differences. Differences are acknowledged. But their complementarity does not consist in each one's exercise of an antecedently determined role. On the contrary, each member is a full-fledged, autonomous member. Each member is above his or her difference, and does not enter into the make-up of the community on the strength of this difference. A man, then, does not enter the community on the strength of his gender; nor is his activity therein defined in function of his gender. Neither is a woman defined by her gender. The complementarity of men and women is not that of two halves of a whole; rather, both are the new person, and therefore equal persons, in a renewed human existence. Of course there are differences. And the differences are maintained. But they are maintained in reciprocity. The differences are not reduced to homogeneity; rather, they join one another in dialogue.

The Christian community thus becomes the scene of a community life of all sexes, races, cultures, educational levels, talents, and natural gifts. No single model is sought, some vehicle of a universal synthesis. No edifice is constructed in which the role of each member would be determined in advance by that member's particular condition and attributes. No particular role is assigned to men, women, indigenous people, blacks, whites, orientals, scholars, or illiterates. All are involved equally in everything. It is this dialogue of differences that establishes the rhythm of our coexistence. A constant circulation, an interreaction, is maintained among all differences. The new Christian community is living proof that the seemingly irreducible conflicts that permeate the human condition—conflicts among the sexes, races, cultures, peoples, speakers of different languages, and nations—can somehow be overcome in concrete reality.

The communities also show that conflict cannot be resolved through isolation. They prove that the sexes, races, and cultures are not made safe by closing off their boundaries and avoiding contact with one another, but by reciprocity, common life, and voluntary exposure to their correlatives. Neither homogeneity nor isolation, but only acceptance of the constant provocation of difference, guarantees the resolution of conflict and the integrity of difference itself.

Someone might object: surely these communities are capable of solving small-scale problems, but they can scarcely furnish solutions for human problems on a large scale. This is a new question, to be addressed in the next section of this chapter. For the moment, suffice it to say that a seed of newness has been sown, and that, ever since Christ became one of us and sowed the seed of a new humanity, he is found precisely in efforts mounted to renew community.

(b) Concrete Missionary Model

(i). Historical Circumstances. Christian newness is too concrete not to be incarnate in an absolutely new and unique type of community. This community presents itself in various historical expressions, but its novelty always lies along the same lines, so that its historical expressions are all basically similar. The unifying thread in the community fabric is the Christian missionary or apostle. The New Testament traces the outline not of a universal person, but of a very particular kind of person. The same model is reproduced in various exemplars: the Twelve of the Synoptic Gospels, the deacons of the Acts of the Apostles, Paul,

the prophets of the Book of Revelation. Contemporary historians have shown that even the human figure of Jesus was sketched after the resurrection—it was drawn from the standpoint of the concrete experience of the life of the first Christian missionaries. In a sense, the entire New Testament is a direct or indirect portrait of the missionary model.

The first Christian missionaries were conscious of constituting, in their life and action, the incarnation and active presence of Christ and his gospel (see EN 41). Socially they were almost marginal. They dissolved all bonds and ties of family, culture, and people, as far as they possibly could. They were completely dedicated to their Christian mission. They had no social authority. They may have had no authority whatsoever in the church. Not even the church formally defined them, and they themselves resisted attempts at definition through which authorities tried to close them in preestablished schemas.

After the missionaries of the first generations, we have little documentation on the evolution of the missionary model. There is everything to indicate that the missionaries of the first centuries were lay people, and poor. There is no evidence of any institution devoting itself to mission, along with every indication of the presence of countless missionary enterprises. Missionary activity was intense, but it was assumed by very simple persons. The pagan philosopher Celsus ridiculed Christianity as a movement propagated by slaves, including women, and by other unlettered persons. And this, of course, is precisely what it was.

But the communities were more than missionary societies. They were always communities as much as they were missionary, and this is the most stable constant of the new person. The missionaries appeared precisely within the community. They were not members of the hierarchy, although members of the hierarchy might also have the gift of the apostolate.

Later, in East and West alike, the mission was taken up by monks. In the East the monks came to be acknowledged as authentic leaders of the Christian people, as during the controversy over images in the Byzantine Empire, or in the glorious centuries of the Russian *startsi* (fifteenth–sixteenth centuries). In the West we need only recall the role of the Irish and Anglo-Saxon monks in the implantation of Christianity in northern

Europe. Here the model, as it were, was created by Sts. Francis and Dominic, the precursors of the vast missionary movement of the twelfth and thirteenth centuries. Of course, all centuries since have had their missionary movements. But rarely have they attained to the perfection of their first exemplars.

The evangelization of the Americas was undertaken by a host of missionaries of exceptional competence, especially during the first century of that evangelization. There were hundreds, thousands of illustrious names, especially of Dominicans, Franciscans, and Jesuits, as well as members of other orders. They were all typical representatives of the new person, whom we might call *homo Christianus,* the type and model that appears anew in each century to constitute the Christian yeast in the dough of the world.

The Iberian cultural context did not accord women the freedom to exercise evangelizing roles in America on an equal footing with men. In Christian antiquity, as in the Middle Ages in the West, there was no dearth of women whose social activity was equal in stature and intensity to that of their male counterparts, despite the restrictions imposed by the dominant civilizations of those times on the freedom of women to ply the highways and byways of the world. Often confined to the four walls of their houses or convents, they nevertheless managed to extend their activity to the political arenas of their time. Examples are Hildegaard of Bingen, Elizabeth of Schönau, Marie of Oignies, Hedwig, Catherine of Siena, and Teresa of Avila, all of whom discharged a role on a par with that of the greatest missionaries of all times.

Later centuries in Latin America no longer saw missionaries of the stature of those of the first hundred years of our evangelization. Part of the reason for this is that the missionary charisms were snuffed out by the formalism and the decadence of the religious orders, and the discredit into which these orders fell throughout Western society.

(ii). Free and Slave. St. Paul has explained more powerfully than anyone else what it means to be a missionary. His descriptions remain unsurpassed even today. The missionary is a free being. And Paul presents himself as a free being—indeed, we might even say, as the very prototype of freedom. He is free

politically; he submits to no political authority. He reserves the
right to pass judgment on the Roman power itself. The price he
pays for his political freedom is imprisonment. Paul is free even
in chains.

He is free economically. He has made his living by the work
of his hands, making no appeal to his right as a missionary to
be supported by his communities. One can be too dependent on
one's rights, as has happened so many times in the history of
clerical institutions. In order to maintain these rights many a
priest has condemned himself to subordinating others.

Paul is culturally free. He has rejected his entire previous
rabbinical training, his whole conception of life. He clings to
none of his old ways of thinking. He has jettisoned the frame of
reference of all of his thinking, which was a Judaism on the
rigoristic, rigorous Pharisaic model. He has renounced the
source of his personal security, the wellspring of his personality,
with its framework and support, the Law. He has given up the
social framework of the people of Israel, with its customs and
way of life, its canon of scriptures and traditions – the ideological deposit of Israel. He has emptied himself, the very thing he
proclaims of Christ. If Christ has become nothing – entirely
empty of all that makes for a human face in society – then so
has Paul, and so must every missionary (Phil. 2:6–8).

"Although I am not bound to anyone, I made myself slave of
all so as to win over as many as possible" (1 Cor. 9:19). The
missionary embodies this portrait of the community. What does
it mean to be the "slave of all"? Paul expresses the same reality,
in different words, when he says, for example:

> It was through the law that I died to the law, to live for
> God. I have been crucified with Christ, and the life I live
> now is not my own; Christ is living in me. I still live my
> human life, but it is a life of faith in the Son of God, who
> loved me and gave himself for me [Gal. 2:19–20].

"To me, 'life' means Christ" (Phil. 1:21), he cries.

In later centuries these words were given a purely mystical
interpretation. In Paul's statements, however, "Christ" always
has a realistic meaning. "Christ" is Christ present in the Chris-

tian communities. "To me, 'life' means Christ." This means: my
life is totally dedicated to the Christian communities. Life for
Paul is not a mystical experience divorced from his devotion to
the community. It is precisely his dedication to the community,
as he labors for the creation, progress, and future promise of
that community.

Missionaries no longer have a private, individual life. Their
life is completely public, steeped in social relationships. In missionaries, all thoughts, sentiments, concerns, the whole series of
faculties that make up human beings, are reserved for the communities. This is to live in Christ, and to live by Christ: to live
as a servant, a slave. Paul is a slave: his life belongs no longer
to himself but to his communities. Person and society, the individual and community, have come to be identified in his life.
The conflict between the social and the personal has vanished.
The individual has become person and society in a single movement.

Service to the communities calls for complete flexibility. Missionaries must become, so to speak, a different, specific personality in each community they serve. They become a multiple
personality. They no longer have a personhood of their own.
They have as many personhoods as they have communities.

> I became like a Jew to the Jews.... To those bound by
> the law I became like one who is bound.... To those not
> subject to the law I became like one not subject to it....
> To the weak I became a weak person.... I have made
> myself all things to all ... [1 Cor. 9:20–22].

"Who is weak that I am not affected by it?" he cries. "Who
is scandalized that I am not aflame with indignation?" (2 Cor.
11:29).

(iii). Weak and Strong. Being free and yet a slave, the missionary is weak—the weakest of beings. Missionaries experience
the weakness of the poor. They enter into the condition of the
poor. They do not explicitly seek poverty. They ascribe it no
value. But it is the price of their freedom and their service.
Attributing a value to voluntary poverty is dangerous. We may
come to think that poverty is something good in itself. This is

the familiar theme of certain philosophical schools, as also of certain schools of spirituality coming to us from the East. Poverty is never idealized in Christian sources. For that matter, while the first Christians were poor, it would never have entered their heads that poverty might have something positive to be said for it. However, it is the price the new person must pay for the privilege of loyalty to God's calling.

Here too, Paul has said almost everything about the weakness and strength of the missionary that could be said. Paul had no political or economic support. Even his family had disappeared, as far as he was concerned, despite its geographical proximity, just as was the case with Jesus of Nazareth. Paul cut himself off from his cultural roots, which could have been his mainstay. For established society, he must have been an object of suspicion, to say the least. He fitted into no defined social roles. This alone made him an enemy of law and order, in every meaning of the expression. He accepted no social role. Then he had to pay the price.

Marginalized by society, missionaries are also frequently marginalized in their own churches — suspect even in the eyes of the communities they evangelize. They can be without friends even among their fellow apostles. Unity is not easy among apostles. Paul was constantly at odds with the other apostles. Missionaries are radical individuals, and this can estrange them even from their colleagues and collaborators (see Phil. 1:15–18; 3:2–3, 17–19; 1 Cor. 1:10–13; 4:14–21; 2 Cor. 11:1–15).

> As I see it, God has put us apostles at the end of the line, like men doomed to die in the arena. We have become a spectacle to the universe, to angels and men alike. We are fools on Christ's account. Ah, but in Christ you are wise! We are the weak ones, you the strong! [1 Cor. 4:9–10].

Missionaries are acutely aware of their frailty. Their lives are lives of constant danger. By virtue of their mission, they may not look for a safe refuge. They must face their enemies. They must defy the world, the communities, and their own friends. They cannot always avoid obstacles: on the contrary, they are here to attack obstacles and remove them, precisely in order that their communities may continue their journey in greater safety. The terms in which Paul describes the difficulties he encountered are valid for all times and places. And the same difficulties dog our steps today (see 2 Cor. 11:21–33; 1 Cor. 4:9–13; 2 Cor. 4:7–15).

The prospect of martyrdom is never absent from the missionary's horizon. Here is the supreme expression of a missionary's weakness. Throughout the New Testament, the fate of an apostle is martyrdom, and the same has been true throughout all the centuries of Christian history. There were martyrs in the evangelization of the Americas. In recent decades, martyrdom has reappeared in Latin America, and it is growing more and more frequent. The martyr has always been an essential feature of the face of the new person. The cross of Christ is the brand on the forehead of the missionary. Paul sees himself as "crucified with Christ" (Gal. 2:19).

The missionary's weakness, however, is accompanied by new strength—another characteristic, and an outstanding one, of the newness of the new person. The new person is an individual (or group) of unparalleled energy.

The strength of missionaries is in their word. Words might seem to be the weakest means of action a human being could employ. What could be more fragile than a bit of air wafting from the mouth? And yet the word of Christ and his missionaries is robed in strength. It is feared. It is hated. It arouses persecution. It is a sign both of weakness and of strength. Paul lifts his voice daringly. He fears no authority. His judges in Jerusalem are thunderstruck (Acts 4:13). How often the enemies of Christians have been similarly astounded through the ages! And their astonishment continues today. How dare these ignoramuses, this riffraff, shout in the faces of their implacable persecutors and publish the truth?

The word of the missionary has the force of life; it maintains the communities in existence. What the whole Johannine corpus proclaims becomes living reality: the word of Christ, the word that is Christ, the word pronounced by the disciples of Jesus, gives life. Here is a word that is the energy of life. Of course, it is not the syllables that have this power. Still less is it the ideas the words represent. A word is the act of the one pronouncing it. Those who set forth and assert the words of Christ's truth offer their lives as proof of those words in the very act of pronouncing them. The word is a public presentation of the person of the missionary. It is on this account that it is the strength of life.

Now we understand the celebrated Pauline portrait of the missionary:

> This treasure we possess in earthen vessels, to make it clear that its surpassing power comes from God and not from us. We are afflicted in every way possible, but we are not crushed; full of doubts, we never despair. We are persecuted but never abandoned; we are struck down but never destroyed. Continually we carry about in our bodies the dying of Jesus, so that in our bodies the life of Jesus may also be revealed. While we live we are constantly being delivered to death for Jesus' sake, so that the life of Jesus may be revealed in our mortal flesh. Death is at work in us, but life in you [2 Cor. 4:7–12].

(iv). Missionary and Community. The primary role of the missionary is to be a source of community energy. In founding their communities as in supporting them thereafter, missionaries act by the strength of their faith. Their faith is vitality, and this vitality is prolonged in hope. A Christian community is an impossible task. It is missing from the register of the economic, political, and social powers of the world. Statistically it is a most unlikely phenomenon. It cannot appeal to the motivations that normally rouse folk to action. It subsists by virtue of the faith of the one who is at the origin and beginning of its renewal. The faith of the missionary is not only the community's fulcrum, but its sole security, as well.

Second, the missionary is the living memory of the community. A missionary is not an archive, stuffed with records of dead facts, but on the contrary, the one who always returns and who says to the community, "Back to basics!" The missionary is the person who reminds the church of its first fervor, its projected goal. Any community will tend to yield to the pressures of the society in which it is living and with which it is communicating.

Instead of evangelizing, a community might be itself reabsorbed into its surroundings. The missionary denounces the reabsorption. The role of the missionary is like that of the prophets of the Old and New Testaments. The missionary word is like the letters in the Book of Revelation. When the community deviates from its objective, when the salt is losing its savor, the force of the missionary word thrusts it back to authenticity. Paul's letters did the same.

Third, the missionary provides the element of detachment so essential to discernment. Missionaries step back from things. They are the first to notice things that will alter situations and cause new problems. They are the first to perceive the signs of the times, and to discern potential responses to new challenges. They discover and arouse the vocations and charisms that prepare the members of the community to continue the struggle in which the missionaries themselves have been engaged.

The community has lost its vitality if it begins to repeat the same responses everlastingly. It has ceased to speak if it learns a discourse by rote and places its confidence in that discourse. The missionary calls for needed reforms, and proclaims the urgency of these reforms for the community's continuance in a genuine Christian life.

On the other hand, there are no missionaries without community. A motor without a clutch will spin until it burns out. A missionary can act only in communication with one or more communities. Without them he or she will be in danger of falling into eccentricity, ineffectiveness, or permanent ill humor. Without their communities, missionaries are helpless to act in the world. Not that community is a tool of their activity. The community must never become the unquestioningly obedient agent of its missionary's projects and plans. The missionary has no authority to require strict obedience. The community multiplies and diversifies the inspirations it has received. It humanizes them, and propagates them. It rescues them from fanaticism or radicalism. It snatches them from a flight into an abstract voluntarism.

Missionary and community are correlatives, then. They complement each other. The missionary guides the community, and the community guides the missionary, albeit in different ways.

The role of the missionary is analogous to certain other roles in ancient and modern society. Missionaries are like prophets, priests, mandarins, gurus, bonzes, and so on. In particular, they resemble the intellectuals of Western civilization, the Enlightenment intellectual. However, there is a difference, as well. Intellectuals draw power from their knowledge. They have authority in society. Intellectuals possess a knowledge that enables them to maintain the social cohesion of complex societies. Missionaries have no utilitarian knowledge. They have no power to keep a complex society united. They act on a popular community level. Their knowledge has no social utility.

When the church transforms itself into a mighty social institution, it has need of members with the intellectual wherewithal to organize a complex ecclesiastical society. And so it creates for itself theologians, canonists, and a corps of bishops and priests. These theologians and canonists work alongside or within the organization. Some of them may be apostles and missionaries, as well. But if they are, they will suffer a loss in esteem for their talents as bishops, priests, theologians, or canonists. Missionaries have no intellectual power. Their power resides in their personal charisma, their intuition, and their radical fidelity to the novelty of the gospel.

(c) The New Practice: Evangelization

(i). Historical Situation. Evangelization is of prime interest to our local and regional Christian churches today, as witness the Roman Synod of 1974, the apostolic exhortation *Evangelii Nuntiandi* of Pope Paul VI, which emerged from that synod, and the bishops' conference at Puebla, which took as its theme "Evangelization at Present and in the Future of Latin America." Evangelization may be called by other names—the apostolate, for example, or mission. But by whatever name, evangelization is the great concern of the church of the twentieth century. This demonstrates the resurgence of Christian vitality in our century. After all, evangelization is part and parcel of the core of the novelty of Christ. The new person acts. This action is called evangelization. Evangelization is the new practice inserted by the new person into the history of humanity.

But what is evangelization? The popularity of the subject in our local and regional churches has resulted in the assignment of the name "evangelization" to the most diversified of activities. All church institutions now feel they must define their activities as evangelization if they hope to justify their existence. Evangelization can even mean the undermining of evangelization.

The first Christian generations felt no need to define evangelization, or mission, or the apostolate, as a specific activity. They evangelized simply by existing. The very existence of Christian communities—comprised of slaves, foreigners, the poor, and other marginalized, all scorned in the profoundly corrupt milieu of the Greco-Roman world of the day—was evangelization enough. The communities made no attempt to live a cozy life, to keep to themselves. Spontaneously, they sought to spread. The courage of their convictions, and the joy of belonging to a free people of sisters and brothers, radiated a dynamic that could only mean expansion. In the early Christian *Letter to Diognetus,* for example, evangelization consists in a proclamation. We are a new people. We are horrified by established society, and we reject it. We proclaim a new world. We have the energy to renew this old world and transform it. This is our good news, our gospel. To the Roman elite, it seemed absurd to have to listen to such nonsense from the lowest strata of society. It was a mighty claim, however, and a positive response was everywhere forthcoming. To evangelize was to invite others to become a part of this new people, this new community, and to begin a life of freedom and communion.

Later, when Christianity decided to include the whole of society—the social structure, with its elite, who dominated the others, as well as the traditional peasant masses with their ancestral religions—evangelization tended to become confused with the transmission of established religion, doctrine, structures, and all. In the intellectual milieu that maintained or had recovered the legacy of the Greek intellectual world, evangelization now fell into idealism. To evangelize was now to initiate a series of intellectual exercises calculated to foster the ascent of the mind to God by way of the intelligence.

There were protests, naturally, and they were raised in every generation. Prophets, missionaries, and communities sought to be delivered from the burden of religious structures, and to return to the gospel. From the third century to our twentieth, local and regional churches have resounded with the cry, "Back to the gospel!" For the ancient monks, such as St. Anthony, the earliest known monk, for Francis of Assisi and his companions, for the sixteenth-century Catholic or Protestant reformers, to evangelize was to return to the gospel, break free of established traditions, and propose a new way of life—one that responded to the calls of the gospel, new and fresh again. Evangelization was conceived first and foremost as an intra-church activity. There were "foreign" missions, but these were marginal, and their purpose was to propagate abroad whatever reforms might be under way at home. This was the missionary effort of the Franciscans, the Dominicans, the Jesuits.

The Jesuits, however, who were missionaries in China, in India, and in the American reductions from the sixteenth century to their extinction, were the forerunners of evangelization in the twentieth-century sense. With them, evangelizing was no longer an intra-church activity. To evangelize was to act in a non-Christian world, a world whose structures had not been taken up and transformed by Christianity. In the world of the twentieth century, the challenge of evangelization is once more that of the first centuries. Few, however, have come to perceive this new situation. Most of us still live in the refuge of our parishes, which are more the relics of an antiquated Christianity than the first fruits of a new people won for Christ in the midst of today's world.

The Puebla Document, and the apostolic exhortation *Evangelii Nuntiandi,* stand as invitations to us to reflect on the duality of our churches today. As official documents of the Roman Catholic Church, they are fraught with an intrinsic ambiguity. They are open to different readings, since they were written with different meanings in mind. The bishops who approved these documents did not all wish to say the same thing. These documents mark the dividing line between two eras.

(ii). The Objective Facet of Evangelization. Like any other organized activity, evangelization comprises intellectual elements. Its content is partly conceptual. It is knowledge. It is not primarily an activity of the transmission of doctrines, however,

because it is not simply the reproduction of the social consciousness or ideology of a society. Evangelization transpires on the level of the begetting of life. Evangelization is a life-creating activity.

To evangelize is to communicate human novelty. The evangelizers are the communities and missionaries who show forth in their own persons the advent of a new person. They assert the presence of this new person within the old human condition, and as a struggle between the new and the old. Thus, to evangelize is to call other persons to enter into a war of the worlds. In the interim between two eras of peace—the peace of the old societies tranquilized by domination, and the future peace of a world destined to transform all dominations—a struggle is being waged: the combat of the present.

In its most radical, naked form, considered apart from its cultural or intellectual trappings, the gospel is the hue and cry of oppressed peoples. The gospel is the cry of the poor. From ancient times, the poor have resigned themselves to their oppression. Or at most their rebellions have been limited to the quasi-biological reaction of organisms struggling not to die. They have mounted no project, entertained no specific purpose, striven for no organization. The cry heard by God in the Bible, the cry of the wronged—which it is the sacred right of the poor to raise, guaranteed by the Law—is now the cry of Jesus on the cross, and the cry of the Christian communities, rising to the Father (Rom. 8:15; Gal. 4:6). It is a cry that expresses not only the agony of the cross, and the abandonment felt by someone helpless, but confidence in the Father's response, as well. The very cry of the poor, the very cry of helplessness, is a proclamation of resurrection. It is a cry of victory. It is a victory celebration in the midst of persecution and suffering. Understood in the fuller meaning of the gospel, then, the cry of the poor is the radical vehicle of this gospel, and itself an act of evangelization.

Evangelization stirs to life. It leads persons and communities to a new dynamism. The idle begin to act; the active whose activity has been in accord with the structures of an old, corrupt, unjust world of domination and destruction, begin a new world of new relationships. Just as the first creation was accomplished by the power of a word, the Word of God, so this new word, too, has the power to create—to inaugurate something altogether new.

(iii). The Subjective Facet of Evangelization. Official church documents, and the traditional theology of evangelization, emphasize elements of doctrine and intellectual content, but fail to define evangelization as an act, indeed as a new and original mode of activity in the world. The lengthy Puebla Document, wholly devoted to evangelization, entirely neglected to say what, after all, evangelization is.

Evangelization is activity, and it is witness. As activity, evangelization consists in going out to meet our neighbor, encountering that neighbor in the form of persons, multitudes, groups, and peoples. Be the evangelizer an individual or a community, that individual or community discovers itself, and reveals itself, in the encounter with neighbor, the meeting with the "other." It "invades" the other's world—not in order to dominate and subjugate, however, but in order to give, to serve. It does not invade this foreign territory with its strength, but with its weakness, not with an attitude of superiority, but with an attitude of inferiority. Only in poverty can one evangelize.

Evangelization falls short of its objective if it encounters only the mask, the defense mechanisms, of the other. To evangelize is to contact reality—the level of others' reality. This level remains unknown even to the other, the neighbor, until the moment of its penetration by the evangelizer. Peoples do not know what they are, do not know that they are a people, until the moment the evangelizer penetrates them. Then a complete turnabout is produced.

The Synoptic Gospels call this encounter proclamation. In the Johannine writings it is witness. Other texts refer to it simply as the word. Paul calls it the good news, the gospel.

Evangelization is witness. Its content begins with the content of ancient prophecy: the denunciation of a situation of sin and the proclamation of a new order. And yet, evangelization goes beyond ancient prophecy. It summons its auditors to a new humanity—new, but already existing, already in act.

Once the evangelizer is in face-to-face communication with the interlocutor—that is, with the world, whether in the form of a mass or group, or simply as an individual—he or she issues an invitation. The gates of community swing wide. This act of liberation consists in a call and summons to share in, to enter into, a new world of participation and community.

After all, no one becomes a Christian by intellectual assent. No one becomes a Christian by way of an individual entry upon a new way of thinking or a new style of personal asceticism. To become a member of the new person is to enter into a concrete, particular community. To become a member of the new person means collectively forming a new community, and acting henceforward in communion.

Evangelization is only one part of liberation—namely, its root and origin. But it is Christianity's specific contribution to liberation. The liberation of humanity spans all aspects of human life. The Christian contribution might seem to be the most fragile, the most tenuous of all. The most important thing in life, however, is life itself. No specific vital activity is possible without the presence of life itself. Christian anthropology proposes a new life precisely in the form of a new creation of life.

Evangelization, the Christian contribution, is not a once-and-for-all infusion of life that need never be repeated. Just as biological life, which is also a gift and power that springs into being at a determined moment, must be continually renewed, so with new life, as well.

The first section of this chapter can be summed up with a statement from St. Paul: "If anyone is in Christ, he is a new creation. The old order has passed away; now all is new!" (2 Cor. 5:17). The prophets of bygone ages proclaimed this new world only from afar. The testimony of the Christian communities is that this new world finally exists. It is crucified, it is persecuted, it exists in suffering and struggle, but it exists. Anyone in Latin America can testify to this fact. We see and hear the object of this testimony. This new life is already at work, and mightily. This book is about Christian anthropology. And the very first aspect of this anthropology to be examined has shown that humanity is already in process of liberation—with groans and entreaties, surely, from amidst the torments of the cross, but indeed already in process of liberation.

2. NEW AND OLD

The root, the core, of Christianity is the proclamation of the
new person now living among us and within us. Equally basic to
Christianity is the assertion that the new and the old co-exist in
the same individuals and the same humanity. The new and old
do not constitute two successive histories, or two parallel histories, but a single history, composed of tensions and struggles
between the new and the old at the heart of every people, every
culture, every individual, and the whole of humanity. The new
is liberated from the old in a struggle that becomes the substance
and drama of human life on earth.

In the struggle for the liberation of the new person, the role
of the authentic vanguard, the role of true leadership, falls to
the poor. The poor are the important ones. They have a special
role, and no one can take this from them. On this point the
Christian message obliges us to turn our habitual conceptions
and spontaneous tendencies completely around. The former
person, the old person, refuses to accept this inversion of values.
The old person fails to comprehend the reason for the preferential option for the poor. But the authentic liberation of the
new person is accomplished only under the leadership and tutelage of the poor.

However, the poor cannot conduct the processes of liberation
simply on the strength of their poverty. They have need of the
mediation of all the forces now in the hands of the mighty. They
must subordinate to their own designs the powerful who resist
their actions. Hence the constant renewal of the struggles for
the liberation of the human in the human being—or, in Christian
eyes, the struggle for the new creation of a new humanity within
the old.

(a) The New Humanity in Combat with the Old

(i). Church and World in a Common Destiny. From the earliest
days of Christianity, certain sectarian tendencies have sought to
divide humanity into two separate groups. On one side would
be the saints, the perfect. These completely embody the new

person. On the other side would be the rest of humanity, the derelict masses, the incarnation of the old person. However, the church has always resisted all such dualistic tendencies. They are too obviously opposed to what tradition recalls about Jesus. The parables of the Reign of God teach precisely that the separation between new and old will occur only at the end of history. There is no way to separate the just and the sinful, the good and the wicked, at the present time. We are all the vessels of new and old together, and we all share in the struggle of the new with the old, with the whole of our being, in all dimensions of our existence.

One could think that the realities of the new person—community, the missions, evangelization—would be found exclusively in the church. But if this were to be the case, the church would be the sole depository of the new person. The activities of a renewed humanity would be limited to the explicitly religious activities proper to the church, while political, economic, and cultural activities would be those of the former person, the old person. It is precisely such a notion that is contradicted in the gospel. Human community is seeing the light of day, is being born, not only, nor most typically, in church communities, but principally in all of the new structures and forms of social cooperation created by world efforts for liberation. God's messengers, the prophets and the missionaries, act not only as ministers of the church, but as persons committed to the endeavor, at the heart of the world, to transform all manifestations of human existence. Evangelization consists not only in ecclesial words and signs, but also in the public activity of all who commit themselves to a renewal of human society and its every member.

The New Testament shows us that even in the beginning, for example in the Pauline and Johannine churches, Christianity had members who regarded themselves as already perfect. These persons regard themselves as consummate embodiments of the new person proclaimed by Jesus. They waft above the struggles, above sin and the old person. They live as if the separation of the good and the wicked had already been accomplished. Resting on the laurels of their supposed election, they abandon the world to its condemnation. Such Christians invariably yield to the temptations of the dualistic religious movements of their time—gnosticism and its cousins—and will generate the pseudo-Christian sects.

In nearly every age of Christian history, out on the margins of Christianity, new sects have arisen based on an unconscious resumption of this same distortion of the gospel. In our present century the sects seem more virulent than ever. As always, they reject all activity in the world as a snare of the Evil One.

Another phenomenon that led to various forms of sectarianism was the current known as messianism. There was a long, Western, medieval tradition of messianism, claiming descent from Joachim of Flora, whose adherents waited for the coming of the true age of the Spirit—the age in which the gospel would be genuinely lived on earth in its pure and integral form. This hope divides Christians into two categories: those who believe in this coming of the new world of the Spirit and prepare for it, and those who do not believe in it and fail to prepare for it. Here the expectation of the messianic Reign has already wrought, in secret, the division to be made manifest at its imminent coming: the children of light are already distinguishable from the children of darkness. And of course the self-styled children of light withdraw from the others and condemn their world.

Many historians regard the Western reforms and revolutions as prolongations of these same medieval messianisms. On the one side we have the reformed, who are the new persons, and on the other side the unreformed, the old persons. On one side there are the revolutionary movements, or the new person, and on the other the rest of society, the old humanity. But with the coming of the reform or the revolution, the new person triumphs and fills the earth, while the old person must disappear. A new society is born, the very incarnation of the new humanity.

Whatever may be the overall value of such historical interpretations, there is an undeniable sectarian ferment in modern reforms and revolutions. To sectarian Christianity, it is as if the revolutionary movements were infected with a virus that secularizes the messianic movements the moment they come into being. This secular virus is the main obstacle encountered by these radical Christians who would have wished to collaborate with modern liberal and socialistic movements.

Even the churches are vulnerable to the sectarian spirit. Of old, there was the temptation of the Christian empires. The theologians of the Byzantine emperors, like those of the Germanic or Russian emperors or "Catholic Kings," presented the new society, governed by "Christian princes," as the new Israel, the new humanity, incarnate in the structural totality of a concrete reality. On one side was Christendom, the body of Christ; on the other were all other societies—the Muslim world, or the pagan world, the realm of the Evil One. But the church never ratified these pretensions on the part of the imperial or royal courts.

In the modern era, the sectarian tendency of the churches has been to close the church off from the world. Certain Christian groups today are infected with a "two reign" type of schema: on one side the church, with all its institutions, the Reign of God on earth—the place of the new person; on the other, civil society, which, while not quite the realm of the Devil, is surely not the Reign of God. Civil society may be the place where Christians acquire merit, as they perform the works of faith; but it is not part of the Reign of God.

Many traces of this complex history survive in the minds of Christians of today. Many, for instance, place the church outside human society. They are unwilling to see the church subjected to a historical or sociological analysis. They regard the church, even as a social organism, as an entity belonging to the Reign of God alone, and not to human society. They continue to regard activity in the world as beneath the dignity of Christians or their church, and prefer to devote their efforts to activity within the church. But the Christian message is enunciated by St. Paul in chapters seven and eight of his Letter to the Romans. The whole of humanity is in struggle and tension; it is caught up in the contradictions enumerated in chapter seven. And the whole of humanity is stimulated and moved by the Spirit that engenders the new person.

(ii). Living the Absolute in the Relative. We must face the facts. We are simply unable to perform a totally pure, perfect activity, removed from all complicity with the old world of sin and domination. There is no route straight to the new person without detours. Were there such a route, all would be far easier. But

all paths are ambivalent, and none is the only one. Humanity goes in quest of its liberation along a variety of pathways, each with its defects, risks, and perils, its connections to the old person. But God has the power to lead humanity to its liberation over imperfect roadways.

Empty illusions have such a curious tenacity in the religious mentality. Some pious persons behave as if there were religious or ecclesial paths exempt from imperfection. Some seem to think that activities of the church, or monastic, religious, priestly, and other vocations to service in that church, are exempt from the law of ambivalence. Surely such activities and vocations could never be contaminated by impure political, economic, and cultural motivations! Surely they will have no connection with the sin of the world! Every aspect of them is pure. Others discredit political or social action movements precisely as being too ambivalent. Others, again, scorn any movements not directed by Christians — as if the ecclesiastical domain were exempt from ambivalence, or as if Christian leadership would automatically remove the ambivalence.

All of this purism is consciously or unconsciously inspired by the notion of "flight from the world," which has so long contaminated Christian spirituality.

The truth is that the absolute of the new person cannot subsist except as enfleshed in imperfect, ambivalent actions and movements. Imperfection, far from being a definitive obstacle, is precisely the path chosen by the Spirit of God to reach final liberation.

Similarly, some reject certain kinds of action, certain movements or processes, because they are partial and limited in scope, or because they represent only one of a number of possible options. But why should the diversity or partiality of pathways ever justify abstention? Amidst risks and perils, making options that cannot be appraised without being tested, we seek out our salvation. Those who make partial or hazardous options are then accused of "reducing" Christianity to such and such a political movement, such and such a social action, or such and such a route to liberation. But by the same token, those who receive the sacraments could be accused of seeking to "reduce" the Reign of God to the sacraments, those who choose a vocation in a religious institute could be accused of seeking to "reduce" Christianity to that institute, and so on.

This is the human condition: that every step along the road to liberation is partial and limited, hazardous, affected by sin, and still based on a past of domination and corruption. Not even the most sacred institutions of the church escape this rule. All is relative. But the absolute of human liberation has no other route to follow. Those who would find the pure absolute condemn themselves either to flee this world or to live on illusion.

(b) Priority of the Poor

There is nothing more solid, more constant, or more evident in Christian anthropology than the special place of the poor. The entire Bible is built on the historical role of the poor. Christian tradition takes up the theme again in every generation.

True, this theme contradicts human preconceptions, the collective unconscious, and dominant ideologies. Its reassertion in every generation produces an effect of novelty and revolution. And indeed its expressions vary with the times, but its truth is always the same. In recent times, the popes, from John XXIII to John Paul II, have emphasized a preferential option for the poor and proclaimed a church of the poor. The bishops' conferences of Medellín and Puebla have designated the option for the poor as the norm of all pastoral activity to be performed by the church in Latin America.

But thus prioritizing the poor affects the church far more extensively than if it were a mere internal disposition on the part of the Christian community. On the contrary, the church makes the preferential option for the poor because the poor have priority in the liberation of the world, because they are the actual vanguard of the new person. The poor are not privileged because the church selects them. The church selects them because God has placed them in the forefront of the movement for the liberation of all humanity.

There is no doubt as to who these poor are. They are explicitly listed in the Puebla document: the vast majorities of the Latin American peoples, unable to satisfy their most basic needs of nutrition, health and hygiene, housing, education, and employment. Poverty is understood here in its concrete, material sense. There is no reference to purely internal psychological disposi- tions (Puebla 32–39).

Not infrequently in history, poverty and its privilege have been misunderstood. It has been said, for example, that the reason the poor are in the vanguard of liberation is their political weight, their social or economic "clout." Nothing could be fur- ther from the truth. The poor have no power. Movements that espouse the cause of the poor may have this sort of strength. But the poor themselves, of themselves, cannot constitute such a force.

Others idealize poverty. Only the wealthy can idealize pov- erty. Poverty, we hear, provides the ideal conditions in which to practice virtue, as well as to live a healthy, carefree life, free of anxiety about wealth or preoccupation with material things. Pov- erty is none of this. In itself, poverty is only to be rejected. It deserves only the contempt in which it is held by anyone actually poor. Voluntary poverty is justifiable only in terms of solidarity with the poor, as Jesus entered into solidarity with the poor, learning with them what it means to be in the dependent con- dition of a slave (Heb. 2:15).

Others exalt poverty because, as they explain, God compen- sates for it with eternal salvation after death. As a reward for their resignation in this world, the poor are to receive eternal felicity. It has been thought that this is the way to interpret the beatitudes of the Sermon on the Mount. This was a theme of the pious European middle classes who lectured the laboring class in the nineteenth century.

What is the positive role of the poor in the liberation of the old person and the formation of the new? Their activity has four aspects.

First, the poor act by the simple assertion of their presence. The Bible says that their cry rises to God and is accepted by God. Then God responds by means of human beings. The cry of the poor is the cry of truth. It voids all systems, structures, and processes that fail to take the liberation of the poor as their primary reference. It imposes an indisputable, insuperable ref- erence. Thus, the cry of the poor obliges the whole of society to search, to innovate, to create something new, to burst barriers.

The cry of the poor is an ongoing ferment of destabilization and invention.

Second, the beginnings of human community develop among the poor, where freedom and service are one at last. The poor generate the expressions of communion that constitute the promises of a new humanity.

Third, as the vanquished of history, the poor bear within them the remnants of an ancient legacy of humanity accumulated over the centuries: the legacy of all of history's attempts to build a life of community and partnership.

Finally, when the poor receive the cooperation of the more privileged sectors of society, who help them to organize, they come together in social and political movements, religious and secular at the same time, that are struggling for the transformation of a subjugated humanity. These movements are partial and ambiguous, to be sure. So is every historical reality. But this does not prevent them from expressing, in history, the liberation promised by the Liberator God of the oppressed.[1]

(c) Historical Mediations

(i). The Poor and History. Christianity places the poor at the center of human history. And it does so not only theoretically, but practically. Christianity not only interprets history from a point of departure in the liberation of the poor; it sees to it that the poor become actual agents of history.

Can Christianity program the activity of the poor? Can it create the theory of a new history, in which the poor are the agents of that history? No. Christianity is the church of the poor, and has no more light or strength than do the poor themselves. When Christianity has any additional power, it is a power borrowed from others, from the mighty ones of history.

Of themselves alone, the poor cannot fight their way free. Christ calls the poor to freedom, and the gospel promises them freedom and life, and this not only in the next world. However, Christ does not confer on the poor the historical strength to build a parallel history. He does not give them weapons to conquer this world. He does not remove them from the history of this world to lead them to another world. Christianity under-

stands that the evangelical promises leave the poor in the midst
of this world, and that earlier history, with all of the forces at
work in it, goes on. Then how can the poor ever go free?

Christianity is not a science of history. On the contrary, Christianity is founded on the supposition that no complete, comprehensive science of history can exist. Were such a science to exist,
Christianity would be superfluous.

History would scarcely seem to serve the liberation of the
poor in any way. Are the poor not the great absentees of written
history, precisely because they have always been absent from
history in the making?

History is moved by forces beyond the control of the poor:
military, political, religious, cultural, economic, and so on. History would seem to be made up of the interplay of all these
forces: the rise and consolidation of economic, political, military,
cultural, and religious systems, competition among them, their
destruction, integration, fusion, and so on. History is the story
of rivalries and wars among politico-military and economic systems, new cultures such as new nations and civilizations, struggles among races, sexes, classes or castes, and so forth. The
elements of diversity and multiplicity in history cannot be
reduced to a simple schema.

But Christianity is not compatible with a Manichaean view of
history, in which everything would be resolved in a conflict
between forces of good and evil, forces of oppression and forces
of liberation. True, this is the anthropology that underlay the
Crusades. And yes, the Book of Revelation, the Gospel of John
itself, and various of the early Christian writings on martyrdom,
could be interpreted in this Manichaean sense. But the Crusades
were not an expression of Christian revelation, and the church
did not approve the dualistic extremes of a certain theology of
martyrdom.

If we take the Bible as a whole, and follow the development
of Christian tradition, we observe historical forces that affect
liberation in a positive sense. God uses these historical forces
for the salvation of the poor and oppressed.

The most remarkable of such cases is that of the Persian
Empire, which delivered Israel from the Babylonian captivity
(Isa. 45). Again, despite its negative points, of which Samuel

warned, the monarchy was accepted by the prophets. And despite similar ambiguities, the prophets of Israel were willing to tolerate pagan, Phoenician architects and laborers when it came to the building of Solomon's temple, out of a consideration of their professional and technical skills. The prophets even tolerated Solomon's wealth. Turning to the New Testament, we find no radical hostility there toward the Roman Empire. On the contrary, the empire actually cooperates in the propagation of the liberating message of Christ.

In other words, the authentic Christian attitude has never been one of radical rejection of the powers of this world. The Christian attitude has been one of discernment and selectivity. Particular historical forces are in themselves indeterminate as to positive and negative effects. All have both. We must beware of identifying historical forces as purely oppressive—oppressive by their very constitution.

Frequently, historical forces that develop in the course of a quest for their own grandeur, their own expansion, are indifferent to the lot of the poor. They use the poor in the service of their own expansion, and neglect the priority of their liberation. This can occur, for example, with nationalisms, with the scientific movement, with technology, with the great world religions, or with great economic programs. These forces are not oppressive in themselves. They become so by indifference. The poor are the very weakest of persons. The poor are the utterly silent. Thus, they are the last to be served, and the ones paid the least attention in any social movement. But there is no radical, essential antagonism between forces seeking to oppress and exploit the poor, and forces seeking to liberate them.

The forces of liberation themselves are never absolutely unambiguous. As forces, they have their internal dynamisms and their own ends. The mighty, liberating activity of a historical movement frequently conceals the rise and ambition of a new controlling class. But this second fact does not necessarily cancel out the first. Only, we must take reality seriously, and exercise discernment.

Of course, we have a problem. On the one hand, the poor are caught up in this old, existing world, and the new humanity arising in their midst can grow only with the help of the historical presence of this old world. On the other hand, every historical force has its own trajectory, its own dynamisms, determinisms, and conditionings, and refuses to obey either ethical considerations or the aspirations of the oppressed.

The old world we live in is the legacy of a past that cannot be suppressed. Voluntarism has no voice in history. In our collective heritage, historical forces have acted more often to oppress the weak than to liberate them. The challenge, then, is to take the tendencies of this world and turn them upside-down.

Christianity has this to say about humanity: a transformation is possible. An inversion of history, however partial, fragmentary, or incomplete, is possible. The old world is not governed by blind fate. The human condition has never frozen stiff.

In the Third World, especially, this confidence in the possibility of transforming the condition of the poor is a new phenomenon. The defeated peoples of history have lost any memory of their victories. Their memory preserves only their defeats. This is why the first step in their liberation must be the proclamation of that very liberation. Yes, the new person is really possible.

The poor can now burst in upon history. Not that they have received some magical power to transform the world by a simple act of the will. They must look for their opening; they must find the hidden entrances, the cracks and fissures in the old structures where they can work their way in. They can act in history only by way of historical forces. History does not follow rigid determinisms. It has more flexible lines. It has its weak points, its indeterminations.

The poor can ally with historical forces. The objectives of various groups can partially coincide. The poor can receive the help of certain elements more powerful than they, but who for one reason or another have been converted to their cause. The leaders and activists of popular organizations often come from the cultural or economic upper classes. The poor can profit from the divisions and internal struggles that weaken their oppressors. The old colonial empires were defeated primarily by the mutual destruction of competing colonial powers.

(ii). Discernment. The crucial importance of historical mediations leads us to a consideration of another central point of

Christian anthropology: the importance of discernment in the selection of our mediations.

The church of our times never tires of reminding us that Christianity proposes no program of historical action. Indeed, we need only read the New Testament to see that it offers no program for the liberation of the oppressed.

Over the course of time, however, many Christians have been unable to accept the facts. They have tried to establish positive ties between their particular social programs and the gospel. Despite all historical disillusionment, the temptation is an everlasting one. Even in our day, some of the very Christians who deny that the church has a program still seek to force their fellow Christians into some specific program in the name of Christianity. No Christian era has been exempt from this inconsistency.

The Christian response to the challenge of history is discernment. Here is the core of the Christian message when it comes to action.[2] History is the matrix of what we call signs of the times. History is always at least somewhat open to the promotion of some element of the Reign of God. And not only is it open to such opportunities, but, to the eyes of faith, the signs of the times are clear about these opportunities.

Why discernment? Because there is never a perfect correspondence between end and means. The new person must be constructed with the materials of the old. There are no ideal historical means. There is no ideal political party, no ideal business enterprise, no ideal labor union, no ideal political ideology. All of these are imperfect and inadequate. But action is absolutely necessary. Option, therefore, choice, is likewise necessary. This is why there is no science of liberation. There is no such thing as a homogeneous praxis of liberation in which the desired end would proceed immediately from the means employed. There are only fragments of knowledge, and a multiplicity of practices of renewal.

Confronted with this situation, Christians do not react by flight from the world, as they may at times be tempted to do. Christians react with an act of discernment among available mediations.

Who is responsible for this discernment? When all is said and done, only the people themselves, only the poor, can make these choices. There can never be specialists or experts in this area. Why? Because there is no such thing as a science of discernment. Discernment is an art and an intuition. The self-styled experts are never the ones who will have to pay the consequences in case their recommendations fail. The "experts" always tend to confuse their "science" with their particular class interests. The intervention of various kinds of experts is useful and necessary. But the definitive options must be made by the interested parties themselves.

It is extremely difficult to allow the poor to exercise their own discernment. A long clerical tradition in the Roman Catholic Church finds priests the most qualified to exercise discernment in the name of the poor. And we find this clericalism reincarnate in the "nomenclatures" or official leadership of the liberation movements. In the laissez-faire systems of capitalistic liberalism, the bourgeoisies regard themselves as the only qualified guides of society's movement, and they manage to gain control of the popular movements. The "vanguard" role to which the Communist Party tenaciously clings shows the same process at work in self-styled socialist systems.

The signs of hope for new, decisive steps in the direction of genuine liberation are therefore those of a broader and more intensive political and social participation on the part of the popular classes, and a greater exercise of their own political and social initiative. The mediation of historical forces, however, is as necessary as ever. The signs of the authenticity of this mediation will be in its awakening of the poor.

3. CONCLUSION

What Christianity brings to the world is not primarily a doctrine, but new facts, new human realities from out of the heart of the old humanity: communities, missions, and a practice of evangelization.

These realities have no power to overcome the world. They are poor, frail yeast, present in what is weakest in the world, the poor. This yeast, however, this ferment, is sent to the world to awaken the new person in all peoples. Will it be subjugated and reconquered by the old person? This danger is always present. But there is also the promise of the transformation of this old person.

Christian hope does not flee the world. Christian hope does not reject humanity for its sinfulness and corruption. Christian hope is not sectarian. It accepts historical forces in all of their power for good.

The task of liberating the world has been entrusted to the poor — to those with the least power to accomplish it. The option for the poor is the great Christian anthropological revelation. Historical forces cannot simply be rejected on account of their imperfections. There are no adequate means to the end of preparing the new person. The poor will know how to practice discernment, on condition that we respect their intuition, decision-making capacity, and initiative. Their liberation will not come from without. No one sets another free. Only those who liberate themselves are free. Christianity offers no leadership in history. It offers Christ and the Holy Spirit to lead the poor along their path. It manifests discernment, that the new humanity may bring itself into being by the power of the Spirit. This new humanity cannot be created by others.

CHAPTER II

Person and Body

Two themes stand in intimate interconnection in the Christian message concerning the human being and humanity: the person, and the body. It may seem paradoxical, but the paradox is Christian through and through: a defense of the value and dignity of the human person requires the defense of the value and dignity of the body. The dignity of the human being is that of the human body.

From time immemorial, Christians have had to defend their assertion of the value of the body against other conceptions prevailing in the world, including their own theologies, which are continually seduced by the notions of the world around. Once more in our own day, and especially in the Third World, where the body is most threatened, Christians have to struggle against the incursions of a dualism that exalts all that is not body, a dualism that condemns or ignores the body.

In their confrontation with today's totalitarianisms, all through the course of our century, the local and regional churches have come to rely more and more on an appeal to the dignity of the human person. Official church documents have been no exception. In Latin America, the theme of "the human" has always been one of the principal weapons used by the church to confront the national security regimes and all the threats of totalitarianism.

1. THE HUMAN PERSON

It is not the task of theology to develop a philosophy of the person. Philosophy follows its own path. It will have many points of contact with the development of theology. Theology will receive the inspirations of philosophy, and philosophy will feel the repercussions of the theological pilgrimage of the people of God. However, the eminently legitimate and useful efforts of philosophers need not be rehearsed here. What I wish to do is point up certain recent developments in theology from a point of departure in the practice of the Christian people and their communities.

(a) The Dignity of the Human Person

When we consider the development of the doctrine of the Roman Catholic Church over the course of the present century, it becomes clear that the theme of the dignity of the human person is the core and fulcrum of the "social teaching of the church." What does the social teaching of the church say in this area? The essentials are contained in certain propositions in the Second Vatican Council's Pastoral Constitution on the Church in the Modern World (*Gaudium et Spes*).

(i). *Absolute Superiority of the Human Being.* First, the social teaching of the church, and Vatican Council II, maintain that there is nothing superior to the human being. Everything in society and in social institutions is to be subordinated to the good of human persons. The human person "stands above all things" (GS 26). "The disposition of affairs is to be subordinate to the personal realm and not contrariwise ..." (ibid.). "The beginning, the subject and the goal of all social institutions is and must be the human person ..." (ibid., no. 25).

In the last fifty years, the Roman Catholic Church has spoken out with increasing emphasis on the subject of the human person and the dignity of that person. The main current of thought guiding this presentation of the theme of human dignity has been the option of open confrontation with the "totalitarian society" condemned in *Octogesimo Anno* (no. 54) and then, more and more frequently, in subsequent documents as well.[1] By "totalitarian society" today these documents doubtless understand the communistic society of Eastern Europe, together with the dictatorships, especially the military ones, of the world of capitalism.

However, the dignity of the human person has also been a key theme of the hue and cry of the Catholic worker movements, such as Workers' Catholic Action. Here the defense of the dignity of the human person takes the form of a denunciation of the inhumane nature of the capitalist economic society in which these movements arose.

(ii). Human Rights. Second, the theme of the dignity of the human person has become ever more closely linked with that of human rights. For nearly two centuries, the Roman Catholic Church had been all but allergic to the subject of human rights. There were two reasons for this. First, the French Revolution had published a Declaration on the Rights of Man and Citizen directed not only against the absolutism of secular monarchs, but against the rights of tutelage claimed by the church over society (rights since formally renounced by Vatican II). Under these conditions, the human rights ideology constituted an assault on the position of the Catholic Church in the world. On the other hand, human rights were formulated in a context, a vocabulary, and a philosophy of the exaltation of the individual over society. But the Christian message of the new person is essentially communitarian, and so was unrecognizable in the liberal individualism of the Declaration on the Rights of Man and other documents on the subject.

But in 1948, the United Nations General Assembly unanimously approved a Universal Declaration on Human Rights. Could the Catholic Church long remain aloof? Fifteen years later, Pope John XXIII broke the silence maintained by his predecessor and published, in the encyclical letter *Pacem in Terris,* a list of human rights practically identical in content with the Universal Declaration, thereby all but officially recognizing and accepting the latter (PT 8–27).

However, *Pacem in Terris* likewise insisted that certain duties corresponded to these rights (ibid., 28–38), and Catholic social teaching has fought for this view of human rights ever since. This is how the church has managed to come down on the side of human rights and yet maintain the Christian position vis-à-vis liberal individualism. Human rights may not be invoked against social solidarity. The common good has priority. Community comes first.

The problem of human rights became more complex when the rights of individuals came into competition with the "rights of peoples." The United Nations also published a Declaration of the Rights of Peoples, which found a more limited acceptance among member nations. There were many problems here. The "rights of peoples" stirred conflict not just with empires, or with the domination exercised by more powerful nations, but also with the rights of wronged minorities (or majorities) in the individual states, as well as with the rights of individuals. Which has precedence, the rights of individuals, or the rights of a people calling individuals to loyalty and sacrifice?

At all events, the human rights theme is the ideological proclamation most representative of Western society as over against the communist model. Communism suffers from a kind of inferiority complex in the area of human rights. True, it has been constrained to sign various international treaties on human rights. But communist society responds by denouncing the purely "formal" nature of the rights proclaimed by capitalist societies, calling attention to the material reality of the gains made by the citizenry of their own societies as a whole. To hesitate to acknowledge formal rights, these societies allege, is a small price to pay for such gains.

The liberal ideology conquered Latin American society and the state in the second half of the nineteenth century, leaving a legacy of enormous frustration. The subsequent movements for formal rights constituted no obstacle to the manifestation and reinforcement of a traditional society of inequality in which rights are de facto reserved to a small minority of persons. The majorities were not even informed of their new "human rights." Hence the frequency with which, before the appearance of the national security regimes, the formalism of human rights was denounced by Latin American movements of transformation.

There has been a considerable evolution since then. The revolutionary movements have discovered a certain positive content in human rights, and have begun to defend these rights no longer out of pure tactics, but as a constitutive element of the new society. The same era has seen a gradual demystification of "real socialism," with a discovery of the structural incompatibility between individual rights and actual, real socialist societies. In "socialism with democracy," however, human rights are acknowledged. As for the local and regional churches, they have polarized the theme of human rights in their manner of confronting the new authoritarian states. The subject of human rights has come to have a place all its own in the Christian denunciation of the evil of this world. We need only read the Puebla Document, or any of the innumerable other episcopal documents and declarations of the past decade.

(iii). Human Dignity Calls for Freedom. Third, the dignity of the human person requires freedom.[2] The new insistence on freedom coincides with the contemporary content of "democracy." Freedom demands that "men should act on their own judgment, enjoying and making use of a responsible freedom, not driven by coercion but motivated by a sense of duty. The demand is also made that constitutional limits should be set to the powers of government, in order that there may be no encroachment on the rightful freedom of the person and of associations" (DH 1). It belongs to the dignity of the person to be able to act freely, without coercion, and to be protected from the tyranny of authority. Without protection there can be no freedom.

The Roman Catholic Church resisted the advent of modern liberties for an entire century. As the nineteenth century dawned, there appeared, on the margins of the church, a "liberal Catholicism" that managed to survive until the accession of Pius IX. Then came the ultramontane tide of antiliberalism, and it prevailed. Here too Vatican II sanctioned an about-face, endorsing the posthumous victory of liberal Catholicism. At Vatican II, the church sanctioned democracy. Freedom has become constitutive of the human person. That person's freedom requires the recognition of the inviolability of the individual vis-à-vis any and every institution or power.[3]

Protestantism has not had the same reasons as Catholicism

for doing battle with the modern freedoms. For Protestantism, the human person is a moral agent, the subject of a responsibility. If each of us is responsible before God, then we must have a dignity as persons. Each of us is a consecrated person in the eyes of God, who confers on each of us an inalienable responsibility.

So in its most visible elements, the most universal teaching of today's Christians concerning the human person appears in the acknowledgment of the values of modernity: an affirmation of the individual in the face of all arbitrary exercise of power; the assertion of the priority of individual rights vis-à-vis society and its structures; an affirmation of the inviolability of the individual and of that individual's will not to be coerced—that is, democracy, individual liberties, and constitutional guarantees.

Today the Catholic Church recognizes a Christian authenticity at the basis of many modern aspirations for freedom. It warns, however, that Christianity is far from endorsing all of the still too liberal and individualistic content of the constitutions, declarations, and laws of so-called Western democratic societies. Why? Because these documents and statutes are almost completely lacking in a sense of solidarity, community, and the priority of the poor.

(b) Points of Contact with Philosophy

There was no room in the Greek world for the development of a concept of the human person. Vis-à-vis the family or the state, the individual had no rights. It was unthinkable that an individual could have more value than the "people," the *laos,* the city-state. Not even philosophy offered a route of access to the inalienable value of the individual. The universal, and the universal alone, was the object of philosophy, not the individual.

Greek philosophy regarded itself as the movement of a universal intelligence that was the same in all individuals, a movement acting through ideas that were independent of individual particularities. Philosophy could only see all philosophers joined in a single movement consisting in the thinking of the same ideas.

In Christianity, the conceptualization of the human being as person originates in the Old Testament, having been proclaimed there in the prophets and the wisdom literature. In the Old Testament, God's interlocutor is the concrete people of Israel as a historical people. It is from among this people that God singles out the prophets, who contract a unique, exclusive relationship with their divine appointer. God renders the prophets autonomous at the moment that they become the servants of the divine mission. For their part, the servants of wisdom receive their wisdom from God, and transmit it to their entire people.

In the New Testament, the person par excellence is Jesus Christ. Christian personalism arises from the figure of Jesus. Just as Jesus enjoys a unique and exclusive relationship with his Father, so each Christian likewise receives a unique, exclusive mission that constitutes him or her as a person.

But let us notice: in the New Testament the Father's interlocutor is the individual precisely in community. The reality of person, of mission, is not defined apart from the individual's subordination to the communities.

Biblical personalism was lived and transmitted by Christian practice. Even today there is no adequate theological treatment of biblical personalism. In the West, classical theology adopted Boethius's definition, repeated it, and endlessly commented on it.[4] It went no further. The authentic Christian conception of person must be sought in a practice to which Christians have never managed to give theoretical expression. We can discover it implicitly in certain positions so vigorously defended by active Christians without their implications awakening any interest on the part of theologians: for example, the position that the ultimate principle of all moral activity is the decision of the individual conscience, from which principle we may infer that every Christian stands in a unique, exclusive relationship with God.

Classical theology was thus the unwitting precursor of modern individualism. It failed to achieve a genuinely integrated view of person and community. True, it saw the Christian only in the church. But that church was now more an institution than a community, and the individual was no longer emancipated. The emancipation of the individual came with the Reformation, that first step in the direction of modernity. Then the Catholic Church followed.

In the twentieth century, one of the most important philosophical currents has been that of personalism. Its most outstanding representatives are Jews, although there have also been Christian personalists.[5] Personalism is a reaction against the extravagant individualism of the earlier centuries of modernity.

The Jewish philosopher Martin Buber presented an anthropology founded on what he called the "I-Thou" relationship. According to Buber, the human being is constituted a person in that relationship, and not in virtue of any relationship with the material world. The "I-Thou" relationship is one of reciprocity: a person arises only in response to the stimulus provided by another. And each person is immediately present in the other. What the "I" discovers in the "thou" and vice versa is not the subjectivity of the other, nor the projection of the subjectivity of the "I," but really the other, by virtue of a certain immediate communication.

Another, more recent Jewish philosopher, Emmanuel Levinas, broadens the perspective. His chosen adversary is the subjectivism born of modernity. Ever since Descartes, moderns have understood the person as consisting in consciousness, and the assertion of the same. This conception makes the person a reality of power, developing by and in power. This conception of person is at the basis of the modern human being, the conqueror — a "person" swept up in a continuous rivalry, implacable with enemies, experiencing the need of a powerful self-assertion in order to be convinced that he or she exists. Levinas attacks the implicit conception of person that has de facto prevailed in the modern West in contradiction of the whole biblical tradition.

For Levinas, human beings come to discover what they really are, discover themselves as persons, only in the revelation of the other. The material world, including human beings as agents of production or power, merely reflects the will to power. In these relationships human beings cannot discover their truth. But the other, the utterly different, obliges them to adopt another attitude. Human beings become real human beings, become persons, when they are converted from their subjective assertion and their will to power, to accept the interpellation of the other and look at the face of the other: the victim, the poor, the widow, the orphan, in biblical terms. The poor reveal the reality of life and of the human being, and thereby transform all attitudes.

It is interesting to note that Levinas's theme of the face of the poor was adopted by the bishops at Puebla, if only implicitly, in order to explain the awakening of personhood (Puebla 32–39).

The viewpoints of the twentieth-century personalists are interesting, as they furnish material that complements the traditional theology of personality. They show that personality is not something fixed, not the classic substance of Greek and early Judeo-Christian philosophy. Personhood is a living reality. Human beings are not simply persons; but to be a person is an opportunity offered to human beings. A human being must be born as a person; and this birth is accomplished only in communication among persons—in the reciprocity between person and person.

On the other hand, the person appears by way of a conversion of the individual, by way of a negation of oneself as isolated subject.

Finally, the themes of personalism encourage a reflection on the mutual relationship between person and community, as it shows that the person exists only in correlation with other persons.

(c) The Person in Latin America

What about personalism in Latin America?

(i). The Conquistador Today. Latin America as we know it was shaped in the era of modernity, and on the basis of an exaggeration of all of the characteristics of that modernity. A particular human type was imposed on our culture, an obligatory model for all, a hero who demands unconditional worship: the conquistador type, an individual of the male sex, white, holder of an almost unimaginably exclusive monopoly of all political and economic power, living in total subjectivism, a self-awareness surrounded by the submission of all the world beside, able to live only on the basis of relationships of superiority, steeped in a sexism combined with racism and the idiosyncrasy of the aristocrat who spends more than he has (although he has every-

thing), ostentatiously wealthy. Behold the dominant Latin American human type.

The type of the conquistador has been rather adequately supported and reinforced, as it happens, at least in many respects, by the Latin American immigrant. The immigrant had been poor. All roads had been closed to him in the world of his origin. Now he discovers a world of open spaces, and he too becomes a conquistador, if one of more modest means. He is eager to imitate the original conquistador, and furnish him with social reinforcement. He is male, he is white. The politics of the whitening of Latin America, as symbolized by the figure of the Argentinian poet Domingo Faustino Sarmiento, is a fine expression of the mutual cooperation of our two types of dominators.

Under these conditions, any abstract or universal representation of principles or definitions of the human person is in danger of evaporating into thin air. Now personalism will be just another cultural element imported from Europe to adorn the mansions of the dominators. As for the implementation of personalism, the conquistador, whether of the older type or an immigrant, can little imagine any bearing personalist themes might have on his way of life.

An effective proclamation of the human person consists first and foremost in knowing to whom the definition of person applies. It will consist in knowing this and stating it. More important than explaining what makes a human person is saying that he and she deserve the title and dignity of human person.

(ii). The Church and the Oppressed. The basic document containing the message of the church regarding the human person is Paul III's papal brief, Pastorale Officium, of 29 May 1537, addressed to the Cardinal Archbishop of Toledo, Juan de Tavera. The pope says that "the Indians, even those outside the church, are intrinsically free beings, and may not be deprived of that freedom, or of the possession of their goods. They are human beings, and therefore capable of faith and salvation" (DS 1495). The Dominicans had asked anyone with any power to speak out on behalf of the oppressed Indians, and this was the pope's response.

The message of the church regarding the human person is: "Indians are persons." That message was first proclaimed on the

famous Third Sunday of Advent of the year 1511 on the island
of Hispaniola, when the Dominican friar Antônio de Montesinos
stated in his homily: "I am a voice crying in the wilderness of
this island . . . and I shall proclaim to you your sin against the
Indians. . . . You are in mortal sin by reason of the cruelty with
which you treat this innocent race!" Montesinos's was only the
first of many voices to shout that the Indians were human beings
and that they deserved to be treated as human beings.[6]

The Indians were truly the "other," in the most complete
sense of the word encountered up to that time. They were the
survivors of another age. Their culture placed them thousands
of years behind the invaders. There was no way for them to
resist the conqueror; the Indians were the weaker, and so they
lost. Not even their bodily organism was prepared to offer any
resistance to the new microbes that came in with the conquistadors. On one side was the almighty conqueror, asserting his
strength and existing in the assertion of that strength. On the
other side was the defenseless Indian. There was no concrete,
realistic opportunity—in the absence of a conversion—that
would enable the first to recognize human personhood in the
second.

It has been said that the Christian missions, and the new local
churches created in the Americas, failed to take up the defense
of the blacks as they had of the Indians. This is not actually the
case. There were great differences, this is true. But Christianity
was not absent or silent in the face of black slavery. Various
circumstances explain the differences. In the first place, there
was far more resistance on the part of the civil authorities and
conquistadors when it came to eradicating black slavery. Both
groups could accept the Christian defense of the freedom of
Indians, who had taken refuge in unproductive and unused
lands. They could not accept the preaching of the freedom of
the black slaves who toiled on their plantations or in their mines.
The papal bulls that championed the cause of the black slaves
were simply never published in the Spanish or Portuguese
empires, and preachers who spoke out against slavery were
forthwith expelled.[7] There were such preachers, but they all
found themselves sailing back to Europe before their defense of
the blacks could even become known.

In the second place, unlike the oppression of the Indians of Latin America, black slavery was spread over a number of continents. There were black slaves in Europe at that time. Black slavery was widespread on the old side of the Atlantic, part of European and Arab culture. It was far more difficult to battle a centuries-old and far-flung institution than a new oppression like that of the Indians.

Circumstances in Latin American society today are still basically the same. On one side, an elite minority continue to regard Latin America simply as a continent for them to exploit, a land of promise, a source of fabulous wealth for the shrewd and the doughty. On the other side are a mass of men and women even weaker and more backward than the Indians of earlier times, without a culture, without traditions, without schooling, without means of production, heaped up on the outskirts of big cities in concentration-camp conditions—millions of unemployed human beings with nothing whatever to look forward to in life. The Latin American masses are simply marginalized and ignored. They are not even always exploited—only when their labor happens to become useful, and this is something that occurs with less and less frequency. What is the role of the theology of the person here?

(iii). The Human Person Today. Today the "absolute other" dwells in our midst by the millions—the ostracized, exiled human being, expelled in every sense of the word, expelled from everything, the leftover person, the one never mentioned lest the nightmare be recalled, the leper of modern times, forbidden to appear in the public square, persecuted by legal and illegal police forces alike. As Levinas himself has said, what is missing is not the private acknowledgment of this person in individual encounter; what is missing is the public acceptance of this person. To acknowledge the human person is to act in such a way that these strangers, these strange others, these poor, whose cause is proclaimed by Medellín and Puebla, be allowed to enter social life, to speak (whether or not they can express themselves correctly), to manifest their existence. Anything less will leave this human person repressed and rejected, denied. This human person is present in the practice of the advancement of Sar-

miento's "barbarians." Who is this human person? Any of these barbarians.

Some church institutions stand for the practice of their advancement: the Vicariate for Solidarity and the Vicariate for the Working-Class Ministry, both of Santiago de Chile; the Peace and Justice Service centered in Buenos Aires and directed by Adolfo Pérez Esquivel; in Brazil, the Land Ministry, the Ministry to Native Americans, the Justice and Peace Commissions. Again, many an individual promotes the human person. We need only recall the names of the three bishops who were murdered for having defended the human person against the tormentor: Oscar Romero, Enrique Angelelli, Gerardo Valencia.[8]

The problem of human rights has come to a head with the appearance of the national security regimes. The problem is not the assertion of universal principles. Our continent is awash in principles: all of the oppressive regimes have officially recognized the Universal Declaration on Human Rights. The local and regional churches have now taken responsibility for actually denouncing violations in individual cases—for asserting the rights of the particular, concrete persons who are the victims, persons who have been enemies of the regimes, suspected enemies of the regimes, or simply members of certain groups with which the regimes are uncomfortable. It is one thing to defend human rights in general, to condemn torture in general, and something else again to defend the rights of this or that particular individual, by name, when the very defense of this person is regarded as hostile and subversive and is therefore subject to the penalties that hang over the head of anyone placing "national security" at risk. It is one thing to condemn torture in general, and quite another to denounce facts that compromise this or that altogether specific organ of the intelligence community.

There have always been Christians, of every class and calling, who find that the role of the churches ought to be limited to a definition of moral principles, without entering into the particularities of individual cases. Christianity should only be universal, we hear, and not enter into the concrete particular.

On the contrary, the opposite practice, maintained by many bishops, priests, and laity, affords a practical demonstration that the mission of the word of Christ is precisely the reverse: not the assertion of universal, and therefore ineffective, principles, but action, based on a personal commitment and position-taking. The person comes to realization as such in the act of adopting a hazardous, specific position. A human being comes to be a person in confronting dangers and opposing them. The human person is promoted when the rights of those who have no rights are defended. A person arrested as a threat to national security simply disappears—officially ceases to exist, losing all rights, including the right to burial. The public defense of the disappeared confers rights on those who have no rights. It recalls the name of the now nameless one, the one missing even from cemetery registers, the woman or man who has never existed at all.

Human rights are first and foremost the rights of the poor. The penal laws are not applicable to the rich and powerful. Conversely, no law need be invoked in order to punish the poor. Any pretext whatever serves for their oppression. Daily facts show how constantly this phenomenon has been repeated over the last half-millennium. The defense of human rights consists in publicly asserting that laws are valid for the poor, too, that the poor, too, have rights, and then to be very specific about names and places. But then to defend human rights is to enter into conflict with many institutions, and with all who represent these institutions.[9] "Person" is a dangerous word. It is dangerous to be a person, and it is dangerous to call another a person.

Finally, the human person is free. No one can be called a person who is never invited to engage freely in decision making, who always obeys passively for fear of implacable repression. If the will of the mighty is imposed as an imperative of law and order, without recourse to any kind of persuasion, discussion, or exchange, the interlocutor is being treated worse than an animal. Wealthy proprietors talk to their cows and horses, but never to the peasants they have expelled from all social life. A person is someone whom one would wish to persuade, and not only at gunpoint. The approach that Bartolomé de las Casas shared with his missionaries is valid for all of life: "Divine providence has established, for everyone and for all times, one single manner of teaching men the true religion: persuasion of the understanding by way of reasoning, invitation, and a gentle moving of the will."[10]

So a human person is not to be found in an alienated consciousness. The consciousness of the poor is authentically the awareness of their helplessness, of the permanence of their humiliation. The consciousness of the rich is the assertion of power, self-assertion through "having," the need to multiply assertions of one's power in order to feel that one exists. The human person is still to be born. But it has to be born of the body of the poor Indians of our times: by acknowledging the dignity of that body, by ascribing it rights despite its lack of values, culture, and intellectuality. The person is in the face of the poor, as Puebla declared (Puebla 32–39). It is hidden there, waiting to be discovered. The human person is something that does not exist and ought to. The human person is a challenge.

2. THE BODY

Almost all of humanity's great cultures have held the body in contempt, regarding it as a kind of prison in which genuine humanity is trapped and seeing genuine humanity as something to be measured exclusively by intellectual values. Historical Christianity has rarely done much better; nearly always, it has fallen into the same distortions as have the other great cultures. But the Christian gospel knows no separation of body and soul, nor any contempt for the body. We might even say that human beings are their bodies, and that in their bodies is everything that gives them worth and value. Of course, we must have a clear understanding of the nature and value of the human body.

(a) Corporeity in the Christian Message

(i). Greek Anthropology versus Biblical Anthropology. Studies in both biblical and systematic theology evince the stark opposition between the biblical and the Greek representations of the human being. The present pages are not the place for a rehearsal of what the reader can find in any library. Greek philosophy did not acknowledge the unity of the human being. Why should it have? The end and aim of Greek philosophy was to

deliver the intellect from the fetters of the flesh. What bestowed worth and value on human beings was the intellect. The Greeks knew no interrelationship between body and intellect. They were ignorant of the functions of the brain and the nervous system. They regarded intellectual activity as absolutely autonomous. They were uninterested in language, or the function of words in thought. Hence they concocted an anthropology of a dolorous, burdensome co-existence of two or even three principles, of which the body was the lowest, and without value, at least for philosophers.

These assertions do not apply to Greek civilization across the board. I am speaking of Greek philosophy. What influenced the later development of Christianity, however, was Greek philosophy, and not the rest of Greek culture, which certainly cared about the human body. Greek art, for example, exalted the body, to the point of seeming to offer it divine worship. Greek medicine was very advanced, and testified to a passionate interest in the body.

What underlies this philosophical contempt for the body? Would it not be in part the reflex of a society based on slavery? Manual labor was the work of slaves. Hence manual labor could only be held in contempt.

In Israel, and for the first Christians, things were different. Biblical men and women were manual laborers and free persons at the same time. Jesus and his disciples were manual laborers, unacquainted with any organized intellectual activity. They had no schooling in our sense of the word. For them, thinking was no more and no less than something naturally accompanying manual activities. To them, it was clear that the human being is one. The Bible has no concept of a "body" or a "soul" that would be distinct from its counterpart. The Hebrew words we translate as "body," "flesh," "soul," or "spirit" denote not distinct parts or constitutive elements of a human being, but different aspects of the human totality. The New Testament writers, while using Greek words, use them in the sense of their Hebrew equivalents. "Flesh," for example, does not mean the body as distinct from the soul, but the entire human being in his or her weakness, mortality, and temptation to sin. Thus, "flesh" is more a matter of the intellect and will than of matter.

Human beings are carnal, fleshly, in their thoughts to the degree that they place their confidence in those thoughts and seek their salvation by means of them.

For the Christian gospel, everything in the human being is corporeal, everything is spiritual, and everything is soul. There is nothing in the human being that is not in the body. Even the spirit is in the body: spirit is the human body as directed and moved by God.

For the Greeks, the body isolates human beings, separates them from one another. Matter is the principle of individuation. Not so in the Bible. On the contrary, it is by their bodies that individuals are joined to a clan, a tribe, a people. After all, the entire body comes from other bodies: a human being is the bodily offspring of other human beings. All members of the same clan are the bodily offspring of the same ancestors. It is the same with the tribe. And the people of Israel are all bodily offspring of Abraham; thus, all Israelites are united in Abraham. Finally, all human beings are bodily offspring of Adam, and hence all relatives. By their bodies, all human beings are intimately united. These ties are not juridical or formal. They are bodily. Far from founding individualism, the body establishes community.

(ii). Incarnation of the Son of God. The most radical expression of Christian anthropology is the doctrine of the incarnation of the Son of God. Philosophers of other cultures could have imagined the presence of a god or a word of God in the human intellect — for example, in the form of an illumination or inspiration of the intellect. But they never suspected the greatest wonder of all: God actually becoming a human being, entering into the human condition through a conception and birth, becoming the offspring of a genealogy reaching back to Adam. The Son of God lived in a human body, a weak, mortal body. The Second Person of the Divine Trinity made no attempt to conceal the weaknesses of his body, or to be exempt from them. Indeed, here was a God willing to be nailed to a cross like a slave (Phil. 2:7–8). That the bodily condition of God might be evident, this incarnate God performed manual labor. The signs he gave of his mission and dignity all relate to the body. As if to show that his world was a world of bodies, he healed the sick.

He healed them to show that the Reign of God and the salvation
of women and men was in the concrete reality of the health of
the body. The evidence of his corporeity was so powerful that
his disciples, the original authors of the Gospels, not only could
not conceal it, but felt obliged to emphasize it. Still, pressures
in the opposite direction – the temptation to spiritualize the figure of Jesus – were not lacking. The movements of the Gnostic
doctrinal deviations, from the close of the first century, show
what was to come: the Greek religious world would exert every
possible pressure on the churches to bring them to adopt a less
material, more heavenly, more intellectual savior.

(iii). Resurrection of the Flesh. All salvation doctrines posit the
essential element of their message in some final liberation. We
need only examine what they propose as the terminus of the
liberation process. For Christians, the terminus of the liberation
process is the resurrection of the flesh. In the Acts of the Apostles, Luke shows us how altogether unintelligible, how completely foreign, such a message was to all Greek humanism of
the time (see Acts 17:32).

Far from thinking of final liberation as that of a soul at last
delivered from its bodily chains, Paul proclaims an eternal life
in the body itself. The body itself can live forever. The body can
be spiritualized. Body is not incompatible with spirit. On the
contrary, spirit animates the body, to make it one with it, to
form a single life.

Salvation doctrines accommodate their temporal salvation to
their ultimate salvation. A doctrine proclaiming the ultimate
deliverance of souls from the fetters of the flesh must necessarily
exalt an intellectual life in the present life, an ascetical process
of neglect, to the limit of the possible, of the needs of bodily
life. By contrast, if final deliverance is in the body, today's path-
way will be bodily as well: we reach our last end and condition
by way of the full acceptance of our bodily condition, and by
way of an activity calculated to transform precisely the body, as
Jesus acted to transform and save bodies.

(iv). Bodily Works. From Christianity's first beginnings, down
through all the centuries since, the life of church communities
has been marked by every sort of initiative on behalf of the body.
The practice of this concrete charity is the finest testimonial to

a Christian anthropology that one could ask. Millions of vocations, male, and especially female, have arisen, throughout all the Christian generations, in response to the need to attend to all forms of material, bodily misery. During the centuries of Christendom, the church always insisted on, and made a point of assuming as its own task in society, the alleviation of all bodily suffering. Today the state has taken over this function. But for eighteen centuries it was performed by the Christian communities. Even today, when social welfare programs officially claim to respond to all the ills of poverty, Christians cooperate, voluntarily and at a sacrifice, always and everywhere.

Action for the defense of human rights, as well, has always been primarily the defense of humiliated, destroyed bodies:

> Failure to find fulfillment as human persons with fundamental rights begins even before birth. People are encouraged to avoid conception of children, and even to interrupt pregnancy by means of abortion. Lack of fulfillment continues with infant malnutrition, premature abandonment, and lack of medical attention, education, and housing. This fosters an ongoing situation of disorder, which not surprisingly leads to a proliferation of criminality, prostitution, alcoholism, and drug addiction. . . . Assassinations, disappearances, arbitrary imprisonment, acts of terrorism, kidnappings, and acts of torture throughout the continent indicate a complete lack of respect for the dignity of the human person [Puebla 1261–62].

(b) The Struggle with Dualism

(i). Challenge of Ancient Dualism. For the Bible, a human being is a unit. A human being is that actual being whom we see in this particular body. And then this body is also spirit, living soul, thought. The problem arose when certain Christians came in contact with Greek thought, and with the Eastern religions at work in the Greek world at the time of Christianity's first appearance. From that time until the modern age, Christian theology—not the Christian communities—has been obliged to try to express a unitary conception of the human being in con-

cepts drawn from Greek dualism. Rarely has it succeeded in doing so.

Greek philosophy tends to propound a soul-body dualism. Soul and body are distinct substances—joined together, yes, but each with its exclusive network of activities. Indeed, the soul must struggle with the body. The soul performs its autonomous activities, and the body performs others. But then the problem arises how they can be joined together. Philosophy must attempt to explain their unity.

This is not the place to begin to trace the whole evolution of theology with regard to the soul-body relationship. Suffice it to recall that classical theology, whether Platonic or Aristotelian in its inspiration, failed to acknowledge the worth of the body, or genuinely unite it with the soul. Theological teaching considered soul and body to be two substances, or quasi-substances, associated in a union that was never harmonious. The body was scorned for its material make-up. How could it have been otherwise, with matter itself being held in contempt? Worthy, dignified activities could only be those of the soul. The soul manifested itself in the intellectual life and in acts of the will— in consciousness and conscience. Only in the soul and its activities did theologians find the image of God. What was worthy of respect in human beings was their consciousness. And theology fell into idealism.

The body was thought of as the instrument of the soul, the vehicle of the soul's activity in the world. Transitive activities, however, were inferior to immanent ones. The actions of the soul without the concurrence of the body—the activity of thinking, for instance—were superior to others. Intellectual activity was divorced from bodily, manual activity. Manual labor was inferior to contemplation.

For centuries the only theologian to emphasize the importance of avoiding an anthropological dualism was St. Thomas Aquinas. In St. Thomas's teaching, the soul is the only substantial form of the human being, and hence the substantial form of the body itself. The soul has no kind of existence apart from the body. The human being is composed of matter and form, not body and soul. Form and matter are the indissoluble components of any material substance. The body is matter, but it is also form or soul; and the soul is form, but it is also matter, or body. The body is soul, and the soul is body. But not even the Thomists remained faithful to their great doctor's teaching.

The upshot was that the Christian intellectual world implicitly inclined to a mitigated dualism, and lost interest in demonstrating the strict unity of the human being. Even Saint Thomas's doctrine was disregarded in practice. It was their theological dualism that made it so easy for theologians to justify the torture inflicted by the Inquisition, or slavery, which was a universal practice, or the reduction of the Amerindians to a condition of servitude, which many theologians attempted to justify as late as the sixteenth century. All of this was possible only because, for theologians, the body was not the real human being. To torture the body, to deprive the body of its liberty, could be justified, since the body was somehow external to the human person, and its mere instrument.

(ii). The Problem of Sects. From remotest antiquity, Western history testifies to the constant appearance of spiritualistic sects. Part religious and part philosophical, some have persisted to our own day, and new ones are constantly arising. All are founded on a radical dualism: the human being as the locus of two contradictory realities, one good, proceeding from a good God, the other evil, and proceeding from a principle of evil. The body emerges from evil and returns thither, taking the soul with it if it can. The soul, on the other hand, is naturally good. Salvation, consequently, consists in an emancipation from the body and a life adapted to the nature of the soul. Among innumerable variations on the theme is a moral perversity consistent with such a low esteem of the body or its importance for salvation. After all, if the body is evil it is already condemned, and it matters little what it does. The soul wafts above all this, uncompromised by sins of the flesh. At the other extreme, members of sects frequently practice high virtue, and offer the example of a heroic ascetical life.

History's best-known sect, owing to the repercussions it has had beyond its time and place, was that of the Cathari (the "pure"), also called Albigenses after their illustrious center at Albi in southern France. By the early part of the thirteenth century the Cathari movement had won over a great part of

Christendom. Indeed the Albigensian crisis can be said to have occasioned the creation of the Inquisition, the Dominican Order, the Kingdom of France, medieval canonical legislation, and the Crusades against the heretics. It provoked the convocation of the Fourth Lateran Council, which was for medieval Christianity what the Council of Trent was for the modern Catholic Church and what Vatican II is for our immediate future.

The core of the Albigensian sect and of all similar sects was their anthropology and their rejection of the body. The intervention of the council was meant in part to defend the value of the human body and to reassert the tradition's teaching on the issue. The fundamental support of the orthodox doctrine on the matter was the dogma of the incarnation of the Second Person of the Blessed Trinity. If the Word of God had assumed a human body, then this body pertained to the very essence of the human being, and ought scarcely to constitute an object of contempt.

The Fourth Lateran Council defines that God is the creator of all that exists, and not only of spiritual reality, as the sects insisted. Among the creatures the council mentions by name is the human creature, "constituted at once of body and spirit" (DS 800). The intent of this conciliar definition was to attribute the origin of the human body to God and thus to endow it with positive value. The same text cites the unity of the human being. Nowhere is that being said to have two "parts" or two "substances." On the contrary, the council insists on the community, the fusion, of body and spirit. The First Vatican Council likewise speaks of God as creator and the human being as God's creature, citing Lateran IV verbatim.

In the era of the Enlightenment, various philosophers were seduced by a fundamentalistic interpretation of Aristotle, and abandoned his Christian reading at the hands of the thirteenth-century Dominicans. The Enlightenment philosophers concluded from the text of Aristotle that the soul is mortal. After all, the soul is the substantial form of the body, or better, the substantial form of the matter of a human being; when the matter corrupts, then, its life-giving form, too, must have died.

St. Thomas himself, in the course of his defense of the human being's composition not of two parts, but of matter and form, neither of which has an independent existence, had already encountered this difficulty. His solution had been to treat human beings as a special case. The human soul is a case apart, by divine privilege, in its very creation. Another difficulty had been that the followers of Aristotle held the existence of a single human soul for all members of the human species. If the soul is the principle of reason, and reason is the same for all, then there is no basis for positing a multiplicity of souls. The principle and origin of individuation is matter, not soul. The Fifth Lateran Council condemned these notions, defending the individuality and the immortality of the soul. It did not attempt to explain why the soul is immortal. But least of all did it propose a dualistic view of the human being in order to justify the immortality of the soul. "We condemn and reprove all who assert that the intellective soul is mortal, or single in all human beings," it says (DS 1440). Fifth Lateran was simply defending the human being's continued existence after death. Something makes it possible for a human being to keep its identity after death, and we call this something the soul.

In these documents the church does not pretend to explain what the soul is or give it any philosophical explanation. What it means by the word "soul" is simply that the principle that bestows identity upon a human being continues to exist after death, awaiting resurrection. Not everything in us purely and simply disappears.

(iii). Human Nature as Experienced by a Christian People. The notion the Christian people have held of their humanity, a notion handed down to them from generation to generation, is not easy to ascertain. Documents are few and far between, and those that exist have as yet been insufficiently studied by historians. Still, certain statements can be made.

First, the popular Christian conception of the human being is manifested in images. Paintings and sculptures of men and women, images of human bodies, have been accorded an important place in Christianity. Christian art gradually detached itself from conventional, abstract shapes, then from figures of animals and plants, to show the human body in an appreciative, idealizing way. Why? Because of a Christian faith in the incarnation of the divine Word, which implies a positive appraisal of the human body. There have been Christian iconoclastic ("image-breaking") movements in East and West alike. But the Catholic Church has always reacted vigorously against them.

Could we measure our faith in the worth of the human body by the quality of its images, we should have to acknowledge a deterioration in that faith over the course of the twentieth century. Popular taste is now very strongly attracted to more conventional, less "human," images. And there is the great popularity of the sects with so many of the poor, in the traditional severity of peasant culture.

In the West, this traditional, rigoristic attitude toward the body acquired an even broader base in the "penitential movement" that enjoyed such popularity in the church from the Middle Ages to the beginning of the twentieth century. The penitential movement has been studied by various scholars, including the French historian Jean Delumeau. It was one of the dominant elements of Western culture, penetrating all social classes. It was characterized by an intense sense of sin, coupled with a deep desire for purification. Crusades, indulgences, auricular confession, penitential practices, scourgings, ·penitential processions, penitential orders of men and women, penitential pilgrimages, were all in the forefront of the practices of the Christian people of the West.

Popular preachers seized on this movement as a tool for their task of guiding and inspiring the Christian people. They both used and abused the sense of sin and the desire for purification it instilled in simple persons. Their sermons rang with a collective and individual indictment for sin. They were well aware of the people's openness to this kind of self-incrimination, and the penitential movement seemed to be the handiest means of improving the popular soul.

It was the body, first and foremost, that was incriminated. There were of course other sins—pride and gluttony, especially—but sexual sins were really the ones to worry about. Thus the body fell under a heavy indictment. It was the body, then, especially, that had to do penance. This was evidence of a potentially healthy Christian realism, but it also tended to impugn the value of God's creation, and to divide human beings into a more sinful bodily part and a less sinful intellectual part.

In any case, the penitential movement and its cult of self-incrimination have disappeared over the course of the present century. The culture currently prevailing in North America has introduced a new anthropology, one which goes in the opposite direction and empties both consciences and customs of the last vestige of personal guilt. The stern indictment of the body of a hundred years ago has been succeeded by a boundless glorification of it now. Will this new excess then be followed by yet another crisis, in the form of a new incrimination of the body?

(iv). Modern Dualism. The modern age and the scientific movement have saddled Western civilization with a new anthropology. Human beings have become the object of scientific research. But as objects of scientific research, they are no longer living, breathing human beings. Science observes human beings with the same detachment as it observes a stone or a tool, progressively reducing human beings to the quantitative predicates of their "objective" being.

Once the physical sciences began to dominate our culture, human beings began to be regarded simply as marvellous machines, governed by the same laws of physics and chemistry as the rest of the material world. Then came the biological, psychological, and social sciences, and other models were created, but still in function of objective forces. Human beings continued to be merely the objectively observable human organism. Scientists came to the conclusion that there was no such thing as a soul, because there was nothing in their observations to warrant such a notion. Everything about the human being, we were told, could be explained by the action of the countless external forces to which this being is subject.

One reality, however, was admittedly left unexplained: consciousness. Some scientists concluded that consciousness was only an apparent reality, not an actual one—a reflection of actual reality, surely, but in itself a mere product of the imagination, generated by biological functions for the sake of a greater functional efficiency. These scientists were generally of a materialistic tendency.

Others concluded that, in view of the importance of human consciousness, human beings must be composed of two parts. One part was scientifically observable, and analogous to other natural objects: the body. The other part, not available to external observation, but present only to the subject, is called consciousness. We might well represent consciousness here by Descartes's basic evidence: I think. Consciousness was the awareness of the thinking "I," and, as objectively unobservable, must be independent of the body. These scientists tended more to the side of idealism. The problem was how to explain the union of body and consciousness. How could consciousness act on matter, and vice versa?

Idealism held that consciousness somehow acted on matter, indeed that it was the principal mover of culture and history. Materialists denied that consciousness was ultimately capable of acting on matter; indeed, they insisted, it was only a reflection of material forces.

The idealistic position, modern scientific soul-body dualism, generated a conflict between idealism and materialism. At the level of philosophical reflection, however, this antagonism has been overcome in the twentieth century, although there are still broad sectors, especially of persons with a smattering of an intellectual background, who find it necessary to take sides, either with idealism or with materialism.

Some philosophers claim to be able to deduce, from the premise of materialism, the nonexistence of God and the mortality of the soul. In Pius IX's *Syllabus of Errors* (1864), and at the First Vatican Council (1869–70), materialism was condemned (DS 2958). Later, when communism claimed to have destroyed all religion in the name of materialism, materialism was once more condemned, by Pius XI in his *Quadragesimo Anno* (1931, nos. 117–19).

Up until modern times, then, the great problem for Christians was idealism. But then scientism appeared, and with it a new apologetics. Now the threat came from the absolutist claims of so many scientists. It was not true, Christianity insisted, that the human being was nothing more than what "objective observation" could verify. Scientism furnishes a pretext for all manner of manipulation of human creatures: manipulation by the state, by ideologies, by systems of communication, manipulation by medicine and genetics, manipulation by educational systems, and so forth. If human beings are no more than objects, like the other objects of science, then there is no reason to limit this manipulation. At bottom, the Christian rejection of materialism is the rejection of all manipulation perpetrated for objective, "scientific" reasons.

(c) The Human Body

(i). Objective Body and Real Body. The objective body is the body as perceived by others. However, others cannot know exactly what makes my body my body. Others do not see my suffering, my emotions, my desires. They glimpse only the wrapper. They do not see what that wrapper contains. Nor, therefore, do the sciences know the reality of my body. Scientists can make a great many observations, and thanks to these observations solve a great many problems encountered by my body throughout the course of my life. It is not the task of theology to review, discuss, approve, or reject scientific observations and techniques of activity on the body, so long as these observations and techniques do not bear on what is most important of all about my body. But, for example, since it is my body, I am unwilling to accept its subjection to biological or psychological experimentation — however much it may be in the interests of scientific institutions so to subject it — if it might prove to be prejudicial to my well-being.

Clearly, a human being is not the objective body the scientists study, although all such investigation bears on human beings in some way. After all, scientists will never be able to discover what my body is as I experience it. If they could, they would discover who I am. A patient is correct, then, to approach physicians a bit gingerly, especially when they do not know the patient on a personal basis. No physician can know what I feel, unless I communicate my feelings to him or her.

The real body is my body. Through my body, I am present to the rest of the universe. I know that I am only a part of the universe, but my body makes me the center of that universe. It enables me to situate myself as, and feel myself to be, a center of impressions, actions, and reactions. In a way, my body is a mere element of the whole, as I regard the lower animals to be. But it is the human body that makes the subject be. With a body run down by disease, a person exists the less. An invalid has already undergone a partial death.

My "I" is not my consciousness, least of all a consciousness separated from my body. My "I" is my body. I am this body. But this body of which I have a living experience is not this body as seen from without. Consciousness is a function of the human body. Consciousness is not the soul. The soul is the seed of eternal life. The soul is what is eternal in the human being. The soul is that which stands in a relation with God. The soul is what subsists after death. We have no consciousness of our soul. Consciousness is too superficial for this. Consciousness affords no authentic knowledge of a human being. It is not by consciousness, but by charity, that we attain to this truth.

My consciousness divides me from others, positing me as an isolated individual. My body, however, joins me with other human beings, since my body is a means of communication and a common life. My thought separates me from others. But my body unites me with others, and this by innumerable avenues. Two bodies side by side communicate. Two thoughts side by side are reciprocally opaque.

This is the approach taken by a good many philosophers today, and it expresses more felicitously than earlier philosophies did what is included in the Christian concept of the human being.

(ii). The Brain. Of all of the results of scientific research on human beings, none has been of more importance than the gradual elucidation of the function of the nervous system, and particularly of our tripartite brain. The human body is primarily its brain. It is of course also the instrument and tool of the brain — hands and muscles. But hands and muscles can largely be replaced by other instruments, giving the brain proportionately more importance.

Before production techniques reached their present state of development, the major portion of human life was devoted to muscular activities: the heavy work of farming, crafts, and industry. Gradually, however, more and more people have begun to spend their working hours performing functions with their brains, rather than working with their hands and muscles.

The brain consists of about fourteen billion neurons, or nerve cells, capable of storing many millions of bits of information. The brain is so complex and rich that no individual could con-

ceivably make use of all of its capabilities in the course of a
lifetime. The brain is a gigantic memory box. The human subject
may receive tens of thousands of pieces of information in a day.
Depending on the surrounding culture, depending on the multiplicity of human contacts and transmittals of information, the
human body becomes humanized, sometimes a great deal, sometimes only a little.

At the same time, billions of connections are possible among
all the data that have thus been preserved. Consequently, the
brain is capable of billions of expressions, which in turn can
represent billions of possibilities for action. The creativity of the
brain is virtually unlimited. Actual human subjects cannot implement so much as a small fraction of its creative potential. Hidden
among its manifold recesses, millions of potential desires and
aspirations stand ready to emerge.

Thanks to a complexifying nervous system, human beings
mold their own bodies. They change their bodies. The body
today is no longer "natural." It is now the product of a long
"cultural history." From the prehistoric primates to homo sapiens, evolution proceeded slowly. For five million years it mean-
dered. Then, some forty thousand years ago, homo sapiens
appeared, and the velocity of human evolution made a quantum
leap. More and more, human beings create themselves, and they
do so in their bodies.

(iii). Conscious and Unconscious. The human body is a fantastic memory machine. But only a minute portion of its memories ever reach the conscious state. All the rest remain in the
unconscious. The psyche of each of us, then, carries about an
immense unconscious component, moving and directing our
lives, not always very well, but always. Consciously, none of us
could possibly solve the thousands of problems that daily challenge the body. The systematic discovery and investigation of
the unconscious is one of the great contributions of the contemporary psychological sciences. From time immemorial, on a pre-
scientific level, however, men and women have known the
importance of dreams, myths, and animal life for an understanding of human nature.

The unconscious is the product of the accumulated experience of all of the ancestors of homo sapiens over the course of

five million years and of homo sapiens themselves over the last forty thousand years. Human aggressiveness, the will to live and to dominate, sexuality, the will to procreate, our desire to project our concern with the mysteries of life (especially the mystery of death), as well as with the forces that guide the universe — all of this lies hidden in the unconscious, acting upon our bodies in the dark, but acting most effectively. Indeed, the unconscious acts not only upon our bodies, but is intimately intertwined with our entire environment and culture, for over a good part of the life of homo sapiens these past forty thousand years the unconscious has been projected upon cultural objects that today make up civilization and direct the internal thrusts of our bodies by furnishing these dynamisms with external targets. However, although we project the unconscious upon these cultural objects, culture itself remains stored for the most part in the unconscious — it is part of the storehouse of the inner brain. A person who feels any need can rummage about in the unconscious and come up with the necessary elements to solve the problem of that need. Of course, the process is incomparably more complex than pulling something down from the shelves of the corner grocery.

(iv). Expressions of the Body. The body lives by expressing itself. The human body differs from the bodies of the other animals precisely by its activity. It is caught up in a continuous self-expression. The brain is constantly inventing new expressions. When certain work methods oblige us to repeat the same activity endlessly, we have the sensation of being reduced to the condition of a brute beast. We achieve our being by inventing our own expressions.

Our relationship with the material world, then, important as it is, is not the most human thing about us. The highest level of our being, the level destined to grow without ever stopping, is that of our relationship with others. Our relationship with matter requires little expression. But our social life multiplies its expressions by the millions.

The following chapters will deal with the principal kinds of bodily expression. On a lower level, the body expresses itself in order to communicate purely functional pieces of information. Numerically, these expressions are far and away the most important. Qualitatively speaking, however, there are more complex, inventive, and meaningful expressions, charged with more content than functional signs could ever contain, and these expressions are of incomparably more specifically human value. These are our expressions of emotion or eros, artistic expressions, and expressions of worship.

(v). Knowledge of the Body. Scientific knowledge, being objective and external, fails to grasp the basic makeup of the human body. Scientific information is an enormous help, once it is subordinated to an overall view furnished by other sources. From the moment it is practiced exclusively, however, scientific knowledge of human beings leads to the manipulation and destruction of the human element in them. Besides, there is no such thing as pure scientific knowledge. Scientific cognition inevitably contains the reflection of the observer's viewpoint. Objective as they may seek to be, scientists never disappear from their scientific observation. All science comports a coefficient of ideology. Again, science easily becomes the expression of a will to power. Thanks to their science, scientists are an elite. They have the weapons needed to subjugate the human beings they observe. They can use science to serve these human beings, of course, but they can also use it to dominate them, and to win social privileges for themselves. And the first of these social privileges is a sense of all-conquering individualism.

We shall never be able to dispense with the cognitions furnished by myth and symbol, which integrate and express traditional wisdom based on a long experience of life. The ultimate reality of the human body will never be an object of science. That reality does not permit science to "get that close." And the only remote knowledge it permits is gained precisely by means of symbolical cognition.

Christianity rejects none of the value of myth and symbol. Quite the contrary. Of course, Christianity knows the value of scientific knowledge, which develops by means of objective observations, in which the human body is taken as an object of observation like any other body in the universe. But in scientific knowing, I prescind from the fact that the body under observation is my body. In other words, I prescind from the most important thing about that body. I prescind from what makes that body my body, the body by which I live, by which I am a real existent in the world and not a pure phenomenon, since I exist by that body and no other.

This is why the ultimate ground of the human body will always be an inexpressible mystery. However, it is possible to intimate something of this mystery through analogies and comparisons. This is the role of both myth and ritual. The Bible, too, transmits myths it did not create, but received from its cultural context, that of ancient Semitic civilizations. But the Bible purifies the ancient myths of the Near East. It modifies them, and only then incorporates them into its conception of being human. The biblical myths contain a part of the truth about being human—a part that will never be expressed in scientific concepts. Always open to new commentary, the biblical myths constitute an inexhaustible source of reflection on the human condition. Bible history is chock-full of myth. Not that biblical myths are the only ones of any value. The myths of other civilizations, as well, shed light on the human mystery. In this sense, the ancient bodies of wisdom contain a message about being human that will never be out of date. Marx himself, modern as he was in his view of humanity, admitted that the ancient Greek myths continue to have their instructional value, still have something to say to us.

It would be a mistake, then, to think that the human sciences render ancient wisdom superfluous. Myths constitute a valid avenue of cognition. Of course, we cannot expect them to offer scientific cognition. The type of cognition they present is of another order. Yesterday's conflicts between the sciences and the traditional anthropology of the churches arose from a confusion. Both Christians and their critics regarded the myths as the equivalent of science; but as science they were erroneous; hence myth must be falsehood—it does not tell the truth. In reality, of course, there is no incompatibility between myth and science. They do different things. The account of our first parents, Adam and Eve, is still a source of knowledge about ourselves. Of course, it does not provide scientific knowledge.

On the other hand, we do not come to know what being human is by words alone, but by our own actions, as well. Work and other activities furnish a direct, immediate knowledge of being human, however little this knowledge can be conveyed in words. Side by side with activities guided by reason—work, for example—other, nonrational, activities exist: for example, ritual. Ritual is also a means of cognition. Christianity has accepted ritual, as well, and this from the beginning of its history. Christianity does not accept just any ritual. It subordinates it to its essential message. But it knows very well that there are profound human cognitions that penetrate the knower only by way of gesture and rite. Human beings learn to discover and to know themselves through bodily expression—for example, through gestures and rites of adoration, thanksgiving, supplication, and satisfaction. In such gestures, they discover the dynamic reality of God, neighbor, and self, in one fell swoop.

(d) Sexuality

(i). Significance of the Fact of Sexuality. The Bible wholly accepts the fact of human sexuality. God created human beings not primarily as individuals, but primarily as a couple. "In the divine image he created him; male and female he created them" (Gen. 1:27). And throughout the rest of its pages, the Bible rather consistently maintains the validity of this observation on the part of the author of the Priestly account of creation. There are two ways of being human, male and female. Of course, the Bible does not favor us with any scientific knowledge of sexuality. What it does tell us comes either from ancient myths, perhaps corrected or transformed, but still in the category of symbolical thought, or else from the common experience of the sexes in Israel or among its neighbors. And yet, even by means of such fragmentary instruments, it does shed a certain light on the subject.

It is not the place of theology to explain sexuality, even by way of a repetition or condensation of the body of knowledge of sexuality that we possess today. The responsibility of theology is to transmit to human beings today certain teachings and insights emerging either from the Christian experience of the past two millennia, or from the experience of ancient Israel, the forerunner of Christianity and a particularly precious font of Christian knowledge for all time to come.

Up until the twentieth century, human ignorance of sexuality was all but beyond our imagining today. As late as about a century ago, no one understood the fertilization process. Therefore no one understood the precise roles of male and female in conception. Nor was anything known of the physiological and psychological development of sexuality in the maturation of the individuals of either sex. All that was known about sexuality came either from a wisdom based on the actual experience of sexual relations, or from a projection of desires and obscure dreams projected into myth, traditional sexual customs, and sexual institutions. Peoples carried out male circumcision and female excision, rituals of adolescent initiation, marriage rites, birth rituals, and so on, without knowing why they were doing so. Their motivations were unconscious. Individuals felt bound by the obligation of these rituals, but could not have said why. Sexuality was, par excellence, the reign of the unconscious – of rigid, incomprehensible obligations, of taboo and mystery, and, finally, of silence. It was the region of human existence to which one referred only by innuendo, mostly for lack of anything approaching a rational way of expressing the content of this area of human concern.

To be sure, ancient societies were deeply impressed, and very frightened, by so many of the possible manifestations of sexuality, and especially by the havoc sexuality can wreak in individuals, families, and societies. Accordingly, these societies sought to confine the exercise of sexuality within rigid institutions. But sexuality is an anarchical factor in human relations, and sexual institutions had to struggle with forces of dissolution. Every new generation threatens the existence of traditional sexual institutions.

These institutions made no attempt to explain the inexplicable. They only sought to secure a common end: the survival of their society or human group. They knew that sexual deviancy placed the survival of the social group at risk. Roman society finally ceased to procreate, thereby preparing its own ruin. All ancient cultures were aware of this danger, and sought to curb it by controlling their sexuality. They knew that permissiveness means suicide.

But they had no scientific knowledge of any of this, and modern rationalism saw this as enough to justify condemning them.

Nowadays the members of industrialized society know a great
deal about sex. But this does not make them wise. On the contrary, it seems to make them more foolish.

Christian institutions took extensive inspiration from those of
the peoples who adopted Christianity as their religion. They
took up both the end and the means of these erstwhile pagan
institutions: the end was the survival of the people, the means
was procreation and the family stability required if children are
to have a wholesome upbringing. Without a stable family, society
fails to transmit cultural values across the generations. Christian
institutions were created by and for poor peoples. Royalty, the
nobility, the wealthy and powerful, have always regarded themselves as exempt from the precepts of common sexual morality,
and have managed to maintain a deviant behavior that could
not harm the people because it was inimitable. In vain have
Christian preachers denounced the sexual vices of the high and
mighty.

Thus, sexuality was far more thoroughly institutionalized than
understood or interpreted. Traditional peoples have often been
reserved when it comes to poetic or other literary expressions
of sexuality, and the other arts follow the same pattern. Amidst
curiosity on the one hand, and fear on the other, sexuality has
frequently acquired a special, and specially protected, status of
semi-clandestinity. Prostitution, sacred or secular, has held an
ambivalent place in most societies. Tolerated, and systematically
developed, it has remained on the margin of established societies, maintaining itself by its own devices.

Christian peoples have found little difficulty in maintaining
the practice of the monogamy prescribed by Jesus. The vast
majority of the poor have never had a choice. And monogamy
was the only regimen compatible with the survival of the family
and a wholesome upbringing of children. Polygamy and other
institutions contrary to monogamy have been the privilege of
the powerful. The latter have never submitted to the sexual
restraints imposed on the poor and weak. Thus in the past, the
governing classes of Christian societies often found themselves
marginalized from the rest of society, if not indeed publicly
excommunicated by the church. But these classes constituted a

small minority, and their behavior had no effect on the great masses of Christian people.

When slaves abandoned monogamous marriage, it was because their owners, in contravention of all the laws of the church, forbade them to contract marriage at all. But here once more the ruling classes refused to accept church discipline, and willingly lived as outlaws in the eyes of canonical legislation.

All peoples adopting Christianity were patriarchal societies. Men dominated women, and they did not abandon the structures of this domination when they adopted Christianity. The Bible itself, in its institutions as in its accounts, reflects the male domination of the peoples who made up its society. Christian institutions are still steeped in patriarchalism, although Christianity has provided women with an opportunity to exercise their freedom to a degree to which they had rarely or never before been accustomed.

Ancient societies dealt with sexuality in terms of their family-oriented or marriage-oriented institutions. Genuine sexual love was not unknown in Christian societies, although it could come to expression only within the bond of holy matrimony. But sexual love was regarded as dangerous in the extreme. The love-life of the Western world has transpired in terms of the myth of Tristan and Isolde: love and death are inextricably intertwined. Love is a death-force. It does not follow the rules. It knows no bounds. Sexual love is insatiable desire, and behaves aś if it were quite determined to destroy all that lies in its path. This was the attitude not of monks or nuns, but of mothers and fathers, and it endured for centuries. Love literature has always been frowned on by the church, and God forbid it come near hearth or home. It, too, was the privilege of a social elite above the law, then.

All of this prevailed in a context of the traditional Christian teaching on sexuality. Christian peoples were precious little interested in the "meaning" of sexuality. They knew its immense strength, and did their best to confine it to manageable channels.

The history of Latin America is a dramatic demonstration of the extent to which human sexuality is branded, traumatized, and distorted by social sin. In subhuman conditions of material destitution, in a situation of social dissolution and extreme oppression, sexuality binds neither a balanced, harmonious couple, nor a family capable of rearing future generations. The spectacle of sexual misery on the plantations (of sugar and cocoa, for example), in the mines, in the shantytowns and slums, among the itinerant populations, leaps out at even the most casual observer. Sex has become completely isolated from the building of human persons and communities.

(ii). Equality of the Sexes. The Bible provides a solid foundation for the equality of men and women. True, the Old Testament falls short of perfection here. In establishing circumcision as the sign of adoption as children of God, the Old Testament proclaims an absolute privilege of the male sex. Men are members of the people of God more completely than are women. The radical New Testament difference is the suppression of circumcision. And with circumcision, all other signs of male dominance go by the board. The path to salvation is faith, and the Gospels present as many examples of women's faith as men's. Neither sex is any closer to faith and salvation than the other. Accordingly, baptism is administered to both sexes without discrimination. And of course there is no other condition for membership in the people of God. The eucharist unites women and men in a single community, unifying them to a new, perhaps unique degree in the history of cultures, in all simplicity and absence of differentiation.

True, at the institutional, organizational level, certain male privileges reappear — for example, in the selection of bishops and presbyters. But this is precisely institutional and organizational, and to that extent superficial. We do not know what the future holds for women where church ministries and church government are concerned. Women may win the battle for access to these ministries, as they may indeed then go on to transform them in depth.

True, there is a fragmentary theology of the sexual relationship in certain New Testament Letters. Best known are certain passages from Paul, which come in for so much criticism by women's liberation movements today. Paul's speculation almost always appeals to Genesis 2–3, a text which maintains a frank inequality of the sexes, although there is some attempt on the part of the sacred writer to attenuate this inequality as it may have existed in the original mythical sources of this narrative.

At all events, Paul, in taking this passage from Genesis as his point of departure, is caught in a vicious circle of sexual inequality. But precisely because he structures his speculation in terms of these passages from Genesis, we cannot ascribe a dogmatic value to his assertions. The argumentation he bases on the analogy of the body and the head do not constitute divine revelation. They constitute mere theological reflection, and are conditioned by their sources. We may not simply invoke these Pauline texts as the basis for a theology of the sexes. On the contrary, we may safely set them aside. They represent an admirable effort for the time, but they must be complemented. Jesus went further, and without becoming lost in involuted speculations on the story of Adam and Eve and the details of their creation. The Christian theologian need attribute no more authority to the Pauline passages than Paul claimed for them. And Paul's only intent was to consolidate certain structures common to the various groups of his time and place, and to provide a theoretical basis for the practical behavior of Christians living within these structures. But Christian behavior went beyond the Pauline theology, and women and men were invited to collaborate in the building of the Christian communities on an equal basis.

The norm of Christian behavior with regard to the equality of the sexes consisted first of all in the conditions specified by Jesus for membership in the community of the Reign of God. But even more important were Jesus' own attitude and behavior toward women. The Gospels emphasize Jesus' dealings with women, which are never accompanied by the least suggestion of male superiority. When it comes to marriage, Jesus prescribes a strict equality between the rights and duties of husbands and those of wives. Old Testament prescriptions favoring men over women were owing, Jesus explains, to the hardness of people's hearts.

The history of Christianity is the scene of an ongoing conflict between the inspiration of the gospel and a civilization based on male dominance. Female theologians today are in the process of unearthing the colossal corruption of a two-thousand-year-old Christianity by pagan, patriarchal structures.

Meanwhile, let us note, women managed to create for them-

selves certain areas of freedom and equality. The condition of
widows in the primitive church, or the freedoms and power won
by women in the Middle Ages in the church, are phenomena of
scant consistency with the prevailing ideological line among European peoples. Although the Catholic hierarchy—made up
entirely of individuals of the male sex—strove to subject societies
of women religious to a canonical status of dependency on their
"counterpart" male orders, women's orders long managed to
maintain a certain independence. It was only in the wake of the
Reformation that an almighty patriarchalism once more raised
its ugly head in the church, the dominant classes in society having taken advantage of the weakening of the church to impose
their own particular dominion and regime. It was the ruling
classes that imposed cloister on women who wished to serve God
and neighbor without being hampered, and, to this purpose, to
be able to move freely about in the streets.

Despite the brake applied by the male element in the church,
women can appeal to evangelical arguments in support of their
struggle for equality of dignity and rights.

As for the division of labor in the traditional family, the conclusion is scarcely warranted that women are thereby necessarily
in an inferior position. In the traditional peasant family, which
has included 90 percent of all the Christians who have ever lived,
roles have indeed been rigidly distributed. However, the authority of women in the home is total, and it has been typically they
who have exercised all authority in family matters, precisely by
virtue of their authority in the home. Women have always made
many of the major family decisions on their own authority.

Then what is the source of women's condition of inferiority?
The Bible teaches that male supremacy is a consequence of sin.
Just what is this sin, and just how should women combat it?

Women's subjugation has economic and social roots. It is in
bourgeois culture, however, that these roots are deepest. If a
woman stays at home and produces nothing for the economy,
she automatically finds herself in a condition of social inferiority.
This has not been the case with the traditional peasant woman.
For other women, the solution consisting of opening the labor
market and the professions to women has partially solved the
problem. But it has not effected any radical modification of their

condition of inferiority. Why? Because, in addition to their work outside the home, women must still assume the greater share of responsibility for domestic tasks and the rearing of children. In practice, women's access to employment outside the home, involving as it does the necessity of competing with men, has obliged them to renounce childbearing, or to be content with one or two children. After all, the right to work outside the home obliges women to compete.

The roots of sexual inequality are cultural, then. Male and female roles do not spring from a so-called human nature, but from culture. They reflect a culture. Our cultures tend to produce models of female dependency because they are impregnated with patriarchalism. The cultural battle is slower and more difficult than the struggle with economico-social structures.

Finally, the relationship of domination and subjection is expressed in the physical relationship of the two sexes. Here is its deepest root. Here, only the re-education of both sexes will be able to advance the process of women's liberation.

Of old, many sought profound reasons to justify a regime of sexual inequality. They called these reasons philosophical. They appealed to considerations drawn from the bodily or psychological life of the sexes. This was pseudoscholarship, and only hardened already imbedded prejudices. It appealed to a supposedly predominant role of the male in procreation, a male superiority in size and muscularity, and so on.

Contemporary sciences have swept away a good many pseudoscientific prejudices. The specifically human organ in the body we call the human being is the brain. But the male and female brains are identical. This fact of course has only recently begun to sink into the thinking of the church. Even St. Thomas said that a woman was the ideal companion for man only for procreation, and that for any other activity a male companion would be preferable (*ST,* I, q. 92, a. 1). This is a particularly striking example of pseudoscholarship. St. Thomas is contradicting holy scripture itself. In his defense, it might be observed that no one seems to have objected to his thesis.

Sexuality includes far more than merely our genital functions. Men and women are sexed beings from head to foot. All activities, from thought to manual labor, can be done in two ways:

masculine and feminine. Human existence plays in two different keys, and they harmonize in every chord, and not just in the act of procreation. Both ways of living life, the masculine and the feminine, are of equal value. Both are fully human—better, both together constitute the authentically human way of living.

(iii). Sexuality and the Person. The physiological and psychological sciences of this century, especially the investigation of the unconscious psyche, have revealed new aspects of sexuality, thereby opening new horizons for an understanding of the role of sexuality in the constitution of the human person. The science of the unconscious typically begins by examining the ancient myths. It is not an exact science, but a knowledge that is partly symbolical, partly scientific.

We are gradually acquiring a better understanding of the stages of the formation of the human personality, a process which begins in earliest infancy, indeed, during gestation. A child's relationship with his or her parents, as well as the relationship between the parents themselves, exert a decisive influence on this development. As for sexuality, it is present right from the start, in the child's relationship with the parents. Sexuality is a crucial factor in the discovery and constitution of the personhood of any individual, male or female.

The psychological sciences demonstrate the ambiguity of the sexual relationship. On the one hand, the reciprocal desire and approach of bodies in a love relationship awakens personhood—makes a human being a self-conscious "I" capable of acting in the world. At the same time, it is only by distancing ourselves from our mother and father, the two objects of our infantile sexual desire, that we are constituted as persons. An understanding of the interplay of withdrawal and approach helps us to a better understanding of the twin aspects of human personality. The person is an autonomous, isolated, inaccessible, incomprehensible being, who must withdraw in self-affirmation, in an assertion of self-sufficiency, maintaining a sufficient distance from others. In order to be a person, one must be one's own person. On the other hand, personhood arises from a cognitive identity, on a visceral level, with other persons. It arises from the contemplation of another person, from love, from physical contact with another. Child development is a particularly clear illustration of this phenomenon, whose reality is lifelong.

Psychoanalysis, beginning with its discoverer, Freud, far from attempting to inculcate a pansexualism such as has de facto invaded the Western world in its name, has shown very well that culture and civilization require a distance, an adequate separation, from sexual practice. Even the development of sexuality requires an alternating withdrawal and approach.

Sex that becomes the be-all and end-all of existence, destroys itself. Sex is among the human experiences that can arouse unlimited desires, desires that reality is unable to satisfy. If we allow such desires full rein, we shall have to flee reality and practical existence. Thereby we shall destroy the self, and end up in nothingness. This is what is meant when sex is described as an idol.

(iv). The Catholic Church and Sexuality. For twenty centuries, 90 percent of the Catholic Church has been composed of rural families living the gospel and looking for a compromise or reconciliation between that gospel and the customs, traditions, and institutions of patriarchal civilizations. However, there are other elements to be considered, as well, in the Catholic attitude toward sexuality.

First there was the influence of monastic life. The monks, through the centuries, had precious little means at their disposal for an interpretation of the problems and inner struggles they experienced in their attempt to live a life of continence. They expressed their problems in ideological schemas that condemned or at least spurned sexuality in general and the female sex in particular. They projected the source of their sexual temptations upon the opposite sex. And they took their inspiration much more from the themes of dualistic, spiritualistic oriental religions than from the gospel. They furnished the Christian world with its vast corpus of literature condemning sexuality and incriminating and rejecting the human body.

The extraordinary importance of the monastic life in the church as a whole from the fourth century onward explains the powerful influence exerted on the laity by this monastic literature. Doubtless these ascetical approaches have been of some help to us in bearing up under the tribulations of family life. But they have not inspired us to foster a harmonious develop-

ment of the values of sexuality. On the other hand, the impact
of monastic spirituality on the peasantry who made up the great
majority must not be exaggerated. The harm was done to the
sons and daughters of the privileged classes educated in religious
colleges. It was they who suffered from the contradiction
between what they learned in school and the lifestyles of their
society.

Nor must we forget the great offensive that has been waged
ever since the Gregorian Reform of the church of the West
(since the eleventh century, then) to force, as it were, the world
of the laity to observe the precepts of the gospel to the hilt. It
was with the Gregorian Reform that the Western church began
to demand, by church legislation as well as through the support
of civil governments, a strict application of the principle of
monogamy and the absolute indissolubility of marriage. Canon
law, the practice of auricular confession, and a campaign of the
incrimination of sex through special emphasis on sexual sins,
were the weapons by which the Catholic Church attempted to
reform and perfect the family. And this "family ministry" was
pursued unflaggingly for eight centuries. Only today has it begun
to yield to the triumph of secular Western civilization.

The family campaign waged by the church encountered terrible obstacles, especially among royalty and the nobility. And
in the seventeenth century the bourgeois entered the lists on
the side of the social elite. The latter pushed for the legitimation
of divorce, along with more premarital and extramarital freedom. The church resisted desperately. It excommunicated kings
and princes. It lost England and its possessions for refusing to
grant Henry VIII a divorce. It waged countless battles, and with
considerable success in the area of divorce, until the eighteenth
century. Only today are the last bastions of the church beginning
to crumble before the bourgeois onslaught.

As might be expected, eight centuries of such persevering toil
largely succeeded in forming a stable, virtuous family life, the
mainspring of the Christian community all through those same
centuries, though less effectively at the top and bottom of society.

The marginalized of society were often without a family life.
The very poorest, the unemployed, thieves, and prostitutes were

excluded from the family. And the campaign never managed to have much influence on the ruling classes, who maintained only a façade, in the hope of escaping ecclesiastical sanctions.

But this pastoral approach to the Christian family eventually provoked strong reaction. With the coming of the modern age, bourgeois culture began to expand, and to adopt the values of the old aristocracies, by then in decline. Thus, over the course of the past hundred years or so, accusations and campaigns against the church have been multiplying in extent and intensity. Campaigns for divorce, sexual freedom, and more recently, for contraception, sterilization, premarital and extramarital sex, and the suppression of social barriers to the free expression of sexuality, have undermined efforts to maintain a traditional Christian sexual morality. The Catholic Church has been seen as an obstacle to sexual liberation.

Of course any recourse to coercion, the use of pressure tactics in order to impose church discipline, and the abuse of guilt feelings in preaching to the people, aroused reactions difficult to regard as altogether illegitimate. With the triumph of bourgeois Catholicism, the legacy of the old Catholicism in the area of sexuality seems a heavy burden to bear. The unpopularity of the church with the masses in the Western world is due mainly to a general revolt against this legacy.

But we must observe that this reaction is typically bourgeois. The mass media are controlled by a bourgeois culture. It was through the media that bourgeois opposition to traditional Christian morality spread to the popular classes. The latter, however, have not manifested the same degree of resistance to this morality, in part because they have been less likely to allow it to oppress them.

The atmosphere of sexual freedom prevailing among the Western bourgeois classes is one of the prime components of the devastating modern movement of individualism. Sex is regarded as an individual right, simply. It has ceased to be the mystery of two persons achieving personhood together, and has ceased to be a way of shaping human community through the reciprocity of persons. The individual claims the right to self-assertion as an individual through a view of sex as merely one means to self-realization among so many.

The resistance of the Catholic Church to modern sexual morality cannot be understood apart from its struggle with the individualism so typical of modernity. Even at Vatican II, when the bishops introduced "conjugal love" into a consideration of the meaning of marriage, they did not mean "love" in the superficial modern sense. The church understands love as a community phenomenon. Love is what joins spouses together and constitutes them complete human beings. The modern demand for sexual freedom is bound up with a broader individualism. The church seeks to defend the community, along with all community limitations on individual rights. For the church, sexual love is first and foremost a community phenomenon, charged with meaning for the community and the whole people of God. The good of the individual is not excluded. But it is found precisely in the individual's bonds to the community.

The church can be criticized, however, for its persistence in seeking to impose by political and social means the ethic of the gospel on great masses of people who have now rejected Christianity and given their allegiance to modern individualism. The church is also open to criticism for its intransigence in limited cases. Since the time of the Gregorian Reform, the Roman Catholic Church has been the scene of an intransigence that surprises and frightens both the Eastern and the non-Catholic Western churches.

(e) Death and Life

(i). The Meaning of Death. No event in human life is more important to us than death. The earliest evidence of the appearance of homo sapiens on earth also reveals that new being's concern about death. Human beings have been thinking about death since the dawn of human culture, then. Death is of terrible significance for the human being.

Other animals die as we. For the human body, however, death has a meaning it does not have for other animals. They live "punctually"; they exist entirely in the present moment and have no reflective memory. By contrast, the human body is a body manufactured by its knowing subject. Over the course of the years, we have enriched our brains, we have stored up millions of bits of reflective information, we have done thousands, millions of things in a state of reflective awareness. We have constructed an immense inner edifice. We have accumulated wisdom, science, and experience. We have acquired an ability to act, to speak, and to love. After a lifetime of such acquisitions, the human body is an infinitely complex organism, and a unique, irreplaceable accomplishment. Death is an irreparable phenomenon. A subhuman animal can simply be replaced by another just like it, and it will occupy the same place in history and do the same things. This does not happen with human beings. We have self-consciousness, we are self-aware, and hence are conscious of the irreparable loss of death. Death is the realization that the immense effort of a lifetime is suddenly empty and useless. Bearing the fullness of that effort and knowledge, the body dies. All that has been built up with such persevering patience is destroyed. The children will not continue the work of the parent, but go on to do something else.

Reflective consciousness has made it possible for the body to become attached to life, to conceive a tenderness for things and persons. Suddenly all of this is in vain! Death turns life into a practical joke, and one in the worst taste. All things conspire to make us take life seriously, and when we have finally done so, it vanishes. The scandal of this has impressed the whole of humanity, as all cultures have abundantly documented. The Bible, too, decries this condition. All wisdom traditions, all philosophies, all religions and salvation messages have sought to attenuate the scandal, to find a rationality in death. And some have enabled us to die with dignity. But they have not resolved the enigma.

The Old Testament wisdom literature describes the death of a patriarch full of days, come to the end of his life's course, surrounded by his children, grandchildren, and great-grandchildren now, weary of life and satiated with its fruits, resigned to leaving a world in which he has lived life to the full. Death is life's culmination and crown. And he dies. Then his corpse is described, and we are struck by the horror of death all over again.

In modern times, Western culture has done its best to forget death—to live as if life were sheer progress, pure forward movement. But we have only succeeded in numbing our awareness, becoming so absorbed in external things that we have forgotten ourselves—and brought Western civilization to the brink of annihilation. The human condition cannot be denied with impunity.

While it occurs only at life's end, death dogs our steps at every moment. Children learn of death early in their own lives, and thus come to realize that their lives culminate in an incomprehensible *absurde*. We are aware of death every waking moment, and many a sleeping one. We find ourselves unable to detach our final moment from the present one. Death is likewise present to us in our awareness of all the dangers that beset us, which can bring death upon us in the twinkling of an eye. The masses of the poor have to live with the specter of starvation— that ever-present, everthreatening symbol par excellence of death. Only the wealthy can afford the illusion that they have come to dominate death and life. For the poor, death is ever real because it is ever visible—death from hunger, thirst, work accidents, traffic accidents, armies, police, death squads.

We live life under pain of death. Death is the condition of our existence. When mortal danger does not actually loom, still there is the threat of disease, poverty, unemployment, war—all the mini-deaths that prepare the way for the genuine article.

Death is at the center of Christianity's salvation message. Death has always been of great importance for Christian peoples, precisely because they are Christian. True, the preachers of penitence have at times dramatized death in questionable taste, for the sake of a more powerful effect on their hearers. Still, we cannot deny that death is at the center of the New Testament. The Gospels are built on the proclamation of the death and resurrection of Jesus of Nazareth. The great fact of Jesus' earthly life is his death. The eternal Son of God takes flesh: therefore he must die. To be human is to confront death, and, far from fleeing this condition, Jesus accepts it from the beginning. The Gospels present the whole of Jesus' life under the sign of his death. The dynamics of the christological hymn of Philippians (2:6–11) clearly demonstrate the link between Jesus' incarnation and his death. In his incarnation, Jesus delivered himself up to death.

Thus, human freedom will have meaning only if it includes a response to death. Were there no resurrection, says St. Paul, our faith would be in vain.

Death is so repugnant to us that St. Paul attributes its origin to sin, recalling the creation account of Genesis with its tree of life and punishment of Adam. That death does not belong to the human condition in God's original intention, but, mysteriously, is a consequence of sin, has been the constant teaching of Catholic tradition, as recalled, for example, by the councils, especially the Council of Trent (DS 1511). In other words, like sin, death cannot be attributed to the creator, but is the consequence of some occurrence among human beings. The point, however, is not what the destiny of the human body would have been according to God's original plan. What Christian teaching intends to convey is the *absurde* of death, and its incongruity in a world fashioned by the God of life.

(ii). Death and Sin. The New Testament consistently links death with sin. The essence of sin is precisely the will to kill. Sin reaches the nadir of its expression in the death of Jesus: wicked human beings murder the source of life itself (Acts 3:15). Jesus' death has revealed the nature of sin: now sin has really shown what it can do, St. John explains (John 8:37–47). In Pauline theology, sin is the cause of death: death is what sin is all about.

Murder is not constituted solely of acts that directly destroy life. There are many ways of destroying life. Jesus says that one who insults a brother is moved by a will to homicide (Matt. 5:21–22). Whatever destroys human life is sin. Behold the paradox of human existence: we aspire to life, therefore we kill. Life kills precisely for the purpose of preserving, or increasing, itself. The life of some is enhanced by the death of others. Hence the spiral of violence so often denounced in Latin America in recent times.

Weapons are not the only killers. Hunger and poverty are killers, too. Hence the tripartite circle of violence cited by Medellín and Puebla and originally denounced by Dom Hélder Câmara: the *institutionalized* violence of injustice, oppression, and poverty (the condition of so many peoples, particularly in Latin America); *revolutionary* violence, which seeks to undo the first kind of violence by force of arms; and *repressive* violence,

which seeks to undo revolutionary violence by means of an inten-
sification of the original institutionalized violence, and the circle
begins all over again, but this time in a higher key. In this circle
is the problem of sin (see Medellín, Peace, 15–19; see also
Puebla 509–10, 1259).

(iii). Life. As with death, so human life is radically different
from the life of other animals. The latter are simply carried
along by life. They merely follow its inner movement. Life is no
problem for them. All is "programmed" for them. Life is not a
task to be taken up and discharged.

But for human beings, life is task and responsibility. A simple
biological dynamism is not enough. Other animals do not commit suicide. But the human being is capable of suicide when the
will to live fails. Life is first and foremost a personal will, taken
up, fostered, and developed. Accordingly, there are different
qualities of life, of living. Some persons live more intensely,
others less. At the basis of the will to live is a faith in life, a
faith in the future. Faith is the bestower of life. Without faith,
no one lives.

Christian faith is not radically different from this common
faith of all men and women. On the contrary, Christianity is
concerned to reinforce this basic faith. It merely instills a greater
confidence, based on a higher knowledge and a higher strength.
Christian faith itself is a will to live, enlarged—and then guided
by these more open, wider ends and horizons. Faith in Christ
and faith in life are the same. Faith in Christ is faith in life
enhanced and confirmed by the security and the promise that
come from God, enlarged by the Spirit, and guided by the light
of Christ. Christ cannot be divorced from life. He is life—the
life of the body, the bread that nourishes the body, the water
that slakes the body's thirst.

Human life, furthermore, is preparation for a future. A person without a future is not alive. To live is to project ourselves
toward the future, to experiment, to struggle, to prepare, to
construct our future. In a word, life is hope. Here again, Christian hope is not radically distinct from the vital hope that animates all women and men who resolve to live. On the contrary,
it enlarges this hope of theirs, then makes it clearer and brighter.

Finally, we do not live alone. We are not alive if we do not communicate with others. In total solitude, we die. We lose our reasons for living. Life is being with others, and building with them. To live is to share faith and hope in community. There is no life without a minimum of community. Life, therefore, is solidarity—called *agapē* in the New Testament. Christianity is not alien from the solidarity that obtains among human beings. On the contrary, Christ comes to bring this solidarity in faith and hope to its culmination. Thus, Christ is life, and the life of faith, hope, and solidarity can never die. It rises again, to live forever.

(iv). Struggle. All animals struggle to live and survive. They struggle with the material world, they struggle with accidents of nature. They struggle among themselves for a greater quantity or better quality of the limited goods around them. The winners survive, and the losers either die or eke out their existence with the bare necessities of life.

With human beings, struggle has a different meaning. Raw struggle is an ever-present threat. Individuals can easily find themselves in a kill-or-be-killed situation of danger and competition. Modern society has not succeeded in eliminating the extreme forms of violence constituted by war or individual self-defense. But human life is also the ceaseless striving for a state of peace—a state in which conflicts may be resolved without recourse to violence.

Struggle is necessary not only because goods are limited, but because the diversity of conditions and qualities of life increases freedom. The mightier manage to eliminate their competitors by ever more subtle means, and succeed in monopolizing more goods and services than they have need for. They also manage to subjugate the weak, and now the weaker are forced to perform the work of the stronger. With the human animal, the field of struggle is incomparably broadened.

The humane solution, however, the human solution, consists in channeling struggles and conflicts in such a way that they do not lead to total death. The human solution is to channel an aggressiveness that, of course, can be far greater than that of the other animals.

Modern civilization, with its fabulous growth in technology, has increased competition, individualism, aggressiveness, domination, and the exploitation of the weak. The victim peoples who, in the modern era, have been swept into the cycle of colonization have been withdrawn from the sources of life as from the resources needed to improve life. Hence the inevitable, necessary struggles that, for lack of structures of dialogue and the peaceful solution of injustices, cannot always be held within the bounds of nonviolent means.

The Bible is the book of Israel's struggles for survival. The New Testament is the book of the struggles waged by Jesus and the Christian communities. Jesus' violent death is at the center of these struggles. Jesus came, as he himself said, to bring not peace, but the sword (Matt. 10:34). St. John shows us a world divided into two irreconcilable parts (John 12:37–50). St. Paul lived a life of tireless struggle.

While Christians have always sought to rise above violence in their struggles, they have not always been able to flee it. In the age of Christendom, Christians very often abused recourse to violence, to the point of undertaking "holy wars," such as the Crusades against the Muslims or the "heretics."

One way or another, life is struggle. However, it need not be a struggle against others, in which some may die that others may live. The objective of life's struggle is community—the organization of a common life. Instead of seeking all available goods for ourselves, we can seek a kind of life in common in which all may share. To live is to share, and to struggle for a just distribution of goods.

3. CONCLUSION

Nothing is clearer in the Bible than that we are our bodies. Indeed, the Christian life, as St. Paul says, is "to offer your bodies as a living sacrifice holy and acceptable to God, your spiritual worship" (Rom. 12:1). Yes, the body is a spiritual sacrifice. "You must know that your body is a temple of the Holy Spirit" (1 Cor. 6:19). A clearer definition of the human being could not be desired.

After all, the human body is different from the bodies of other animals. The human body is first and foremost the brain. The human brain is capable of maintaining a reflective consciousness and thus confers a different value on existence than a brain incapable of such consciousness. So human life, and death, as well, are different from the life and death of other animals. Each individual has an irreplaceable value. Each is destined to exist forever. With homo sapiens, no longer is an animal merely one more link in the chain of evolution of a species. Now each individual is unique.

How does human personhood develop? In interchange with others. In this interchange, sex occupies a central place. Children come to be adults in sexuality: their own, and in relation to that of their parents. In sexuality, children learn to live and to be for the sake of, and in dependence on, another. They also learn, however, the importance of taking their distance from others. The person is the one who achieves a balance between autonomy and communion, solitude and fusion. This is what we call community. There is no such thing as a person apart from community. Christianity has always opposed individualism. Western modernity has been a cataclysm of individualism, ever victimizing the hapless masses of the earth. The answer to this individualism will not be a collectivity armed only for struggle. The answer will be the end of struggle. The answer will be sharing, and community.

CHAPTER III

Human Beings
in the World

Human beings are creatures of space and time. But human space and time are different from the space and time defined by scientists, the matrix of the phenomena they observe. Human space and time have enabled humanity to spread across the face of the earth down through the centuries. This spatial dispersion has generated a multiplicity of cultures and civilizations over the course of time. Nowadays these cultures enter into more intimate, more frequent contact. But no new humanity is being formed. Only more and more confusion is generated. What, then, is the destiny of this manifold humanity condemned to live henceforward in a limited space and time? Conflict waxes apace. So does the number of questions. Where is this humanity headed, with all of its different peoples crammed up against one another? Peoples, and generations, are swept up in conflict. Will "peaceful coexistence" be the last word—the best that can be done? Or will a universal polity one day literally realize the dream of *oikoumene* —the project of universality, the dream of ancient empires? What is the Christian message regarding the future of this humanity, so one and yet so many?

1. HUMANITY IN SPACE

(a) Humanity and the Earth

(i). Earth and Space. Humanity was born on the surface of the earth. So far, it has known very little else. As for the ancients,

the only part of the earth they knew was the land in which they had been born, and certain other regions of the earth of which they had heard people speak. Up until the sixteenth century, no one imagined the vastness of the earth. Then suddenly it seemed enormous. Since that time, exploration has proceeded beyond the earth: thanks to new technology, applied in astronomy, we have discovered that our earth is but an infinitesimal speck in a vast ocean of universe.

Earth is one of the planets of one of the seven billion stars that dot our galaxy. But we now know of dozens of billions of galaxies. The distances separating them exceed all power of imagination. We receive signals from points in our expanding universe ten billion light-years away. By contrast our sun is a mere eight light-minutes distant from the earth.

And all of this enormous quantity of matter is but one of the lowest strata of the primordial element of semi-matter/semi-energy that forms the ground of the universe.

Confronted with this immensity, some of us feel simply annihilated. What are we in comparison with this colossal mass? What can human beings mean in a space and time that infinitely transcend their paltry dimensions? A first response is that we are insignificant. Smaller than a grain of dust in the universe, we are irrelevant beings.

Others imagine that there must be many human races, perhaps an infinity of them, if there exist so many billions upon billions of stars. But if there is an infinity of human races, then again, what can our own possibly mean? Current findings, however, do not tend to support the notion of a vast multiplicity of intelligent creatures scattered across the universe. For humanity to appear, the conditions required are so many and so improbable that the phenomenon itself becomes consummately improbable. It is all but a miracle that such a thing should have occurred even once. Many conditions were required for the formation of the heavy atoms that compose such a great part of our earth. Then molecules are necessary if living beings are to have cells. Then organic matter will have an infinitude of further requirements. Finally, the likelihood that the human brain should have evolved from organic matter borders on statistical monstrosity. The probability of such a miracle ever recurring seems next to none at all. Our earth is a miracle of nature, and the human being a far greater miracle still. In any case, we have no positive data that might justify our suspicion that there could be beings like ourselves on other planets of our universe. Any such notions will be pure conjecture and imagination.

The grandeur of humanity does not consist in the space and time it occupies, then. Our greatness is not quantitative, but qualitative. It consists in the unbelievable degree of organization and complexity of the material required by the human body. Each of the billions of cells of the human body is an inconceivably complex arrangement of molecules. And every molecule of human matter is a structure of such complexity that even today's microelectronic technology is helpless to decipher it.

Humanity's grandeur lies in its place in the movement of the universe toward an ever greater complexification of matter, as the poet and theologian who has taught Christians to renew their ancient admiration for the works of God, Pierre Teilhard de Chardin, has shown. Our knowledge of matter is incomparably greater than it was in Teilhard's lifetime, but his poetic Christian message still rings true.

Scientific progress has trivialized neither humanity nor the earth. The size of the earth has not diminished, nor has the greatness of the human being. Earth and human beings are still at the center of the universe. We can still say, with the old scholastics, that human beings are in some sense "everything," since the force of our curiosity and intelligence has succeeded in penetrating further and further into the universe, whose inexhaustibility is the only insuperable obstacle it has ever placed in our path.

Earth and human beings remain the end and purpose of all the created universe. The purpose of the huge explosion of the primordial element was not to create an expanding universe. It was to release energies capable of producing a greater and greater concentration and complexification. The concentration of those energies of the universe in humanity remains the end of that universe. Galileo's discoveries have been multiplied by the millions. But neither ours nor his can deprive the universe of its anthropocentrism.

Confronted with the immensity of this space of ours, we hear once more the voice of God addressing Job. The silence of the infinite spaces that struck terror into the heart of a Pascal has only grown deeper. And our response, following the example of Job himself, will once more be one of worship and obedience before the magnificence of our creator (Job 40:3–5; 42:2–6).

(ii). To Fill the Earth. God created Adam and Eve, then said: "Fill the earth and subdue it" (Gen. 1:28). And all humanity seems to have heard these words.

The peopling of the earth, however, was no quick and easy task. If homo sapiens are forty thousand years old, more human beings have lived since the thirteenth century than in all the 393 centuries before. The population of the earth did not reach its first million until the New Stone Age. At the beginning of the Christian era, only some one hundred to two hundred million people lived on the earth. Only in the twentieth century were there a billion of us. The human race today multiplies more in two generations than it did throughout all its first forty thousand years. The injunction laid upon us, "Fill the earth," then, has been accomplished, but only in our own twentieth century. We are on the way toward a certain "balance" that experts estimate in the vicinity of fifteen billion inhabitants—one hundred persons for every person alive at the time of Jesus. In numbers as in everything else, evolution is in the midst of a fantastic upward swing.

The population of earth has done its best to fill that earth. Here again, occupation of the land is the great task of the twentieth century. By far the greater part of inhabitable territory on earth remained all but uninhabited up until a few centuries ago, and population remained at a very low density until even more recently. The first region of the earth to reach a population density of forty persons per square kilometer—the concentration estimated to be required for an acceleration of history—was the region between the Rhine and the Loire in the thirteenth century.

The first human beings needed a great deal of space in order to survive. For them there was no farming, vegetable or animal. All regions of the globe were inhabited before the invention of agriculture.

Long journeys, with their exploration of unknown territory,

were an early phenomenon, and we have never tired of them. In fact, they have become longer and more important. Exploration of continents, the investigation of natural resources, of animal and vegetable species, and of all the phenomena that affect any region, were early under way. Humanity seems agitated by a thirst for movement. We "just can't sit still."

The Christian missions further stimulated this agitation, and from the very beginning. Missionaries were not so eager to discover the universe, however, as to unify it, to establish communication links among all human beings. Even before Jesus, the missionary movement was prefigured in the Jewish diaspora. There is every indication that Jews soon lived as far from their land of Palestine as India, perhaps even China. We know very little about the first Christian missionary journeys. We do know, however, that Christian missionaries reached India, China, and parts of the African continent very early.

(iii). The First Diaspora. We cannot be certain where homo sapiens first appeared, or where, therefore, humanity initiated its journeys of the exploration of the earth. What we do know is what the biblical account of the Tower of Babel seeks to inculcate: that a multiplicity of human groups appeared, almost entirely deprived of contact with one another, and with very different cultures. Each group had adapted to the territory in which it was established. This dispersal of humanity rendered communication most difficult.

In each culture, the members of a people identified humanity with their own culture. It seemed incomprehensible that strangers, different from themselves, should be human beings too. There was no category for their inclusion in the common life of the body social. In almost every land, the same word served to denote a human being and an inhabitant of that land.

Of the many cultures that arose, many disappeared, while others still survive after a complex evolution. Some have vanished for no apparent reason. Others were destroyed by conquest at the hands of other peoples.

Human beings struck root in the various corners of the earth in such a way that they came to identify with the land. They considered themselves members of that land, bound to it. After all, without it they would be unable to live a human life.

The most powerful myth of a land as belonging to a people, and a people to a land, is without doubt the myth of the land of Israel. The Old Testament has a thousand ways of describing the oneness of the people of Israel with their land, and it attributes this oneness to a decree of the God of Israel, who is also the God of the universe (see Deut. 1:8; 6:10; 7:1; 8:10; 26:9, 15; 34:4; etc.). Yahweh was said to have granted the land of Palestine to Yahweh's people, Israel. This myth is so powerful that even in our day the state of Israel invokes it as the fundamental title to its existence, and on this basis feels justified in having expelled the Palestinians from the land they had occupied for so many centuries.

With Jesus and Christianity, the myth of a people's ownership of a land is nullified. No longer can there be a sacred title or inalienable right to any land. The whole earth belongs to all. Everyone has a right to live on it and enjoy it. There are rules of justice in social organization that ought to prevail, but historical, so-called natural considerations must yield to the primacy of the ownership of all the earth by all human beings. Hence the right of migration and immigration, as opposed to the unbridled nationalism of modern centuries.

We are infinitely far from our utopia—the earth for all. As a remote transition, however, Christians claim the right to free movement throughout the entire world—the right of the Christian missions to proclaim the gospel everywhere, which includes the right to proclaim an age to come in which the world will be everyone's, voiding all so-called sacred possession of specific territories by specific peoples. Christians likewise claim the right to unrestricted immigration and emigration, on condition that these movements do no serious injury to other inhabitants of our common earth (see OA 19).

(iv). Conquest. Humanity's dispersal across the face of the earth has not been a homogeneous phenomenon. Population growth, economic development, political and military development, have all been uneven. For various reasons, certain more powerful peoples have invaded the lands occupied by weaker peoples. History shows that the political factor is decisive. The ability to mobilize many individual persons in view of a common end will generally determine the success of an attempt to control

a great deal of territory. It was the superiority of European political organization that permitted those nations to neutralize the Muslim empires, reshape them, and turn to the conquest of the rest of the earth in two successive waves, in the fifteenth and sixteenth, and again in the nineteenth centuries. European technological superiority was not prodigious. But Europeans had a better savoir-faire when it came to taking advantage of available techniques, adopting these wherever they found them, and forging them into instruments of conquest.

So the empires of the West arose, and the sun has not set on their sway. In our own day the physical conquest of territory has less importance. There are other, more economical, means to control territory.

The first empires appeared some two thousand years before Christ. The unification of Egypt, which occurred even earlier, might also be regarded as the birth of an empire.

Empires need not be unified by military might. The organization of some of them is purely political. Even within national states we find quasi-imperial relationships, in which a more powerful landowner, a more successful business enterprise, will invade the lands of those who work them, evict these workers, and begin to use the land for their exclusive profit.

In Latin America the problem of the land has existed since the sixteenth-century invasions. Our native peoples have been gradually deprived of almost all of their land. The movement is reaching a climax in our era: the Indians' last land is now being violently wrested from their possession. This was the crime of the conquistador nations who made America their empire, and this has always been the crime of the large landowners, who drive out the population, seize the land, and exploit it selfishly, for example by using it as a means to political power.

In the countryside, persons without land are obliged either to leave the area of their birth and ancestry, and submit to a de facto condition of slavery, or die of hunger. Hence the importance attributed by the church to its "land ministry."

Invaders have always rationalized their robbery. The "reasons" they have given for their deeds have always been largely mythical. Conquering armies have invariably claimed that gods had entrusted them with the mission of civilizing others; or else that the forces of nature, or the forces of history, make them the chosen ones of the earth; or they have claimed to find a sign of their imperial vocation simply in the superiority of their race or kind. The mythologies of empire have repeated themselves down through the centuries with very little variation. Conquerors have always conquered by the will of a god.

Underlying the mythological motives, however, is another, more pedestrian rationalization. Invaders accuse the inhabitants of an inability adequately to exploit the land they work. Then they have lost the right to possess it, have they not? Land ought to be in the possession of those who are capable of making it yield the most fruit, the greatest income. This is the reasoning advanced by, for instance, the corporate farms, when they rob small, isolated farmers of their land. Finally, invaders invoke moral motives, accusing the residents of all manner of perversity.

The motivations invoked by the European imperial conquerors since the fifteenth century are an excellent case in point. Their theologians have furnished them the necessary mythical and moral motives. Not all theologians have attempted to justify conquest. But those who have placed restrictions on it have had no power to prevent it, and have been simply ignored.

In the face of these conquests, which are still under way, with new kinds of empires arising year after year—invasion of lands, or forced sale thereof to large multinational corporations, for example—the church has taken the side of justice. The land belongs to all. No one has complete and absolute rights over it, since God has assigned no one any particular tract of land (John Paul II, Opening Address at the Puebla Conference, nos. 3, 4). The land should serve the interests of all, and those who can make the best use of it have the right to use it. But this does not give them the right to evict its former tenants. Conflicting rights must be reconciled. And no one has the right to exclusive ownership of land that he or she does not farm or otherwise adequately utilize. No one has exclusive rights to the fruits of a piece of land. Its produce must serve to nourish all. Nowadays, in Latin America especially, the question of the land is kept alive by the Christian communities, although with limited results as yet.

(b) Geography and Human Beings

(i). A Humanity Dominated by Geography. Until the dawn of our own century, the earth presented enormous obstacles to human enterprise. The wealth it could produce was very limited. Nature covers the earth in staggering variety. And it presents a variety of obstacles. God entrusted human beings with the mission of subduing the earth. But the earth subdued human beings instead.

Land and water lay most inconveniently. Vast oceans resisted crossing by all but the doughtiest, and swallowed up most of these. Mountains and canyons, bush, impenetrable forests, and enormous deserts either excluded the presence of human beings, or rendered their passage, by primitive conveyance, most precarious. Navigation was a deed of the utmost daring. Sea voyages in earlier times were incomparably more hazardous than space voyages are today. Travellers' accounts held a great fascination for peoples, especially as they made no great attempt to distinguish fact from fantasy. For twenty-five centuries the *Odyssey* had fascinated all peoples of the Greek cultural tradition. As late as the eighteenth century, journeys through the Amazon region, or central Africa, or the heart of Asia, seemed the supernatural exploits of superhuman beings.

Climate could be devastating. Droughts and deserts, equatorial heat and humidity provided disease and epidemic with a veritable greenhouse. Malaria, cholera, and the bubonic plague were finally overcome only in our own century. Disease and epidemic decimated whole peoples—our native Americans, for example, after the Conquest. In Europe, the great plagues of the fourteenth century reduced the population of some regions almost by half. The all but irresistible onslaught of the epidemics cancelled countless efforts of development.

Living obstacles were no more easily overcome. In our twentieth century, the beasts of the wild have been so completely contained that it is difficult to imagine the terror they struck into the hearts of our ancestors, who lived with the peril of great beasts who ravaged farms and threatened human lives. Snakes, too, and insects, were a menace to be reckoned with.

Hence the cultural isolation of early humanity. Hence also

the great heterogeneity of the levels of development achieved by our contemporary cultures. Some cultures were centuries, almost millennia ahead of others in their development, as for example the culture of the European invaders by comparison with those of the peoples of America and Africa.

Not only did the numerous human cultures exist in a state of isolation, but, even within a given culture, human beings built rural communities that were practically self-sufficient. They had no choice. Trade was limited to the exchange of a few objects that were regarded as having particularly great value. Before the twentieth century, less than 1 percent of the gross world product was destined for commerce. Each separate community had to face the great challenges of nutrition – and drought, floods, pestilence, and disease – alone.

(ii). The Human Struggle with Geography. The struggle with natural obstacles absorbed the greater part of human energies until the present century. Even today it is the principal task and challenge of a great many people. It constituted the struggle waged by the peasants for twelve thousand years, the battle of miners and artisans to dominate their raw materials, and the struggle of the first political units to dominate the energies of water, wind, and fire.

The collective unconscious of the human race, then, is constituted of the remnants of mighty battles. For centuries, indeed from time immemorial, children's imaginations have fed on sudden, unexpected combats with animals, climate, natural obstacles, mountains, rivers, seas, and foreign cultures. Our collective memory is peopled with the mythical accounts of these events. The human brain carries the memory of forty thousand years of struggle with nature's elements.

Our children today are the first generation to feed their fiery imaginations with a new fantasy: extraterrestrial beings locked in combat in outer space. Here is a unique, totally new development, and one which is sure to produce completely new cultural problems. Indeed, the problems are already here – only, we do not know how to interpret them.

The social institutions of every culture bear the reflection of a particular geography. A hot or cold, wet or dry climate, the produce of the local soil, regional diseases, mountains, rivers, or

the sea, the prairie, the pampa, the rain forest—all such things
have an influence on social institutions and the overall shape of
a society.

For nearly fifteen centuries, Christianity was rural. Faith as
lived in the countryside produced a church structure, a collective
Christian unconscious, as it were, a memory, institutions, customs, traditions, and representations that lose their value in the
modern culture of our cities. The crisis of traditional religion is
bound up with the fabulous changes occurring in humanity's
relationship with nature. The unconscious memory of the church
is rural, although the first centuries of its history were urban.
Ruralism still inspires and limits our anthropology and our practical history.

(iii). Limitations of Earth. After years of ecological campaigns,
humanity is at last beginning to perceive that the earth has limits. Arable land is limited, rainwater is limited, mineral resources
and energy sources are limited. Furthermore, humanity is now
capable of undertakings that can destroy the earth, or sabotage
its future by rendering it uninhabitable. Nuclear energy, industrial and urban pollution, and the destruction of animal and
vegetable species are no longer merely frightful specters, but
reality. Humanity is now capable of creating vast deserts, extinguishing all life in seas and rivers, and making the air unbreath-
able. None of these resources is unlimited—not the air, not the
sea, not vegetation. In a word, with the increase in population
and the disturbances provoked by our anarchical "development," we are witnessing the veritable destruction of our environment.

First of all, we have the uncontrolled growth of our urban
slums. Millions of persons live in the worst imaginable conditions, piled up on garbage heaps like so much human refuse.
The only thing they or their children ever see of the world about
them is industrial waste and litter. A civilization of trash is in
the making, once described by the sociologist Oscar Lewis as
the "culture of poverty." And since his time, the phenomenon
has everywhere spawned its like.

The chasm yawns ever deeper between a privileged minority,
who have access to a nature adapted to their real or supposed
desires (the civilization of tourism), and a majority kept at arm's

length from all that is beautiful and pleasant in the world —
deprived of air fit to breathe, and water fit to drink, without
vegetation, without parks or woods, without access to places of
natural beauty that are now reserved for tourists. The seashore,
the mountains, and the rivers are reserved for a minority of the
privileged. Available resources are swept into the service of the
tourist industry, instead of being applied to correct conditions
of the most abject poverty. Assuredly, the earth today has two
faces, one for the rich and another for the poor.

Further: the rigorous application of the mechanisms of capitalism has radically changed our attitude toward nature. Of old,
nature was dealt with more kindly. An affective fusion prevailed
between human beings, on the one hand, and animals, plants,
and geographical features, on the other. Modern criteria have
dictated a primacy of utilitarianism. Nature is merely a resource
to be exploited. Western men and women have become aggressive toward nature. They have destroyed animal species, forests
and woods, rivers and mountains. They have built monstrous
cities, for the sole purpose of extracting from them the greatest
selfish utility (see OS 21).

(c) Peoples and Their Countries

(i). The Diversity of Peoples. The human beings scattered
throughout the earth have not remained in a state of pure dispersion. They have joined together in clans, tribes, and peoples.
History creates peoples. That is, internal and external struggle,
a constant striving for domination, creates units of persons.
Every people is the crystallized residue of countless wars, conquests, and internecine strife. Ethnic units, as well, have tended
to form political units. These units have gradually come to constitute a certain order of coexistence, despite the interruption
of that coexistence by wars and the domination of foreign
empires. War has become a constitutive element of human units.
No people abides in security. Finally, peoples are tied to their
geographies. It frequently happens that various peoples have
had to share the same territory. This, too, has been a source of
innumerable conflicts. Hence the tendency to identify a people
with a territory.

All peoples have objective rights, just as do individuals. In actuality, however, many peoples have been subjugated and absorbed by other, stronger peoples. They have lost their language. Their culture has melted away into the dominant culture. Thus it was that the sixty peoples conquered by the Roman Empire lost their individuality and acquired the language and culture of the conqueror. Today's national boundaries are the expression of the modern ideal. Nearly always, however, these boundaries injure ethnic identity. History has always been stronger than peoples and their aspirations.

Other peoples have simply disintegrated in history. European colonization, for example, destroyed certain ethnic units forever. The decolonization of the Spanish American empire transpired in a context that favored its pulverization into mini-nations. Many find that, in reality, there is only one Latin American people, which has not yet been able to achieve its unity.

(ii). People, Person, Foreigner. In the traditional world, individuals cut off from their peoples had neither rights nor protection. Only merchants, in quest of fabulous profit, or exiles, rejected by their people, took the risks of expatriation. The Old Testament, however, had laws for the protection of foreigners. The people of Israel had formulated the notion that their respect for foreigners would be one of their distinctive characteristics as the people of God. The myth of Israel's slavery in Egypt before its liberation served as a basis for this respect for foreigners (Exod. 22:20; 23:9; Lev. 19:34; Deut. 10:19; 24:17–18). In the Exile, and the diaspora, the Israelites were the main beneficiaries of their own propaganda on behalf of foreigners. They lived in ghettoes, side by side with other peoples but without mixing with them.

With the advent of the Christian communities, a new reality appeared. The Christian communities arose amidst their respective, very diverse peoples. Each Christian community belonged to its people. At the same time, each belonged to a new people, a vast communion that knew no boundaries. The Christian communities were simultaneously foreign and native. Each people held them at arm's length, closing in upon itself as peoples will tend to do, so the communities were always foreign (1 Pet. 1:1; James 1:1). Yet they belonged to a universal people, and as members of a universal people, they were always and everywhere in their native land.

The condition of exiles is a miserable one. Many exiles today were driven away from the peoples among whom they were born, and from the land possessed by these peoples, for political, cultural, religious, or economic reasons. Just as miserable is the condition of internal exiles—strangers in their own land. And yet all have a homeland—the earth—and all belong to the one people of God.

(iii). Community of Peoples. Christian eschatology promises a future unification of all peoples, all tribes, all tongues, and all nations on earth in a single people in Christ (Rev. 5:9; 7:9). It is clear, then, that a historical people constitutes no definitive value as such. Human beings cannot be defined simply and solely in terms of the people to which they belong. From the Old Testament prophets to the message of Jesus, the call of the neighbor, the other, is addressed to peoples and individuals alike. Individualism in peoples, a collective individualism, is even more stubborn than in individuals. Collective individualism sacralizes itself—enshrouds itself in an aura of the sacred. The individual is sacrificed to the people, in a collective behavior of domination, exploitation, and selfishness.

Christian eschatology calls the peoples of the earth to a discovery of other peoples precisely in their otherness. The unification of peoples is not to be their absorption by a larger totality. On the contrary, the highest common reality is never a closed totality, but always a community. Peoples will unite in an exchange of their differences, abandoning their isolation, and gaining new strength precisely in the exchange. When peoples become nations, the political problem arises, and this will be the subject of a later chapter.

What can we recover from the plane of eschatology and transfer to the plane of history? The Christian contribution to the formation of the community of peoples is the evangelization of those peoples: mission. Whole libraries are devoted to the Christian mission. In our own time, the very countries that have been mission countries for centuries have become the principal missionary countries. Today more missionaries are natives of the Third World than of the First.

There have always been manifold interrelations, and a great deal of intercommunication, between Western explorers and colonizers, on the one hand, and missionaries, on the other. It could scarcely have been otherwise. Having bodies, missionaries had to have themselves transported aboard the seagoing vessels of the colonial adventurers. Belonging to a people, the people of the conquistadors, how could they have been untouched, at least on an unconscious level, by its ambitions?[1]

At all events, the missionaries were ahead of their time, far ahead of it, in their attempts to approach and acknowledge other peoples. They made enormous efforts to learn their languages, their institutions, their wisdom, their religions, and their customs, despite huge handicaps in terms of available resources. Today, a rapprochement of cultures is far more difficult than the old missionaries could have imagined. We are still, in a sense, only on the threshold of this task.

Vatican Council II inaugurated a new phase in the history of the missions. The council openly recognized the legitimacy of a diversity of culture, even acknowledging the vitality of the great world religions bound up with these cultures. Evangelization can no longer be thought of in terms of the strait-jacketing of all human beings in narrowly homogeneous frameworks. True, the procedures of the Jesuits of the sixteenth and seventeenth centuries, like the instructions issued by the Sacred Congregation for the Propagation of the Faith beginning early in the seventeenth century, were forerunners of the new openness, but they were only forerunners.[2]

Christians themselves, such as Eusebius of Caesarea or Lactantius, were seduced by the message of the empires, beginning with the Roman Empire. Three times Christians helped the dying Roman Empire rise to life again. The first time was under Constantine, founder of the Byzantine Empire. The second time was under the King of the Franks, Charlemagne, in a campaign of widely varying fortunes that ultimately failed to unify the West. The third time was with the Russian Empire of the Third Rome, Moscow.

The Roman Empire broadcast a message of universal peace and order to which St. Luke himself was not insensitive. While it is true that St. Augustine called the Roman Empire a great band of brigands, he himself exhorted Christians to defend it against devastation at the hands of the barbarians. The empire forged the unity of peoples, and maintained law and order among those peoples. While the *Pax Romana* was based on domination, at least it brought tranquility. Throughout its various episodes, the empire represented itself as the unity of all peoples. It never came close to accomplishing this dream. But the dream held, as a utopia, and seemed to justify the effort to bring all neighboring peoples under the same domination.

In the West, the collapse of the Germanic Holy Roman Empire was followed by the attempted implementation of the imperial ideal once more. The greatest possible number of peoples would be joined together in peace. Monarchs succeeded in unifying their nations and peoples, thereby laying the foundations of modern nations. Centralization, however, had cost blood and tears. Far across the sea, imperial projects yielded to modern colonialism and modern imperialism.

While the political unification of all peoples was seen to be impossible, Roman Catholics long maintained the illusion that at least they could achieve a "spiritual" unification, under the Roman pontiff. The Latin language as a basis of ideology, scholastic philosophy, and canon law would furnish the basis of the "Catholic *oikoumene*." There was resistance, however, and schism. Today the project is well on its way out of the picture, although it still has its dreamers.

Every people has always spontaneously tended to think of itself as the totality of the human race. Another, neighboring people seems a rival, exclusive unit. The two units seek to destroy one another. They cannot coexist. Actually each people ought to accept the fact that it represents only one collective human experience, conditioned by geography and history. In fact, the genuine human being is to be found precisely in openness to the radically other. It is scarcely easy to accept a member of another people as equally human, equally worthy, and, least of all, as essential to our own human experience. And yet the acknowledgment of the otherness of other peoples is the necessary condition for access to genuinely human value.

We cannot fail to recognize a Christian inspiration in the familiar Latin American utopia, the notion of a complete racial mixture. The *mestizo* would become the fusion and reconciliation of all races. The *mestizo* to be presented to the world by Latin America would be black, Amerindian (the native American), and white, all at once, and even oriental, being descended from Japanese and Chinese as well. Latin America would thereby be offering the world a cure for its pagan racism, in the form of a historically realized ideal: a magnificent commingling of the races, accompanied by a unification of all their qualities in an even more magnificent fusion of individual differences.

(d) The City

Urbanism is a science and an art. We cannot consider the whole gamut of its contributions here. It is not the role of theology to replace the sciences. However, in the Bible as in Christian tradition, cities have a great deal of meaning, which needs to be examined here. The Christian community has close traditional ties with the city.

(i). *The Reality, not the Phenomena, of the City.* Most women and men live most of their lives within the limits of a rather clearly defined space. Leave this space, and you have gone on a journey. History shows that humankind tends toward living an urban life. Even in the Neolithic culture, which was based on farming, people tended to live in villages — the tiny cities of primitive society. But it wasn't until some six to eight thousand years later that the first real cities appeared — the capitals of the first empires. Until our present century, however, the urban population of the globe never numbered more than 10 percent of the total population of the earth. By the end of this same twentieth century, we may expect to see a world society that will be 90 percent urbanized. How so? By way of the massive migration to the city of a rural population of at least five billion persons.

What is the meaning of the city? The city is basically the extension of the body. A country, a nation, a people, are concepts far too broad to stand as objects of immediate vital experience. They are abstract conceptualizations. The city is the space we live in, the space where our body moves, receives stimuli, and produces actions. The city is essentially the meeting place of thousands or millions of persons. If human persons exist only in interchange with other persons, if I know myself, learn myself, and develop only by gazing upon the face of others, where shall I find these others but in the place where I live, in my space, in my city? The city allows the greatest possible number of daily human contacts. The city, then, and before it, to a certain extent, the village, is the place of personalization.

By and large, the city is the product of the development of industry, trade, and the great organisms of production and administration. For their part, the cities promote this same development, stimulating research, science, new technology, and culture in all its expressions. The cities are the places where human evolution accelerates. Villages developed only very gradually. But once a certain population concentration had been reached, the rate of concentration accelerated geometrically.

Again, cities are the birthplace of freedom. A medieval German proverb stated, "Town air sets you free." And indeed, in the countryside the serfs remained under the domination of the landowners. Democracy, human rights, and individual liberties could arise only in cities. While modern police forces manage to keep city life under control in our day, domination is far easier in the countryside.

However, besides being places of encounter, cities are also something built. Cities are objectified culture. The spectacle of the city offers its inhabitants a reflection of their whole culture. Everything is there, and on permanent display. The buildings, their proportions, their divisions, their shapes, tasteful or not, provide a reflection of the individual. How so? Each of us bears the city in our body. Our body adapts to a city, knows it, and is able to use it. It learns with it, and expresses itself with it. The city is the exteriorization of the human being. It is the synthesis of all the arts and sciences, all incorporated, become body. The city is female, then. Thus, as man discovers his face in woman, so also the masculine component of the human being discovers its face in the city. The city is the intermediary of humanity, as woman is the symbolic and traditional, at least in the patriarchal world, intermediary of that humanity.

(ii). Experience of the Cities. The history of peoples is inscribed on cities. They are the outward monuments of all of our struggles, our victories, our defeats. Cities are the memory of peoples.

Among a population scattered across the countryside, everything is gradually forgotten. No dates are carved on country walls, stones, or roadways. No evolution, no development is recorded there.

Conquerors destroy the cities of conquered peoples, and build new ones instead, on the same site. So it was in the Middle Ages, when the Christians destroyed old pagan Rome and used its stones to build a Christian Rome. In Mexico the conquistadors destroyed Tenochtitlán, the Aztec capital, perhaps the largest city in the world at the time, and made of its stones their own new capital.

In Latin America, cities proclaim the distance between the subjugated peoples and the triumphant oligarchies made up of the heirs of the conquistadors. The first colonial cities were created by establishing the power of the king and his administration in a particular locale. Natives were admitted to the cities only under very strict conditions. The ancient inhabitants of the land were kept far off; they were not permitted to create autonomous or quasi-autonomous villages in the countryside. Only in the Jesuit "reductions" were native Americans allowed to create their own cities, and this eventually aroused the fear and jealousy of the dominators.

Until the present century, the majority of the Latin American population lived on large plantations, or near the mines in which they worked. This scattered distribution of the population, under the immediate control of plantation owners, prevented the awakening of freedom. In Latin America, the notion of freedom is entirely new among the rural masses — no more than two or three decades old.

At the same time, the colossal migration from the countryside has occasioned the appearance not of cities, but merely of immense heaps of people, all deprived of anything remotely resembling city life. These are our enormous capitals, with their six, ten, or more millions of inhabitants, made up almost entirely of rural populations who have had to abandon the countryside. They find no decent housing, work, or transportation. A city is communication and human contact. But the contacts maintained by the slum-dwellers, in their shacks, on the buses, on the streets, are the very frustration of the human. A great deal has been written on the great megalopolises of the two worlds, each megalopolis cleaved into two cities worlds apart. The name "city" would be applicable to the wealthy areas, were it not for the appearance of irreality they acquire from their existence alongside huge areas of the most abysmal destitution. Rio de Janeiro is a most typical example—a city of surrealism.

It is not the theologian's task to examine the human problems of our contemporary cities, or the enormous problems with which coming generations will have to deal—future generations condemned to live in inhuman cities which a century of effort will not succeed in making livable. What interests us here is the Christian contribution.

(iii). City of God. St. Augustine takes his inspiration directly from the Book of Revelation when he represents the people of God as a city. The inspired author of Revelation represents the people of God as the new Jerusalem (Rev. 21:1–22:5). The history of God with humanity and humanity in God starts in a garden and ends in a city, then, just as the people of God migrate from the country to the city today. So our thesis of the unification of human beings in cities receives radical confirmation. We perceive a profound movement, and one that finds its meaning in the creator and the savior.

The Book of Revelation is also concerned to demonstrate the culmination of Jerusalem's tragic lot. Jerusalem is the prototype of the city. Awash in ambivalence, it is the city of God, and it is the city that murders the Son of God. It is the city that hears the prophets, and it is the city that kills the prophets. Jerusalem both epitomizes and elucidates the ambivalence of all cities of all times. Jerusalem is the city that founds the people of God, and the city that murders the prophets.

Christians did not characteristically flee cities. Only episodically, in the interests of an interim pedagogy, did monks eschew cities, to which they later returned, refreshed and strengthened. The Christian community typically installed itself in cities (or villages). When necessary, it hastened the rooting of populations in cities. In the cities was a world to be evangelized. After all, evangelization is addressed to collectivities, to peoples. And peoples gather in communities. The gospel is witness borne in cities, in public squares. The Christian communities were the signs and precursors of the great communities which cannot but be cities. The Christian communities show cities their calling.

So the first Christian communities came to be installed in cities. The local churches were organized around the principal cities of the Roman Empire, and even today bishops bear the titles of the cities in which their churches are performing their task of evangelization.

Humanity is not evangelized by fishing for women and men one by one and leading them forth to refuge in the parishes. The gospel is the yeast in the dough of a city, and will penetrate and transform this body of humanity. The gospel strives to make the city into a genuinely human polity, for it is in the city that all sin and all liberation are embodied.

Humanity is an archipelago of thousands of cities, in communication and exchange, just as the church is a communion of local churches. The ideal image of humanity is not a political system, nor an army on the march, but a collection of harmonious, balanced cities, each representing one of the facets of the human being, and all complementing one another.

2. HUMANITY IN TIME

(a) Human Time and the Tempo of the Universe

(i). Place of Human Time in the Tempo of the Universe. The primordial explosion of the universe must have occurred somewhere between ten and twenty billion years ago. The earth is some five billion years old. Two-and-one-half billion years were required on earth for the formation of the first molecule of nucleic acid, the basic building block of life. Another two billion years were necessary for the evolution of life to progress as far as the first humanoids. Only five million years separate us from the appearance of the first animals to walk upright, from which homo sapiens must have emerged. Almost five million years were needed for this prehuman being to adapt and develop to the point of being human in our ordinary sense of the word.

About forty thousand years ago, at a significant point in an extraordinarily lengthy evolution, the first human beings like ourselves appeared. It had taken five million years for the evolution of homo sapiens—more than a hundred times as long a time as all the time that has elapsed since then. But then time began to speed up. Only thirty thousand years were needed for the discovery of farming, so that human beings could settle down in a fixed location. A mere nine thousand years ago, wheat was discovered and planted. Six thousand years ago, the first empires were organized, and picture writing began. We are four thousand years from Abraham, three thousand years from the Phoenician's written alphabet, and 2,500 years from the earliest philosophy. Everything since is relatively recent history.

How much that is new has happened in the last 2,500 years! And yet how much faster time goes today as compared with 2,500 years ago! Indeed, time still marched very slowly until it reached modernity at the close of the eighteenth century. Then it suddenly accelerated. Or again, there is no comparison between the rate of human time from 1800 and 1950, and since 1950. Today humanity transforms the face of the earth more in a single decade than in the course of centuries in bygone times.

In the past, therefore, people were unable to notice changes in the world. Their world was stable. It saw very little change. People were borne forward by an evolution, but by an evolution so slow that they were unaware of it. Today, no one escapes the sensation of change. The immense phenomenon of our migration to cities has sensitized the vast majority of our population to the rapid rate of human change. Of old, men did the same work as their fathers and ancestors, just as women's life was no different from that of their mothers. Today it is rare for anyone to practice the same trade throughout a single lifetime.

(ii). Time of Civilizations and Empires. Human time does not follow a linear pattern. Humanity builds its cultures and civilizations around certain centers. The development of these centers is neither parallel nor simultaneous. The various cultures have developed at different rates, and have been at a geographical distance from one another. Civilizations are mortal. They are born, they grow, they may develop or they may encounter insuperable obstacles, then they triumph or collapse, and eventually all enter the time of their decadence. Six thousand years ago they began to form political empires, embracing vast agglomerations of human beings. Each culture has its time, each civi-

lization a limited span of centuries, if indeed a geographical or historical accident does not abbreviate its destiny. At the zenith of modernity, there were those who thought that modern Western civilization might escape the fate of earlier civilizations. Why should this civilization, at last, not go on indefinitely? It was even thought that our civilization would finally absorb other civilizations that had survived up to that point (the Arab world, India, China, and so forth). Nowadays it is clear that Western civilization is no different from the others in point of defectibility. And today it has reached the end of its course.

Indeed, ancient empires were far more durable. The empires of Egypt, Japan, and China lasted thousands of years. Even the Roman Empire lasted 1,500 years, until the fall of Constantinople. Since then the Arab and Turkish empires, or any of the empires of the West, have survived but a few centuries. The British Empire lasted only a hundred years. History is moving much faster now.

The causes of the rise and fall of empires are obscure. The modern West has decided to disappear by contraception. A civilization is committing suicide. It is likely that similar phenomena have occurred in the past. All indications are that the fall of certain empires and civilizations has been owing to internal deficiencies. Others, however, have been destroyed by conquest, when stronger civilizations have fallen upon them and subjugated them, as occurred with the original American civilizations.

All human beings find themselves integrated into a cycle of culture, of civilization, and, at certain moments, of the rivalry of empires. None of us selects our birth date. We are born into a dawning civilization, a flourishing one, or a declining, decadent, moribund one. The condition of our civilization determines our own destiny.

It was in apocalyptical Judaism that a consciousness of the frailty of empires and cultures, of their succession and of the march of history, was born.[3] St. Augustine saw with crystal clarity that he was living in the era of the fall of the Roman Empire in the West. He could not foresee its thousand-year survival in the East.

Indeed, a radically flawed apocalypticism has always deceived many Christians. Interpreting Daniel's prophecy literally, Christians often think that the coming of Christianity means the end of all earlier civilizations and cultures, and the establishment of a new, unique culture spread across the face of the earth. And behold, the notion of Christendom arises—the idea of a Christian people covering the earth from end to end, heir to the ancient empires. For centuries, Christians failed to perceive that a speciously universal Christendom was but the mask of a specific, particular civilization, as limited and as mortal as any other. They thought that Christianity was guiding the development of culture. Of course, nothing of the kind was occurring. Christ creates a new people of God, a new person, a new humanity, yes. But this does not militate against the fact of a succession of cultures. Cultures go on dying and being born. The coming of Christianity did not alter the fact of the tempo of civilizations. New civilizations have continued to appear, and new civilizations are undoubtedly in gestation at this very moment, destined to replace a Western civilization now in its death throes.

It is impossible for most of those who live in a given age to recognize their particular moment in history. They lack the required historical distance. Who could possibly know what cultures and civilizations are arising in the Third World at this very moment? Most members of a decadent civilization have not the least suspicion that their civilization is even in danger. None of us, indeed, knows what history we are making.

We are all swept along by a culture, a cycle, and a phase of that cycle that we have not selected. We can be diffident, suspicious, or adventurous. And we can be mistaken. Thus, no quest for liberation will eventuate in apocalyptical deliverance. There is no question of founding a definitive civilization. We can only search for justice in the phase of the evolution of civilization in which we find ourselves. Every culture is partial. Each has its values, but each has its immovable limits, as well.

Still, with Judeo-Christian apocalypticism a consciousness both of the limitations of our era and of its destiny appeared. To each era corresponds a destiny—a task to accomplish. It is not a matter of deducing, from abstract propositions, an ideal model of life in common. The community we seek is the one that will be adequate to the phase of development to which we belong in our particular cultural cycle.

When civilizations lived in isolation, each regarding itself as universal and unique, outsiders were never more than "barbarians." To be a human being and to be a member of a particular culture were one and the same. Today we know that all of us are temporary. We represent but a single era in the evolution of a single culture.

(iii). Tempo of the Generations. The tempo of civilizations is different from the tempo of economic, political, or social systems. The social sciences project human phenomena along a uniform, continuous time-line. Thus they imagine social phenomena themselves as continuous, with foreseeable, merely cyclical, changes compatible with an overall continuity. But human affairs are host to a factor of discontinuity — the death of each generation. One generation dies, and another is born.[4]

No guarantee exists that one generation will continue the work of the preceding generation. Things were different when time moved more slowly. When time began to accelerate, a change took place. Nowadays no new generation simply takes up where another has left off. Continuity is anything but a foregone conclusion.

For example, sociologists used to imagine that the offspring of a capitalistic society would adopt the same values as their forebears, and that in this way a capitalistic economy would continue to thrive. They had not foreseen the birth of generations indifferent to all economy. They had not foreseen that, in the Muslim world, young people would conceive a passion for religion. The options of new generations are not predetermined. Parents in capitalistic societies no longer succeed in communicating their values to their children part and parcel. Similar phenomena are observed in the new socialistic societies.

In a certain sense, each new generation "starts afresh," conceiving the projects of its culture and civilization "from scratch." Obviously, the new generation cannot invent everything out of whole cloth. Each begins with the memories of the past that it has received. But then each picks and chooses among those memories. It remembers some things and forgets others. It confers a positive value on certain projects of the past, while leaving others out of account. Accordingly, each generation mounts projects destined never to be completed. Indeed, humanity itself never completes its projects. All its works remain unfinished. Every generation dies with the illusion that the generation to come will continue its work; but once the preceding generation is buried, the next hastens to move on to other projects. Each generation chooses its own future, then pursues this future to whatever extent it can reconcile it with reality. Little by little, however, it must renounce certain projects. It finds itself incapable of controlling history, and finally tries merely to salvage what it can.

Each generation, then, must begin with new blood, a new spirit, and new ambitions. The liberation of the human race is a new task for each new generation. And indeed, each generation is convinced that its discovery of reality is the first such discovery in history, and that it is the first generation to attempt to win its liberation. It is as if, with every new generation, the world begins anew.

Hence the special value of the Old Testament. For Christians, the New Testament represents the definitive, the Old represents the provisional. But the provisional, the transitory, continues to accompany the definitive. Christ is definitive; but Christ lives only in situations as transitory as those of the Old Testament.

The Old Testament shows how each generation in Israel encountered new challenges, found itself in different situations, and sought to accomplish whatever project Israelite society had in view at the time. Despite the Bible's proclamation that the intentions of every generation result in failure, the same Bible likewise testifies to the perseverance of the Spirit of God, who ceaselessly renews hearts and inspires new undertakings. Here the Old Testament is a parable of the entire history of the Christian people, even to our own times. We do not know what the challenges to the Christian communities will be in the twenty-first century, when the superpowers will be the Arab world, China, Japan, India, black Africa, and Brazil. What will be the life projects of the civilizations of the new century? This is a question that we must leave to those who will be there to implement these projects. Our own tasks are only those that we can situate within the development of the empires and cultures of the close of the twentieth century.

(b) Tempo of Individual Existence

(i). Brevity of Life. Even ancient Hebrew wisdom sang its melancholy song of the shortness of life. And today the tempo of human life is far more rapid than it was in the time of the sages of Israel. In those days, the number of projects that could be taken up by a human being was very limited. An individual could therefore, so to speak, finish what he or she had begun. Ancient farmers or artisans could foreseeably bring to fruition in the course of their lifetime all the projects that they had conceived.

Today, however, long-term undertakings can easily be projected for more than the length of time allotted to a human individual on earth. More and more frequently, economic, political, and ideological projects are launched whose realization will require more than merely sixty or seventy years. Decisions taken today may well not bear fruit until much longer than that. Projects of lesser scope, we now see, will change nothing. Important projects now take time. And so, persons come to the end of their lives with a feeling of having accomplished little or nothing.

Our time is short, the New Testament warns (Rom. 13:11; 1 Cor. 7:29; 2 Cor. 6:2; Eph. 5:16). Only a short span has been allotted to us. Only a little moment separates us from the end of the world and the coming of Christ. If "time is running out," then—What ought we to do? We ought to take advantage of the time we have. We certainly may not conclude, from the shortness of time available to us, that "it's not worth it"—that nothing is worthwhile. Quite the contrary, the Christian interpretation of the brevity of time enjoins on us a more intense activity still.

We have the example of Jesus. As the Gospels tell, the Father allotted him a brief time indeed. He died young, after a very short ministry. No one, however, complains or laments that Jesus' life was too short. Why? Because, in that short span, he accomplished all that he had been given to do. Henceforward, then, shortness of time no longer matters. What matters is that the work incumbent on each be done. Jesus' work, the most perfect of works, was completed in the space of a few months. So it is with Christians. Many martyrs died very young, but there was no weeping and wailing over the brevity of their lives. They had done incomparably more than others could do in the longest of lives. They had indeed "done enough."

Christian time is the time of the mission of each of us. What matters is the accomplishment of our mission. The Christian message is not concerned with the quantity of time allotted to the individual. Time lived in Christ has the same dimensions as Christ's own time, Christ's own span of life.

(ii). Time of Preparation. Paradoxically, for human beings to mature, to prepare to act in life, the time of life required is exceptionally long. Individual rearing takes longer and longer. In agrarian cultures, individuals could begin to produce goods and have a family at thirteen to fifteen years if female, at fifteen to eighteen years if male. In a more developed civilization, the preparation time gradually lengthens. A human being today needs twenty-two to twenty-five years to reach maturity. In other words, by the time he or she is mature, a person has lived a third of a lifetime. Once mature, a human being in our society today has only thirty to thirty-five years of active life left, after which society will thrust this human being aside. More than half of the time of one's active life is used up in preparation and training.

And now we are headed for a state of culture in which an ongoing, permanent formation will be necessary for all of us. We shall all be spending our whole active lives in the constant acquisition of new knowledge.

During the time of our active existence, furthermore, more and more time is spent preparing and ruminating our decisions, our various projects. Production time, harvest time, is brief, while the time of preparation grows much lengthier. Human beings have come to be defined as maturing animals. Other animals are ready for all the activities of their species practically the moment they are born. We humans need more and more preparation. Without it, our activity is ineffective. The disproportion between our long task of preparation and the brief time for any effective action not infrequently drives us to impatience. The young do not always accept this limitation, this postponement of their launch into life. Hence the multiplication of failed lives. Too many have wanted to achieve too much too soon.

(iii). Procreation. Until our own day, procreation had never

constituted a problem for humanity as a whole. The number of human ovulations is far greater than the number of conceptions needed to reproduce the human species, while the urge to copulate is so strong that opportunities for these conceptions will scarcely be lacking.

The reason why growth in the human population of our planet has been so gradual over previous centuries has been our adult life expectancy: an average of thirty years. Furthermore, infant mortality has been high. Now, progress in hygiene and medicine has stretched our average life expectancy to sixty or seventy years, and infant mortality has also notably declined. Midway through the twentieth century, Westerners were seized by panic at the population growth of the Third World, and birth-control campaigns were set afoot in Third World countries, implemented by the distribution of artificial means of contraception.

But these anti-birth campaigns have had more effect in the West than in the Third World, bringing the former to the point of its demise. It may be no more than two or three decades now before a liberated Third World will not need much more struggle in order to gather up the legacy and destroy the power of the more developed countries of the twentieth century. Some of us seem to wonder whether procreation is really a human task or not. Birth-control campaigners treat procreation as if it were an irrational instinct to be curbed. They have at least in part succeeded in extinguishing the desire to have children among the governing classes of humanity today. However, they have not succeeded when it comes to the poor of the Third World. Given this multilayered scenario, it may be interesting to consider the motivations that have over history lent meaning to procreation.

The Old Testament esteemed procreation most highly. Sterility was a woman's deepest humiliation; not to have a son was a terrible trial for a man. To suffer childlessness was like having one's life cut off at the root. Sons were their parents' pride and joy. Without sons, existence lost its deepest meaning. Procreation was more than obedience to a precept enjoined by God on Adam and Eve: it was the human being's noblest task. The Old Testament obviously reflects the conviction of the agrarian civilizations of its time. It does not seem likely, however, that the mission assigned by God in the first book of the Bible (Gen. 1:28) can be demythologized as a mere cultural phenomenon.

The New Testament shifts the problem of the transmission of life. Jesus separates the people of God from the phenomenon of physical generation. Suddenly we transmit our faith to another not by generation, as in the past, but by way of word. Word becomes more important than procreation. The apostles were even persuaded to renounce procreation and to devote their entire effort to the service of the word.

However, the service of the word also requires continuity. It is conceived as a task to be handed on and continued. If an apostle procreates no successors, others must. Even in the Christian community, continuity still makes sense. The mission must go on. Consequently, procreation continues to be a basic human calling. We may not conclude, however, that every culture must go on. The task of filling the earth can always be entrusted to other cultures and other peoples.

(c) Time and Tempo

(i). Difference in Times. Human time is not a continuous flux. It is marked by a succession of peaks and valleys, or rather, peaks separated by more or less desultory intervals. The succession of times shapes the structure of existence.

The first factor in the rhythm of times, the tempo of human life, has been imposed by the more perceptible rhythms of nature. Human life follows the succession of days and nights, years and seasons, moons and constellations. Astrology still plays an important role in the life of humanity, perhaps more today than ever. Men and women actually continue to seek solid indications for their lives in the world of the stars, which can seem so much more reliable than this fickle human world. And for all the rest of us, the succession of days, seasons, and years is a major factor in the rhythm of work and social relations.

Second, there is the rhythm of an individual human existence. Birth and death are the fundamental moments of our lives. Between them, we slowly grow old. Each of us is at a particular point on our personal time line. We are closer either to our birth or to our death. This time line is basic for us. It conditions all of our behavior.

We all know how old we are, the number of years we have lived so far. Nearly all of us know the date of our birth. Other birth dates also serve as points of reference for us, as do the deaths of others—our parents, our siblings, perhaps our daughters and sons, and of course those of famous persons. Concrete human history finds its key moments in births and deaths. And we may add our marriage date, which also serves as a reference and framework for life. Those who have never married lack a certain structure or reference, as if life were more fragile for them. Furthermore, those of us who do marry are at present living either in a premarriage or postmarriage moment. Life does not have the same meaning before marriage as after. Finally, the number of years that have elapsed since marriage is also of great importance.

After death, what survives? Three dates on society's registers: birth, marriage, and death. Once we are no longer here, our life is summed up in these three dates.

Once historical societies appeared, new times came to be: dates of the founding of cities and empires, dates of the investiture of kings and emperors. Peoples number the years of their existence from a special date that serves them as a reference: the year since the foundation of Rome, since the installation of the monarchy, the year of the emperor or the king. These dates stand as signs of human liberation. If Rome is at peace in terms of the ideology of the empire, the years of Rome are the years of the peace of the entire world. If the monarch is the liberator of the people, then the date of the accession of the monarch is the date of the liberation of the people.

In the biblical tradition, historical times tend to supplant the times in the rhythm of nature. Passover, which had been a seasonal feast, becomes the festival of liberation from Egypt, and so on. For the people of Israel, time is crisply structured. The past has been a succession of events of liberation. We may safely say that Israel is the first people on earth to create for itself a genuine past. Israel celebrates, in the past, the events that were events of genuine liberation for the people, and not merely events of the installation of a new power, which, after all, is of incomparably greater service to those in power than it is to the people who furnish them with a pretext for the exercise of that power.

The times of Israel's present are the times of the actualization of the victories of the past. Israel can build a future because it has a past. The past is warranty for the future. Popular history was born in Israel.[5]

Since then, peoples molded in the Judeo-Christian tradition have recorded their history. Their historical time is structured. The past sheds light on the present. Without a past, structured out of defined events, what could be the meaning of the present? It would be impossible to single out events of the present as being of particular importance. All would be a sheer jumble of happenings, without any apparent interconnection. The present coheres in virtue of the past. Memory singles out events of profound change in the past and establishes them as dividing lines between historical eras. It places its invisible finger on defeats and victories, advances and retreats, and meaningful forward steps in history.

For us moderns, too, the shape of the past enables us to prepare and define the happenings of the present, and to take a position regarding them all. What could newspapers, commentators, or historians do, in discussing the present, without being able to refer to the past, show an order among events, and thereby organize time? Without the organization of time, no social activity would be conceivable.

Finally, we build the future on the foundations of the past. The future is a projection of the past upon the aims and goals of the present. Just as a future Passover is the projection of the ancient Passover for purposes of present activity, so the revolution of the future is the renewal of the revolutions of the past—their concrete actualization here and now as a goal of present action.

Thus, time is rhythmic; it involves the ascending resumption of a theme. The same revolution is periodically renewed: the revolution of the past has only been the image, the frustrated promise, of the true revolution to come. Each revolution holds for a time, but only for a time, to be transformed into a new, definitive revolution, now in preparation. In order to be altogether human, time must be historical. Human time is the time of human deeds, the deeds by which human communities take their destiny in hand and constitute themselves a community of freedom. The rhythm of history is the succession of those times in which human efforts, after a long, slow build-up, explode and change the face of our human world.

Christian time is signed from beginning to end by one central moment: the hour of Jesus (John 2:4; 4:21; 7:30; 8:20; 12:23, 27; 16:32). The hour of Jesus is the center of the world and of all history. Christ's Passover takes on the meaning previously contained in the world's creation, to become humanity's true foundational event. And again, that same Passover — Christ's death, issuing in his resurrection — in some sense acquires the meaning heretofore monopolized by the end of the world, as well. For Christians, the Passover of the Lord is everything.[6]

Not that paschal time suppresses historical time. On the contrary, it lends it new foundation. Christ's Passover is reincarnate in the Pasch, the Easter, of his people. His Passover becomes historical once more. Nor is it actualized in individual conversions alone. For that matter, individual conversions are not unique moments. They are a simply a multiplicity of times of conversion within the single moment of a basic option. The truth is the other way about: conversion to Christ generates historical events. Peoples are converted, and subsequently undergo transformations resulting from their overall, collective options. Faith in Christ is not an isolated, discrete event. Faith is the act of an entire people caught up in conversion and renewal.

However, human history as such does not simply become salvation history. History is still oppression and liberation. It is not yet pure liberation, or even pure liberation-journey. It is paschal at every step. The options are never definitive, and never complete. History is a combination of slavery and liberation, in an ongoing dialectic of Good Friday and Easter. Even individual events are fraught with ambiguity. In fact, we can say that the time of Christ exposes the ambiguity of the time of history.

Today we are far from the naivetés of the ancient empires, for which history had been redeemed by the empire itself, or by the emperor. There is no liberator but Jesus Christ. All other "liberators" carry the risks of history's ambiguity. Liberation is fated to blaze a dubious, ultimately incomprehensible trail, a trail of permanent challenge to renewal.

(ii). Memory. There is no time without memory. Human memory is not simply a recording device. For one thing, it does not record everything that happens. Besides, a simple recording device can only record noise. It knows nothing of events. Everything presented to our memory is first filtered through our human options, commitments, and struggles. Only then is it possible for us to sort out, in the flux of everyday life, certain events to be consigned to our memory and stored there.

The content of memory is stored in the human brain. However, there are techniques to enhance the function of the brain in such a way as to enable it to reproduce, outside the organism, the content of its memory. Writing, especially, has enabled us to reproduce and multiply our memory of events. And in our own day, new techniques make it possible to enhance the function of writing as well. And suddenly the memory stored in our brain finds its effects on the outside world progressing geometrically.

The first monuments to the memory of particular events were erected by the heads of empires, and for obvious reasons. Means and techniques of memory have frequently been monopolized, and even developed, by the mighty, in order to engrave the foundational events of their own regime, their power, on their people's memory. So the gift of memory becomes the gift of power. That is why the written memory of peoples has always tended to be limited to the particular memory of events regarded as important by the conquerors and dominators. Recorded history is the memory not of history's losers, but of its winners.

There is one great exception: the Bible. The memory preserved in the Bible is that of an oppressed people concerned to record their struggles in their own version — a people who refuse to accept their conquerors' version of history. Vanquished peoples, too, have a memory. They have their own version of things. There are two versions of the 11th of September in Chilean history, just as in Brazil there are two versions of the 31st of March. And so forth. Peoples often keep their memory concealed, in the form of stories, fables, festivals, or rites. But the Bible makes this memory explicit, and bestows courage on the vanquished, since it agrees with the losers and protests the arrogance of the winners.

The Christian communities, too, preserve the memory of their struggles, and find in this memory the starting point they require for an understanding of current events. Now they can mold their projects in a way that will tend to shape a new and different future.

(iii). Celebration and Festival. Festival bestows solidity on the present. A people without festival would be stagnated in the pure repetition of its past. Their memory would be like a broken record that always plays in the same groove. Or else they would be all absorbed in preparing a fantasy future, one destined never to come. But no, there is a time to produce, and a time to consume, and festival is the time for consuming—the time when time stops, or seems to stop, as if it had already reached perfection. After a long climb, you need to stop and rest. Your repose will be brief; but without it, life would never arrive at any kind of fullness. You would always be on the move, always in transit. But there are moments of terminus, of culmination. These moments are called festival, or feast.

Humanity has gradually followed the route of the Bible. It has passed from festivals of nature to festivals of history. True, it has not completely abandoned nature festivals. It still celebrates festivals of birth, death, and marriage, with anniversary celebrations of them all. Primitive societies continue to celebrate traditional feasts of the seasons. Some feasts have lost their reference to the past, and continue simply as festival for its own sake, as, for example, at carnival time.

Festivals gather up, and in a certain sense constitute, communities. Without a common celebration, there can be no community. Festivals are communication, and common expression. Without them there cannot be the common language needed by every people, every city, every community.

When peoples began to record history, they began to establish festivals to celebrate their own history. They celebrated feasts of victory. They even celebrated their defeats—"celebrated" their common shame. They celebrated feasts of the foundation of cities and republics, feasts of the enthronement of royalty or the installation of governors, feasts of popular or trade-union elections, feasts of workers' struggles, of strikes, of protests, feasts of popular uprisings. Then they multiplied these festivals in anniversary celebrations, and the events of the past are suddenly alive in the present. For example, almost all countries celebrate the First of May.

Festivals have always been taken over by the dominators insofar as they have been able. The mighty have always known the importance of festival for the maintenance of a regime "by consent of the governed." The master of the revels is master of the people. During the age of Christendom, a veritable explosion of festival occurred in the church. Medieval Christianity counted as many as 150 "holidays" a year—holy days, or "feast days," by which it transmitted its own interpretation of social life. True, there were excesses, and moral abuses. But the church has always found the advantages far more numerous than the drawbacks.

In today's individualistic, capitalistic Western society, festival is in a state of decadence. Society as we know it no longer has either the motivation for festival or the content with which to invest it. The old feasts have been gradually abolished, and replaced by sheer manipulated consumerism. The best example is Christmas, with its unbridled consumerism bereft of rhyme or reason, its total lack of any interpersonal communication, and its mournful, paltry purpose: that an economic elite may flaunt its buying power. Only traditional peoples still celebrate feast days, and even here festival is being rapidly contaminated by the dominant civilization. Thus are destroyed the last remnants of the old communities.

Properly speaking, Christianity recognizes only one festival, and one which it regards as having been celebrated in all worthiness only a single time: the feast of Easter. And yet it renews this feast continually, at all times and in all places. Christianity celebrates Easter with the eucharist. The eucharist can be celebrated in any circumstances, although historically the official church has tended to divide up both time and space with its festivals and celebrate the eucharist especially in churches and on Sundays—the Lord's Day—along with other special "feast days."

The authentic feasts of the Christian people, however, are

not the Sundays or feast days of the traditional calendar. Christians celebrate the festivals of their peoples and communities. Sundays and the feast days of the church calendar are only signs, preparing for, and bestowing meaning on, the authentic festivals of the people of God.

Christians feel the need of special times for their own gatherings and festivals. They must defend themselves against the pressure of the feast days of the dominators. The poor must salvage some of their festivals. They must gather, in festive mood, to affirm, to themselves, their identity, their will to exist, to defend what they are, to acquire a place of their own in society. The meaning of Sundays and feast days in the Christian community is that of an alternative—a refuge from the life of subjugation, and a preparation for its liberation, a preparation that occurs during the time that the members of the community are kept at a distance from official festivities. A Christian feast is a feast open to the poor and celebrated for their sake. A Christian festival is one in which the poor discover their human reality—discover themselves as the collective subject of an existence and the agent of an activity. Now they can start off on their journey. This has been, and must ever be, the sense of the eucharist, and of the Christian commemoration of Easter.

3. CONCLUSION

Every human being enters history bearing the legacy of an immense world, a tremendously diversified earth. Each of us bears the heritage of somewhere between ten and twenty billion years of preparation. Every human being is an infinitely complex memory, with millions of neurons and billions of life experiences. As humanity multiplies, so does diversity. Ideas become simpler. Moderns have developed simple systems in which to close humanity up. But reality resists and protests.

Humanity stands at the beginning of its history. Its time so far has been insignificant as compared with the time the universe has been in existence. The space it has so far occupied is insignificant in the immensity of existing space. Humanity must endure, and spread out.

Dreams are our projections of totality. Our vocation, however, carries us back to this little piece of time and space in which our destiny is played out. The infinitude of our adolescent desires, or indeed our mature desires, must be reconcentrated on the lowly tasks of every day.

The media tend to make spectators of us. Our real world is being replaced by an imaginary one, in which each of us is offered the illusion of playing a part in the destinies of the entire world. But this is pure mirage. The only way to play a part in the destiny of the world is to accept the time and space in which God has placed us. For this we have been sent. At stake is human liberation.

CHAPTER IV

Human Beings and
the Challenge of Matter

We are matter. We are made of the same matter as the world around us.

It has not been easy for us to discover and accept that we are made of matter, and that our destiny is therefore entirely material. Many myths of the origin of humanity attribute that origin to gods or other superior beings. Many of these same myths present our existence amidst a material world as a "fall." So say the myths of the ancient East, for example — and the Bible contradicts them flat out. What is new in the biblical account of our first creation is that we humans have been taken from the earth. We are dust, and to dust we shall return. We belong to the earth — so much so that the final resurrection of humanity coincides with the creation of a new earth. Consciously and deliberately, the Bible rejected the myths of a "fall," with their contempt for matter.[1]

The destiny of human life, then, is a symbiosis with the earth. Between humanity and matter exists a profound, radical affinity. Humanity and matter compenetrate and cooperate. Human existence is one of real, physical collaboration between the earth and human beings. This cooperation is basically effected by means of science, technology, and work. Other forms of association are not excluded, but they remain secondary to these three. Hence the two sections of this chapter. Science and technology are closely associated. Work is the basic relation, and science and technology are at the service of work.

1. SCIENCE AND TECHNOLOGY

(a) Christianity, Science, and Technology

(i). Historical Situation of Science and Technology. From the very first, homo sapiens had science and technology. Among humanity's great steps forward are certainly to be reckoned the domestication of fire and the invention of the wheel. Agriculture was discovered and developed thanks to constant progress in knowledge of grains, and an as yet anonymous science of genetics. The first technologies of stone and metal required a huge store of scientific knowledge.

During the first human millennia, growth in the sciences and technologies was slow. It accelerated with the foundation of the first empires. But the acceleration was uneven. All peoples had now developed sciences and technologies, but not all had attained that critical mass of scientific knowledge, that level of scientific dynamism, at which each discovery opens the way to new ones.

Only in recent centuries, especially since the seventeenth century, have science, first, and then technology, appeared on the scene no longer in disguise. Earlier science was practically indistinguishable from philosophy or mythology. The first civilizations expressed their self-knowledge through myth. Their myths included scientific data; they were not pure fantasy. But they mixed imagination with reality in such a way as effectively to paralyze the development of intelligence. To the myths, the scientific mentality opposed observation and experimentation, as well as ever more rigorous, and gradually more mathematical, rules for reasoning. At great cost, science learned to prescind from subjectivity, and scientific objectivity was created. At first, human beings projected themselves upon their surroundings in such a way that there was no way to measure those surroundings disinterestedly. Traditional peoples still did their thinking on the basis of observations that projected their mythic view of the world upon the objects of those observations.

Science likewise had to emancipate itself from philosophy. The struggle with myth was also, and principally, taken up by the philosophers. However, philosophers appealed to introspection, and deductive argumentation, as well as to conceptual logic. Ancient Greek philosophy, at any rate, entertained the notion of a universal, total knowledge, and imagined it possible for individuals to assimilate all this knowledge. Ancient philosophers introduced empirical data of genuine scientific value into their systems. However, they sought to deduce these data from their synthetic views, thus distorting the scientific perspective. Later, when new scientific data contradicted their syntheses, they appealed to their intellectual sovereignty to contradict the results of a far more sure-footed science. In fact, the definitive emancipation of the sciences from the fetters of philosophy is a recent phenomenon. Until recently, dreamers still sighed after a total synthesis of all knowing, in which philosophy would wear the crown of absolute knowledge.

Almost up to our present century, technology developed independently of science, more often at the hands of persons directly plying the practical arts. The technology of agriculture, the crafts, and industry was invented by persons who had to respond to immediate challenges. Many inventions were all but accidental. All of them came by way of a happy intuition. Inventors knew that the processes they invented functioned, but they were at a loss to explain how. Science had few, if any, technological applications, and little in the way of theoretical foundations. Past civilizations developed extremely sophisticated technologies. Then these disappeared, replaced by still more highly developed technologies, and today even the latter are more highly developed, and accompanied by all manner of theoretical paraphernalia. We need only think of the use of the energies of water, wind, wood, and coal, the instruments of war, oceangoing vessels, or manufacturing techniques.

Ancient technology had no scientific status, and was not studied in the universities, which were devoted to pure theory. After all, theory seemed superior to practice. Today, technology depends more and more on science — on physics, chemistry, biology, and other sciences. The use of atomic energy, electronic technologies, robotics, information manipulation and storage, telematics, would be simply impossible in the absence of antecedent scientific knowledge. In the same way, a great deal of medical therapy today is based on scientific knowledge. Machinery is no longer built on the basis of data furnished by the eyes. Nowadays it is necessary to know things the eye cannot discern.

The meshing of science and technology is a phenomenon of our own century. It grows year by year. Science can no longer be practiced without the machinery furnished it by a very advanced technology, and technology cannot be practiced except on the basis of scientific knowledge.

This fusion enables epistemologists, or philosophers of knowledge, to make a better determination of the status both of science and of technology. It is becoming ever more evident that the ends of science are not purely speculative. The purpose of science is not to afford a representation of the world. More and more such a representation is seen to be impossible. Science is bound up with technology, and both of these are bound up with work. Science is one of a series of activities bearing on a comprehensive task: to place the material world at the service of human life, to render the material world more viable and habitable for humanity, and thereby to render human life more humane, more developed in all its dimensions.

Accordingly, science has ceased to be an activity monopolized by certain curious minds. Instead of proceeding from curiosity, science is now practiced in view of the task of subduing the world and transforming it—the task of humanity as a whole. Science has become a political problem, and indeed, more and more, a basic political problem.

After all, science has ceased to be an individual undertaking. No scientist of our day can do his or her research with the resources available to the individual. Science requires an enormous outlay, which can be furnished only by the state, or by exceedingly powerful private foundations. The progress of science is a result of political decisions, since it depends on the quantity of resources that a nation decides to reserve for it.

Work, in both its quality and its productivity, necessarily depends on scientific and technological progress. Science and technology have become everyone's problem, then. The life of each and all necessarily depends on the evolution of science and technology.

(ii). The Christian Position. At the time of Christian origins, neither science nor technology was consciously practiced as such. Neither the Bible nor the ancient tradition of the church could have spoken of something that at that point had never attained the level of consciousness. However, there is other content in the Christian message, and indeed in its basic positions, from which Christians can recognize the value of the sciences and technologies.

Contradicting the mythologies that did not dare to posit human origins in matter, the Bible is unhesitating: humanity proceeds from the earth, and its destiny is the earth. We are on earth to cultivate and subdue it. As I have suggested, for the ancient Hebrews and ancient Christians this domination of the earth did not consciously include science and technology, which did not consciously exist. But Jews and Christians were perfectly capable of employing whatever science and technology arose around them.

The people of the Bible had no advanced technology, however, even for the time, and Solomon had to look to the Gentiles for his engineers. Nor did the people of the Bible have scientists. Why? Because God's people were poor, and the poor develop neither science nor technology. However, the poor need not reject out of hand the science and technology used by the powerful to oppress them. There is no such rejection in the Bible. There is no exaltation of an archaic way of life over the use of technological innovations, at least not as a consistent line of thought.

The compatibility between Christian faith, on the one hand, and science and technology, on the other, was based on three very clear arguments. First, Christian anthropology teaches the earthly nature of the human being, and leads humanity to live on the earth, of the earth, and inclined to earth—not with its head in the clouds. Second, two thousand years of Christianity evince the great part played by Christians in scientific and technological discoveries. Numerous priests and monks were scientists and inventors. The role of the monks in the shaping of European history has always leapt from the pages of that history, and with good reason, although of course this scarcely constituted the only factor of progress in the past. Third, science and technology developed continuously, and at an accelerated pace, precisely in Christendom. In other civilizations they encountered obstacles in religion, or in religious philosophy, that stunted their growth. We need only cite the cases of Arab, Muslim, Chinese, or East Indian civilization. It cannot have been by chance that science developed in Christendom. There was conflict, but the conflict did not halt the scientific or technological movement.

Hence Puebla's recognition of the role of science and technology:

We ask scientists, technical people, and the creators of technological society to nurture their scientific spirit with love for the truth so that they may investigate the riddles of the universe and gain dominion over the earth [1240].

The formulation is not faultless, and is still somewhat in debt to the old notion of the speculative end of science that the bishops learned in the scholastic philosophy of their seminary days. But the overall sense is clear.

Pope John Paul II, as well, in his encyclical *On Human Work*, eulogizes technology:

Technology is surely man's ally. . . . Thus, if the words of the Bible, "subdue the earth," addressed to man in the beginning, were to be understood in the context of the whole modern industrial and post-industrial age, they surely would also include a relation to technology—a relation to that world of mechanisms and machines that is the fruit of a labor of human intelligence and the historical confirmation of man's dominion over nature [LE 5].

(iii). Conflicts of the Past. The notion of a compatibility in principle between Christianity and science still provokes bewilderment in many people, especially in Latin America. The intellectual class is still under the misapprehension that science and faith are somehow at odds, and so is persuaded that a scientist

cannot be a Christian. Christianity, the intellectual still feels, somehow places limits on scientific research.

However, this persistent opposition to the church in the name of science comes mostly from people to whom actual scientific research is altogether foreign, and whose investigation into the matter at hand is limited to works of popularization often still reflecting the polemics of a century ago.

In the eighteenth century, a mighty assault was launched against Christianity, and especially against the Catholic Church, in the name of science. The ensuing polemics, limited to the world of academe at first, were popularized at the turn of the century and raged in popular milieus all through the course of the nineteenth century. In Latin America, the social and intellectual elite gleefully entered the fray. They read all the French polemical literature, and accepted all anti-Christian criticism in the name of science as scientific dogma. As it happened, this criticism was a phenomenon of the romance-language countries especially, and of France in particular, and so Latin America was particularly receptive. The new governing classes were striving to destroy the power of the old colonial church. Latin scientism, then, came as a welcome ally of political liberalism.

Actually, a great number of scientists of every generation have been Christians or Jews, loyal to their faith, and finding no incompatibility between their faith and their science. It is true, however, that some measure of justification of the liberal fears was furnished by certain prohibitions and condemnations on the part of the official church, for example the notorious prohibition of the dissection of cadavers, the condemnation of the Copernican system and of Galileo, or the condemnation of transformism.

The church had adopted and perfected the Greek philosophical notion of a total science of all reality. Within this comprehensive science, the sciences of the material world had their place. Thus, they too came to be speculative sciences. After all, they had to be accommodated within the framework of the whole. They too, then, must submit to the deductive method of philosophy and the general propositions held by philosophers as self-evident. Scholasticism's total science embraced, at least ideally, both the concepts of the Bible and the legacy of the philosophers of antiquity. It was with this self-styled comprehensive science that real science entered into conflict, and it was this self-styled comprehensive science that certain elements of the institutional church felt it their mission to defend. In their mind, Christian faith itself called for a commitment to scholasticism.

In that era, however, not even scientists had a clear grasp of the epistemological status of their science. It was not until the twentieth century that science acquired its explicit epistemological foundations, which finally demonstrated the originality of science and its complete autonomy vis-à-vis philosophy. The sciences work out their own methodology. They are not part of a higher, speculative whole. At the Second Vatican Council, the church finally acknowledged the compatibility of faith and science. At last the autonomy of science was unambiguously proclaimed. The "individual sciences or arts" have their "appropriate methods," the council said.

> Therefore, if methodological investigation within every branch of learning is carried out in a genuinely scientific manner and in accord with moral norms, it never truly conflicts with faith . . . .
> Consequently, we cannot but deplore certain habits of mind, sometimes found too among Christians, which do not sufficiently attend to the rightful independence of science [GS 36].

This does not mean that Christians can never find themselves at odds with science. The Christian message insists on the absolute priority of human beings among creatures. In other words, the sciences have their finality not in themselves, but in human beings. To the extent that they depart from this aim, they will meet with opposition from Christians.

Puebla says:

> We ask [scientists] to avoid the negative effects of a hedonistic society and the technocratic temptation; to apply the power of technology to the creation of goods and the invention of means designed to rescue humanity from underdevelopment [1240].

(b) The Agent of Science and Technology

(i). The Scientific Class. In bygone times, scientists were typically marginalized by society as strange, eccentric individuals, devoted to abstruse, fantastic things. Often they were persons of independent means, or were supported by the generosity of a Maecenas, and hence had no need to earn their daily bread. Nowadays the scientific world is a populous one. Scientists number in the millions, and are not only accepted by society, but are actually in the employ of powerful institutions. Their research is programmed either by the state or by other institutions that furnish its capital, even by scientific business enterprises themselves if they are large and independent. Scientists almost always have some association with the state, as well as, secondarily, with other institutions capable of a huge financial outlay. Their services are most highly prized, and they make up a prestigious, privileged class.

If the state programs science, then at least in principle we should expect science to be somehow under the control of the citizens of the state. In practice, however, scientists enjoy an almost total autonomy vis-à-vis the citizenry. Scientists constitute the privileged repository of a treasure out of reach of everyone but themselves. More and more, science separates the knowledgeable from the ignorant. Whenever they wish to defend either their privileges or their preferences, the former can appeal to reasons the latter do not understand.

In practice, the function of the scientific class is often to justify the privileges of the ruling elite and enhance the authority of the state. Further: the phenomenon of science is not evenly distributed throughout the world. Science and technology have managed to widen still further the gap between rich countries and poor ones. A country excluded from the scientific and technological movement may never again have the opportunity of recouping its losses. It is condemned to dependence on other countries, and will have to work with the most backward and least interesting technologies, those that make no contribution to scientific progress itself. Thus, the wall of separation between those who know and those who do not, grows higher and wider.

(ii). The Multitudes without Science. And so the world today

is divided between a minority of persons who have entered the scientific era and a majority still excluded from that era. The underdeveloped nations that are entering the scientific era are themselves divided into two groups: a minority of persons is beginning to share, however dependently, in the benefits of science and technology, while a majority finds itself more excluded than ever. All told, then, a minority of persons in the world practices science, while a majority watches it, in astonishment, on television, if they have television. For the majority of the people of the world, the world of science is another world.

Hence three challenges facing the Third World.

1. Access to more advanced scientific and technological research, lest that research gradually form the basis of a political superiority across the board.

2. The training of the young in scientific skills. Not all will become professional scientists. But in order to have an adequate number of professional scientists, the Third World must train a broader base from which to select the most talented. Without the scientific training of the young there can be no scientific class. But in Third World countries, the pitiful level of popular education prevents all access on the part of the great majorities to the antechambers of the sciences and technologies.

3. Basic scientific and technological inventions require thousands and millions of small discoveries and technological improvements. In the past, farmers and artisans made millions of discoveries. Millions of individuals have contributed, however modestly, to scientific and technical progress. Today, when "development" invades a country ill-prepared to receive it, the result is a total paralysis of the inventive, creative mind. Imported specialists and technologists solve every problem, and no solutions but theirs are seen to have any value. The population is stagnated, and gains nothing, while a minority reaps the benefits of the imported technologies. Here the challenge will be to reactivate the capacity for invention and creation on the part of the ordinary folk of our nations, while shielding them from the premature incursions of a technology or science beyond their abilities or resources. Certain intermediate technologies can guide the masses once again to a state of creativity. Otherwise we shall have reason to fear the continued dehumani-

zation of our marginalized populations. New generations will become accustomed to sitting as spectators at a demonstration of works wrought by others, unable to create anything themselves.

These three challenges may be reduced to one: How are we to enable the peoples to transform themselves into agents—subjects, rather than mere objects—of science and technology?

(c) Dangers of Science and Technology

(i). Scientism. The Second Vatican Council warned against the autonomy of earthly realities: "If the expression, the independence of temporal affairs, is taken to mean that created things do not depend on God, and that man can use them without any reference to their Creator, anyone who acknowledges God will see how false such a meaning is" (GS 36). The council is referring to the old scientism that excluded God in the name of science. The scientism of the eighteenth century actually held that science could one day furnish a complete knowledge of the world, a system capable of replacing all the old systems of representation of the world. A scientific view of the world would now provide us all with a representation that would exclude everything that had not received science's stamp of approval.

Scientism today is different. It no longer lays claim to a total representation of the world. This is not the finality of science. Instead, science today has become an intellectual dynamism which, when combined with the development of a technological, industrial, and economic infrastructure, tends to develop "on its own," without reference to any other instance. Scientists tend to accept no nonscientific norm in any area whatever. Thus, science becomes an end in itself.

Indeed, in various scientific circles, anything other than science is an object of contempt, and certainly not regarded as invested with the authority to function as a norm of the practice of science. The only end of science is its own exercise—that is, its endless growth.

This is the way in which science can become out-and-out ideology. If scientists come to power, they will control a great part of the power of state, and will be able to manipulate the resources of their nation for their own emolument. They will be able to shape the national budget to suit their Pharaonic purpose: scientific growth without limit. In today's world of the collapse of traditional values, little is sacred. One of the few things that is, is science. It could happen that a society would seek its ultimate legitimation in science.

(ii). Human Beings and Scientific Objectification. Indeed, where are the limits of science? They lie in the very reason for the success of science. Science is objective. It has succeeded in observing phenomena in an all but total detachment from any interference on the part of the subject. The world it observes is a world without subjectivity, without even the subjectivity of the observer. At least this is the ideal. In practice, there will always be a remnant of subjectivity. It has been this effort of objectivity that has permitted science to slip the bonds that had tied it first to myth, magic, astrology, and the like, and then to philosophy.

But in their attachment to objectivity, scientists run the risk of forgetting the ultimate goal of all science: the life of all humanity. Unless science improves the condition of all women and men, how can its practice be justified? Scientists live further and further removed from common, ordinary folk. Their projects become more and more fragmentary. How can they continue to keep the ultimate goal in view? The danger is the greater, the more remote the immediate connection between scientific projects and any human good. Scientists forget that their science is, before all else, a political affair.

Further: scientific objectivity increasingly consists in the replacement of material reality by mathematical and quasimathematical schemas and structures. Thereby science gains the increased efficiency it will need if it is to achieve precise, prompt, and numerous effects. But this evolution ought to be counterbalanced by a concern for the primacy of the human subject.

Again, the more nearly the sciences approach the human being, the less exact they become. What are human beings in their subjectivity? Science will never know. Science is perfectly adapted to an analysis of nonliving matter. But when its object is life, it can no longer express the whole of its object. And when its object is the human being, it only scratches the surface. Is this a source of anxiety for science? Not in the least; science as such is not interested in what is most human — human worth and dignity, the freedom of the subject, a community of responsible persons. For that matter, the human sciences are inevitably impregnated with myths, philosophy, and wisdom of a religious origin. But they rarely demonstrate any awareness of this fact. They have sought to be their own exclusive proprietors, after the model of the physical sciences.

(iii). Science and Power. In our day and age, there can no longer be any doubt that science makes for power. Indeed, science will bid fairly soon to become the most important factor in all power. The other factors — natural resources, work, population size, and so on — count less and less as science learns to make more efficient use of them.

In the first place, there has always been a close connection between science and war. Since Archimedes, and surely even earlier, military considerations have always provided scientific research with its most powerful stimulus. And of course this is eminently true today, in our age of nuclear energy, electronics, the mass media, space travel, and so forth. Science enables human beings to manufacture more terrible, more sophisticated weaponry than ever before. The military budget is more and more often the principal terminus of a country's capital, hence the huge proportion of that budget destined for modern scientific research. Nowadays a great deal of such research is done under military contract.

Second, science favors the growth of the state. It favors the development of technologies requiring resources that only the state is capable of supplying or adequately complementing. Science tends to Pharaonic works, and such works reinforce the power of the state. Furthermore, new technologies constantly increase the pressure exerted by the state on the citizenry. Science has abetted totalitarian, tyrannical governments by confining the autonomy of individuals and small entities.

In the third place, science increasingly operates in the interest of the classes in power. Only the latter have the capital to furnish science with its tools, supply it the machinery it needs for research. Thus the powerful are permitted to set science its tasks, problems, and challenges, all of which have less to do with the needs of the impoverished masses than with the aspirations of privileged minorities.

(iv). Science and Social Classes. Science consumes enormous capital. Technology serves only those enterprises with a great deal of capital at their disposal. Groups that control capital can exert strong pressure on science. In societies of the Western type, the state, big business, and science or technology are always in collusion. In the Third World, the large multinational corporations, operating under the patronage of the state, import their own science and technology. So there can be no national science or technology other than that of state enterprises.

Science that develops without any control tends simply to grow—to produce without let or hindrance. This means it must have access to a market of powerful economic resources. In the Third World, only a small minority of persons are in a position to purchase the services of science and technology. The majority are left in the lurch. Under these conditions, scientific development tends to favor that minority and leave the majorities out of account. Science and technology will offer more and more help to the minority, who control such vast resources, and leave the masses of the people to their own devices. Science augments the privileges of the privileged. Science remarginalizes the marginalized. As the Pope says: "Technology, man's ally, can become his adversary" (LE 5).

2. WORK

(a) Dignity of the Worker

The dignity of the worker is one of the most constantly recurring themes in the teachings of the magisterium since *Rerum Novarum* (see, e.g., LE 9). We shall do well, however, to see it in its proper context, especially its historical context. Pius XII still found it unseemly for a priest to work as an industrial laborer. But if work is unworthy of a priest, what dignity will it actually have—all theoretical protests to the contrary notwithstanding? Then Paul VI contradicted his predecessor, actually claiming that it had been the church that had sent priests to work side by side with other laborers in industry (OA 48).

(i). Ancient Contempt for Work. Past civilizations generally regarded manual work as an activity of little value — indeed, as one unworthy of any human being of any real dignity. Work was held in contempt.

In Africa, in many places, manual work is reserved to women even today. Nor is the intent thereby to enhance the dignity of women. Men busy themselves with hunting, conversation, and social activities. With the first empires, and first complex societies, work began to be reserved to slaves, male and female. But slaves were not regarded as human beings. One could ask for no clearer expression of a contempt for work. In the Roman world, the distinction was very clear between the condition of citizens — genuinely free persons who were not laborers, but soldiers, administrators, or slave drivers — and the condition of slaves, who were manual workers. Or at any rate the heavier work was reserved to slaves, while the intermediate classes of the technically free poor engaged in less laborious occupations.

Not all work merited the same degree of contempt. Artistic work could actually be esteemed. But most work of that era was indeed subhuman. Until the advent of recent technology, most manual tasks were genuinely degrading: digging the earth, carrying stones, cutting trees. Work on the land required a great deal of muscular energy, and yielded little by way of results. Only the crafts demanded art, or indeed any intellectual, emotional, or creative capacity.

In India, heavy work was reserved to the lowest caste and to the panchamas, the "untouchable" class that ranked below the lowest caste. In the West, society was long divided into three "estates": those engaged in, respectively, prayer, war, and manual work. The distinction was officially abolished by the French Revolution, but by then the rise of the bourgeoisie had introduced a new element.

Actually, throughout almost all of history, up until recent times, efforts at the transformation of the world by work had not yielded much in the way of visible results. The biblical injunction to subdue the earth by the sweat of the human brow could almost have been taken to be God's sardonic jest. It was nature that dominated women and men in work, rather than they who dominated nature. The purpose of work was either simply to get something to eat, or else to produce sumptuous works and monuments for the mighty, or fortresses or other instruments of power for conquerors.

Work began to transform the world, and human life in that world, only in our own times. Even today, in the Third World, rarely does the toil of the peasants transform anything. Their world has not changed for centuries; they farm the way their ancestors farmed. The only changes have been in the income they receive from what they produce, which is lower, and the taxes and rent they have to pay, which are higher.

No wonder, then, that, in traditional societies of the Third World, the ancient distinction prevails between an upper class, which posits its self-esteem and dignity in not having to work, and a working class, which is treated like a mass of slaves deprived of all dignity. Work is still regarded as unworthy of a human being. Even in a household, the men do no work, believing such work will demean them. Men try to find a "position." But having a position does not mean working. Men look for a "position" precisely in order not to have to do any work. The old structure of a slave or serf society has not disappeared in Latin America. Work is not rewarded; idleness is. The wealthy take pride in having the greatest number of "positions," the greatest number of sinecures.

(ii). The New Dignity of Work. With the advent of technology and science, work has acquired a new dignity. The employee has had to learn technology, has had to acquire an education, has had to learn to operate machines and complex instruments. Work has changed. Its productivity has increased. It has become less wasteful. Heavier work has begun to be done by machines. The gap between intelligence and work has narrowed.

The bourgeoisie were the first to appreciate the new productivity of labor, and its capacity for modifying the external world, human life, and the worker's own way of life. As they were able to exploit this new productivity of labor to their own advantage, the bourgeoisie created an ideology of work, and of a society founded on work.

Workers themselves, however, learned to defend themselves against exploitation at the hands of the bourgeoisie. They won better living conditions, together with the actual dignity that the bourgeois ideology had preached in the abstract. The struggle for the dignity of the working class became a struggle between the working class and the class in possession of the means of production. Workers discovered that work transforms the world, and sought to share in the benefits of this transformation. No one today denies the dignity of work, or of workers, on the theoretical level.

(iii). The Right to Work. But what occurs in practice? With the development of technology, any work task requires more and more expensive machinery. Production today requires little physical toil, and a great deal of capital. Consequently the demand for a work force diminishes. In parallel fashion, the productivity of labor increases, and this is another factor in the reduced demand for labor. Hence the phenomenon of mass unemployment.

The situation is most serious in the Third World. Here there is far less capital available, and workers in industrialized Third World countries typically manufacture products for export, in the employ of corporations whose capital comes from abroad. In Latin America, over the course of the last decade, a systematically applied policy of modernization has eliminated millions of industrial and agricultural jobs. Work has become appreciated and humanizing; but it has thereby become difficult to come by. The countries of the Third World are excluded from the new work. As for traditional work, it continues, but only at a diminished rate, because farming or animal husbandry tends to monopolize the land, and the state, under pressure of more modern and more powerful producers, must sacrifice our obsolete industry, including farming.

By all indications, the right to work is becoming the major problem for labor. What makes socialism so attractive to the Third World is the guarantee of employment. In a socialist society, there will be work for all. Work used to be regarded as an obligation. Now it is regarded as a right.

Sheer subsistence is not the issue. Dignity is the issue. The unemployed, even if they receive enough income to live, have the sensation of being excluded from society, the feeling of having no worth or dignity. They are not regarded as worthy of contributing to activity to transform the world. Nowadays, the dignity of the worker means first of all the right to work, the right to employment (GS 67; LE 18).

(b) Alienation of the Worker

(i). Exploitation of the Body. Any kind of work, as Pope John Paul II reminds us in his encyclical on labor, causes fatigue and pain (LE 9, 27). Some work tasks, however, leave the rhythms of human beings entirely out of account, subjecting workers' bodies to efforts and rhythms that absolutely exhaust those bodies. What a ceaseless struggle on the part of workers has attained in part in certain countries—job safety, better working conditions, housing, transportation, and so on—is still an empty dream in many regions of the Third World. Many workers are the victims of a bodily exhaustion reminiscent of the forced labor of slaves or of concentration camp internees. This is the deepest, most radical, and most destructive form of the alienation of labor.

(ii). The Capitalist System. The second alienation emerges from the capitalist system, especially when that system is applied without adequate control, as so often in the Third World. Workers receive in wages only what is indispensable for their survival. The actual fruit of their labor is confiscated to augment capital. Capital becomes the proprietor of production. Production no longer has the purpose of satisfying the needs of the worker. Now its purpose is simply the increase of capital, in order that the prevailing productive system may enjoy indefinite growth. Marxism subjects capitalism to a radical, exhaustive criticism as a model of society. This gives Marxism great prestige in the Third World. It furnishes a model for criticism of the oppressive established system.

(iii). Construction of a Civilization of Privilege. The third alienation is that workers construct a world destined to remain forever foreign to them. In the Third World, the dynamism of capitalism fails. Here, accumulated capital serves not to enhance the system of production, but to build a world of luxury and overconsumption for the satisfaction of an infinitesimal minority of the population. Labor and capital are both delivered into the hands of an aristocratic minority. This minority, by concentrating

all ownership in its own hands, by having to contribute almost nothing to the common good in the form of taxes, and by corrupting the state from bottom to top, manages to confiscate most of the national product for the enhancement of its luxurious lifestyle. In Brazil, 1 percent of the population controls almost 50 percent of the national product. This gives us our wonderful cities, and makes possible our ostentatious expenditures for a fantasy world built by workers who receive no benefit from it. Workers building the mansions and the banks have not so much as a shack to live in, but simply eat and sleep where they work.

(c) The Gospel of Work

(i). Value of Work. The most noteworthy documents of the church magisterium on labor are the Vatican II Constitution *Gaudium et Spes* and Pope John Paul II's encyclical *Laborem Exercens.* These documents speak for multitudes of Catholic workers. They are the reflection of the persevering activity of the Catholic worker movements and all worker movements. In the Catholic Church, worker movements must wage an uphill battle with the timidity of the church, the formidable pressures of the bourgeoisie, and the prestige of the members of the bourgeoisie who style themselves Christian. Opposition in the church to all forms of defense of the dignity and rights of workers is still powerful in our day. However, at least at the theoretical level, workers have won certain victories with the publication of the documents just cited.

Today, as during all the centuries of the old Christendoms, a contrast prevails between original Christianity and Christianity in its later development. The people of Israel were essentially a people of free workers, who nevertheless had to struggle against every form of domination, external and internal, to maintain their freedoms. Israel made no distinction between a working class deprived of its rights and a class of dominators monopolizing all rights. Even priests, doctors of the laws, and scribes were manual laborers. At no moment was there any expression of contempt for manual work.

Jesus embarked on the life of a manual laborer not because this was an extraordinary way of life, but simply because he was a member of the people of Israel. This caused him no problems. He was not looked down upon as some kind of slave because he was a manual laborer. Nor was anyone who took on manual work regarded as performing an act of humility. Being a laborer did not mean that one was lowering oneself in any way.

The first Christian communities were composed, at least predominantly, of manual laborers, and this lent a tonality to the whole of Christian life. Things changed when the clergy entered the privileged, nonworking class. Now the church recognized a feudal society based on a division into warriors, priests, and workers. From that moment forward, workers were on the bottom rung of the social ladder. The prejudices of Greco-Roman society had invaded Christians' very mode of existence.

During the era of the Christendoms, moral reform invariably emphasized a return to manual work. The old monks and nuns had been manual workers, and monastic reforms sought to return to the original state of things. But pressures in the opposite direction were strong. Francis of Assisi had hoped to be allowed to perform manual work, but pressure from those opposed to the dignity of manual labor proved too strong even for him.

As the laborer's calling became more and more an object of contempt, workers' influence in the church itself gradually diminished. Accordingly, we must wonder about the actual scope of public declarations on the part of the church when it comes to the "dignity of the working class." Might such pronouncements be only a concession to the bourgeois party line? We can in fact evaluate the real scope of these declarations only by examining their practical applications. Here, the problem of the clergy must come first. If the clergy take no interest in the advancement of manual workers, if the clergy are composed of nonworkers, what does this tell Christians about the real value of manual work? At best it says: you can get along without it. Second is the problem of workers' actual influence in the church: What opportunities are afforded workers to make their voices heard in the church? Third, what of the dominant lifestyle, and ideology of lifestyle, in the church? At the moment the prevailing tone is bourgeois, and corresponds to the mentality of the middle classes of the developed countries. When will the voice of the workers be heard in liturgy, in catechetics, in the style of church organizations, and in positions taken by church authorities?

Contemporary documents complacently cite the texts of the Book of Genesis identifying manual labor as a participation in the creative work of God (LE 9, 27). And indeed Genesis concurs with the aspirations of the working civilizations of our day: work transforms the world, and by transforming the world transforms humanity itself. Here we see what work ought to be. Here is the workers' goal, a workers' utopia. Reading the Book of Genesis, workers have always been able to perceive the extent to which their hopes and efforts have been frustrated.

Even today, many tasks taken up by human beings have nothing transforming about them, either of the world or of those who dwell in it, and furnish no image of God's deed of creation. What transformation is experienced by the countless street vendors of the great cities, selling cigars or Gillette blades or aspirins one at a time? What transformation do night security personnel, or hall porters, or sugar cane cutters, or miners, or street sweepers, or an infinitude of other persons doing lowly tasks ever see? Only a minority of persons have the privilege of working at a task either dignifying in itself or in any way reminiscent of the work of creation.

Whenever the Bible shows us the great works of transformation of the world—the Tower of Babel, the pyramids of Egypt, the magnificent works of Solomon, the grandeur of Tyre, the magnificence of Babylon—it denounces them, and condemns the pridefulness and oppression upon which they have been built. The world is transformed at the price of the oppression of the poor. The same image of labor prevails in our world today as well. We are far indeed from the image of work in the creation accounts of the Bible! (See, for example, Gen. 11:1–9; 1 Kings 10:14–11:13; Jer. 50–51; Ezek. 26–28.)

Nor, when the Bible mentions the work of the people, does it ever compare it to the work of God. Even Jesus' manual work in Nazareth is not singled out as cooperation with the deed of God as creator. Nor does Paul appeal to any such consideration in calling his addressees to fidelity to their task, or to justify his own manual work. The motive invoked or underlying is always:

to have something to eat. If one would eat, one must work.

The message of the Bible is precisely that no one has the right to consume what another needs in order to live. Food is the fruit of toil. To devour the food of another is a breach of solidarity among the people. If anyone is unwilling to work, let that one have nothing to eat (see 2 Thess. 3:6–8, 10–12). Work is the collective task of humanity. All must share in it. Those who refuse to do so cut themselves off from community.

Accordingly, when we speak of the transformation of the world, we cannot escape the fact that the basic, primordial transformation of the world is the conversion of matter to food. The purpose of work is to produce food. This finality may have disappeared from the perspective of wealthy peoples. But in the Third World, nutrition is still the basic human requirement, and the problem of labor is still situated at this level.

Jesus himself willed to be a worker. That means he was willing to perform his share of the common task. He did not wish to eat, to live, by the toil of others. But evangelization, too, is work, and here too the worker has the right to something to eat. Workers have their dignity in doing their part in the production of food. Those persons are dignified, are worthy, who eat bread produced by the sweat of their own brow, not that of others.

(ii). Priority of the Worker. Capitalist economy has set the entire human scale of values on its ear. It has promoted itself to the status of the highest value of all. First comes the economy, then those who work in the economy. This inversion of values prevails in the Third World especially, where nations enjoy little or no autonomy in the direction of their economies. Third World economies are swept up in world movements beyond their control. Workers are completely subjected to the economy. Hence the church's forthright condemnation of the capitalist system, culminating in Pope John Paul II's *Laborem Exercens.* True, the pope observes, socialism is exposed to the same danger. In either system, the economy can be directed by a small group of persons who subordinate it to Pharaonic works—weaponry policies, or other policies drawn up without consultation of the workers in that economy and contrary to their interests.

If they hope to subordinate the economy to their own control, workers have only themselves to rely on, through workers' organizations of which they themselves must have charge (see LE 9, 16, 17).

As work procedures become more and more complex, coming to depend more and more on advanced technologies and huge outlays of capital, the danger of an autonomous economy increases. Workers have less opportunity to evaluate the scope of plans and enterprises—less control over where the capital goes. It becomes child's play for the czars of society to deceive them. Only the state grows, as it builds up an economy intended to swell its power to still greater proportions. We are farther than ever from the principle of the priority of the worker. We are faced with a political problem of the first magnitude.

Undeniably, work is dependent on the requirements of matter. Matter does not readily subordinate itself to human preferences or conveniences. Work is a struggle with material forces, especially with the inertia of matter, the law of gravity, the atomic and molecular forces. The finest machinery in the world will not eliminate fatigue and physical exhaustion. However, one must weigh the genuine need a work project may foreseeably fulfill in terms of the common good, against the human price of that same project. Undertakings are set afoot nowadays that take no account whatever of the human cost in terms of lives lost, persons mutilated or otherwise sidelined from the work force, and work accidents of all kinds. Each year more persons die from accidents at work than from all of our wars and criminal acts combined.

(d) Ownership

(i). Triumph of Bourgeois Individualism. With the bourgeois revolutions, on the heels of the triumph of the American and French Revolutions, came the principle of private ownership as the basis of social order. The great texts proclaiming the right to private property were the Declaration on the Rights of Man and the Citizen (1789), the Fifth Amendment to the Constitution of the United States (1791), and Articles 544 and 545 of the Napoleonic Civil Code (1804).[2] All liberal constitutions have copied this legislation.

Bourgeois individualism declares the right to private property to be sacred and inviolable, absolute and inalienable, and per-petual. The right of ownership confers the right of use and abuse without any limitation other than that of public order.

This liberal "right" has served most effectively as a cloak for the expansion of the capitalist system. This is the "right" that still predominates in the Western world, and that now prevails as well in many nations of the Third World, which had never known it until the arrival of the invader.

(ii). Evolution of Official Catholic Teaching. Bourgeois individual-ualism exalts ownership to the status of an essential attribute of human nature. Only someone who owns something is genuinely a human being. Consequently, full civil rights are denied to those who own nothing. The basic relationship between the material world and humanity is no longer the relationship of work, then, but the relationship of ownership. Matter is no longer primarily our collaborator at work. Matter has become primarily the prop-erty of its owner.

Before Vatican II, Catholic social teaching tried to straddle the fence. It defended the bourgeois right to private ownership as a property of human nature itself, and therefore as essential to the makeup of the human being. But it failed to specify the object of this essential ownership. It never made a distinction between proprietorship over goods and services on the one hand, and the means of production on the other. It made no distinction between ownership of a family farm and ownership of plantations, or similar large enterprises, employing thousands of workers. It applied the same principles to both.

Behind this attitude lurked one part ignorance and one part confusion. Moral theologians were so impressed by the argu-ments of the liberal ideology that they forgot the prophetic words of the Fathers of the church. They accepted the liberal principle that promoted private ownership to the status of a necessary condition for economic development.[3]

Beginning with *Gaudium et Spes,* however, the church ceased to view private ownership as constituting an essential of human nature. It was no longer a right guaranteed by natural law, but emerged only from the historical conditions of peoples (GS 71). The encyclical *Laborem Exercens* adopts the same teaching, and expounds a radical criticism of private property. It simply denies the basis of the liberal doctrine. The right of ownership as enunciated in the constitutions of Western countries, and as applied in those same countries, cannot be justified. Socialist regimes do not come in for the same criticism, although the pope does state that it is not enough to nationalize goods and services in order for them to be genuinely at the service of the people. (LE 14). There is no such thing as a right to absolute, exclusive ownership, says the pope. All ownership represents a "social mortgage." People may not do just as they please with their property, or reserve goods for their own exclusive use (ibid.; see Puebla 975, 1224, 1281). In other words, ownership may no longer be regarded as an indispensable attribute of the human being, or as something essential to the dignity of that human being.

Catholic social teaching looks for a third way through the horns of the dilemma of private ownership and state ownership. The pope seems to suggest that the ideal owners would be certain intermediate entities. These entities would not be far from the ancient tradition of ownership of the land by the clan or tribe (see LE 14).

(iii). The People and Ownership. The first need of the poor consists of the necessities of life. Thus the primary right of the poor is not the ownership of anything, but the use of certain things: a house, a strip of land to cultivate, certain work implements, a bicycle, and so on. Further: farmers demand land in order to cultivate it, and workers want a factory in order to work there. It is not private ownership that they seek, then. On the contrary: traditionally, land ownership has been collective, and this has been no obstacle to dividing it up among the members of a community when it comes to actual use.

True, workers have a right to the fruit of their labor. But it does not follow that they have the right to the private ownership of the fruit of their labor. A confusion of these two concepts has lain at the basis of the unremitting liberal claim that proprietors have a right simply to appropriate the products of their lands or factories for their own exclusive use. No, all involved in the production of anything have a right to their fair share of the fruits of this common toil. Work is the collective deed of the human community. There is no such thing as individual work. There is no such thing as work that will produce something by the sole powers of one individual. All work is social. Its fruits must be social as well.

3. CONCLUSION

Human beings are made for a life of communion with the material world, and the basic mode of this communion is work. This is the most profound point of agreement between Marxism and Christianity. Some have even said, with a dash of exaggeration, that Marx was the first Christian philosopher—the first to express in philosophical terms the fundamental principle of Christian anthropology. Before Marx, the philosophies employed by Christianity had all been too idealistic. Not even Aristotle had made an adequate appraisal of the dignity of work.

There is no reason why the Bible should have developed an explicit doctrine of work. The biblical world was a working world. Everything the Bible says refers to workers. As everyone worked, and everything they did was work, there was no need to be talking about workers and work.

The impact of Hellenistic society on the Christian tradition was tremendous. Roman society had no knowledge of work, having reduced it to the status of a subhuman reality. After all, work was done by slaves. Nor has work ever recovered its dignity in the church as a whole. There have always been groups, and prophets; there has always been the silent life of Christians, the vast majority of whom have been workers. Their life and condition as workers did not, however, succeed in penetrating the style of the superstructure erected above the people of God. Today, however, with the coming of the Third World, work may at last have found its historical opportunity in the church. Here, at least, the repository of the meaning of the gospel of Jesus the worker is a people of workers. They know that work is the human calling, and that it is by means of work that human beings both achieve their destiny and accomplish the will of God. Work does not exclude other responsibilities. But it is at the basis of them all. Without work, nothing else is of any worth. Work, and work alone, confers seriousness and realism on all other human endeavors.

CHAPTER V

Humanity and the History of Its Liberation

From the outset, the Christian message focused far more intently on human beings' relationship with one another than on their relationship with matter. Liberation would not be the anguished problem it is if it referred only to our relationship with nature. The problem of human subjugation lies in the relationship among human beings themselves.

Obviously the liberation of humanity must include the conquest and domination of nature. The principal obstacle to this domination, however, resides not in matter itself, but in human beings, who utilize nature as an instrument of domination. By the will of human beings, work, science and technology, and matter itself have been transformed into instruments of enslavement. Our deliverance from the domination of matter, then, can only follow upon our deliverance from relations of domination by one another. The prime obstacle to human liberation resides not in the resistance of matter, but in the resistance of human beings themselves, as we struggle with one another to gain and keep the upper hand over our neighbor.

Otherwise, history could practically be reduced to the progressive domination of matter by the human race. But the reality is far more traumatic. More than anything else, history is the saga of the struggles waged by human beings for the conquest of the world of human beings and matter alike. Material development, then, far from resolving social conflicts, only renders them more extensive, radical, and tragic.

The law of human societies has always been human beings' internecine strife—a struggle of varying form and worth, but a perpetual struggle. The challenge to humanity as the common existence of millions of individuals is the challenge to rise above the struggles that weave the warp and woof of history. Humanity lives amidst constant social struggles. Our endless quest for peace and communion in justice and collaboration has come to constitute our very history. Over and over we try, only to fail once more. Then we begin again. History is woven of human beings' struggles and their attempts to put an end, somehow, to their endless recurrence.

Christianity discerns this self-destructive struggle waged by humanity, singles it out as the special object of its attention, and subjects it to its own interpretation. So reticent on the subject of our conquest of matter, the Bible is filled with the story of our strife with one another. The history of the people of God is the story of the suffering inflicted on them by human struggle. Far from being meaningless, then, human struggles are crucial to Christian eschatology. This is where they receive their deepest value. Christian eschatology interprets history precisely from the viewpoint of these struggles.

A social struggle must choose its means. One means is war. The other is word. Will history finally be made by war or by word? The Christian message includes an answer to this question, as well. For Christian theology, the central thread of history, the core of the life of women and men in society, is the struggle for the liberation of a people of the poor. It is in this struggle that history has its meaning—its link with eschatology, its bond with the coming of the Reign of God. The people of the poor struggle by their word; they express themselves in real and specific historical movements. The people of the poor are struggling in Latin America, and not only in Latin America: when we share in the struggles of the impoverished people of Latin America, our eyes are opened to so many analogues, past and present, of this same struggle. All of these concrete historical phenomena constitute a unity in the eyes of Christianity. Christianity focuses its light on this reality, and shows us ever the same reality: the emergence of the people of God out of the midst of the poor—the birth pangs of a new humanity, born here on this earth to reach full maturity in the world of the future.

In the first section of this chapter I propose to examine the birth of the people of the poor amidst social struggles. In the second section, I shall look at the ways in which the people of the poor struggle to be born and to live in a world that rejects them and refuses to permit them to exist.

Many classic philosophies and theologies were content with principles of the highest generality, having nothing to do with actual human beings. For example: "Man is a social being." From this kind of statement, philosophy and theology went on to deduce a whole series of innocuous, totally irrelevant propositions. After all, what exists is never a "society" in the abstract, but a network of concrete conflicts and struggles. It is here, in the real world of actuality, that philosophy and theology must find meaning and orientation.

1. A PEOPLE OF THE POOR IN A STRUGGLE FOR LIBERATION

(a) Humanity Delivered Over to Subjugation

(i). The Historical Situation of Domination. Apart from exceptional cases, human societies present a superficial appearance of tranquility. Agitations, debates, are no threat to established institutions. Even the spectacle of Latin America, despite the rhetoric of the media, gives the impression of stability. Institutions function, so the people must be cooperating; nations function, with all of the activities of state in good running order; business functions; cultural institutions function. They all function in virtue of a certain consent. And so there is an impression of a predominant stability and harmony. Indeed, the dominant classes are able to point to a certain popular "consent" to prevailing institutions, and thereby "squash rumors" of an underlying conflict.

The continuity of the institutions in question might indeed seem to justify the conclusion that, in the social sphere, integration is mightier than struggle. The most powerful objection to theories based on a class struggle will always be the simple observation of empirical reality. It used to be said that the working class will necessarily be revolutionary, because it is oppressed, and because it is strong. But observers have been on the lookout for this revolutionary working class for 150 years now, and it has not yet put in its appearance. Arguments in favor of institutions — in favor of the nation, business, the schools, and so on — have always seemed stronger than the arguments for the destruction or radical transformation of these institutions. The most visible phenomenon in Latin America is the resistance of established structures to what ought surely to have been the explosiveness of the facts of domination and subjugation.

Why do institutions function? Why does the stability of structures turn out to be stronger than opposing factors? In part, because of the strength of the dominant ideology, which "defuses" any attempt to change things. In part, because of the weakness of factors of transformation. But above all, because of the sheer need to survive. The masses accept the status quo because it affords them minimal subsistence, which they fear they might lose if there were to be a radical change. And the governing classes carefully nurture this fear. Hence there is a certain consensus in favor of the maintenance of prevailing institutions, which fails only in exceptional circumstances, such as revolution, itself due to a complete internal disintegration of institutions.

But then the habitual stability of established societies seems to belie the notion that vast masses of people eke out their existence in a basically unlivable situation of subjugation and oppression. This permits the denial, on the lips of the ideologues of domination, of the existence of any such situation. In Latin America, the dominant ideologies deny any domination exercised by the industrialized nations. They deny the subjugation of the people by the upper classes, by states, by dominant cultures, by the white race, or by the male sex. All "apparent difficulties" are laid to the account of isolated, circumstantial, secondary facts and occurrences.

By their silence, the masses appear to vouch for the reality of a prevailing Latin American social harmony. However, this silence reigns only in the public square, from which the poor are watchfully excluded. It is a forced silence, and a localized one. The poor speak, but in the public square their voice is muffled by the louder noises of the lords of power.

When we come to define the dominant element in the social reality of Latin America, then, we must make an option. We must choose between a view of oneness and harmony, and a view of struggle and opposition. The powerful invariably opt for the view of a prevailing unity. The oppressed select a dualistic view—one of combat.

Medellín and Puebla are the twin directional signs erected for the guidance of the Latin American church in its interpretation of human reality. Both of these great conferences have selected the dualistic view, which is likewise the prevailing view in Latin American theology.

In the West, the dualistic anthropological interpretation, which prioritizes the element of combat, has been principally represented by Marxism, while all or nearly all other philosophies have presented an optimistic view of human society, thereby supplying established societies with their made-to-order ideologies.

Because of this material identity between the respective views of factual reality held by Marxism and Latin American theology, certain critics have pronounced Latin American theology to be based on Marxism. But the argument does not follow. The view of reality embraced by Puebla and Medellín is based on facts. If the facts have been elucidated by theoretical data, these data have been primarily not Marxist, but biblical. And indeed, biblical dualism here is the same as Marxist dualism.

The facts of domination and subjugation fairly leap out at the impartial observer. Of course, the observer must be impartial. The facts are not visible to all. Many have a stake in not seeing them. The steadfast, almost total silence of these persons must not deceive us. They all know very well how human society is constituted, although they do not all believe in the possibility of a change. They know only that the stability of institutions is based on fear. "Consent" here means fear, and the force of arms.

The fact is that human being dominates human being. Society is that space where some persons subjugate others. A minority subjugates a majority. Human society is the vehicle of an inner corruption and basic vitiation. No human relationship is unscarred by the corruption of domination and subjugation.

It is not the place of theology to attempt to describe the forms of domination and dependency prevailing in Latin America today. This is the task of sociology. Theology's function is to examine the scope of this domination and dependency in the light of faith and thereby come to a fuller understanding of the human being.

The phenomenon in question is manifold. It cannot be reduced to a single, basic factor. There is class domination, and there are other forms of domination, which are more than mere aspects of the former. But the basic and most comprehensive domination in Latin America, the result of the original *conquista,* is the domination exercised over the masses by minorities that have managed to preserve the legacy of this conquest and subjugation of races and peoples. Still today whites dominate blacks, those descendants of enslaved ancestors. Whites still dominate Indians, those heirs of crushed peoples. The basic, comprehensive domination that disfigures the face of our continent is the domination of victors over vanquished, of those who have for centuries held military and political power over those who have never held such power. The basic, comprehensive domination that is the scourge of Latin America today is the subjugation of certain peoples, regarded as inferior, by a people regarding itself as superior, precisely in the name of its imagined superiority of race, culture, people, and nation. The real, concrete root of the real, concrete superiority of the dominators is war and military victory. Their domination is a domination founded on war. The face of Latin America is the face of a humanity split between victor and vanquished. If the victors today appear as the prolongation and extension of the dominators of the entire world, this does not militate against, but only confirms, the analogous division of humanity into two contrary poles.

True, there are the *mestizos.* We do have a people in the middle. But this only means that they are caught in the middle.

The *mestizos* avenge their subjugation by oppressing Indians or blacks. Being themselves the victims of subjugation, they subjugate their own victims out of resentment, and in imitation of their own conquerors. The mere fact of the existence of two opposite poles must not hoodwink us into drawing the naive inference that any given individual will ever be entirely on one side or the other of the dividing wall. No, we each belong to both poles, and our lives are situations of simultaneous internal and external division.

Side by side with political and military domination exists a state of economic domination, by way of the exploitation of labor. Obviously, political domination and economic domination will tend to reinforce one another. The defeated will be the most exploited of workers, as in the case of the Indians and blacks of Latin America. However, there can be economic domination without an antecedent military victory. Many poor whites, members of the conquistador peoples, are likewise exploited by the dominant classes.

Again, economic domination assumes a variety of aspects. At the present time it consists in, for example, the marginalization of all who cannot be integrated into the established, dominant system of production. Millions of potential workers sit idle. Either they do not have the necessary cultural qualifications, or else insufficient capital is available to create employment for them. The peoples and groups who monopolize the world's science and technology keep the juiciest pieces of world production for themselves, distributing only the less appetizing portions to other nations and groups. This is how the peoples of the Third World have been excluded from the spiral of genuine economic development. Economic dependency is intertwined with a cultural subjugation. The proprietor of scientific culture becomes the proprietor of the economy.

The majority of the poor of this world do not understand all that is transpiring. But they do know that they are being regarded by others as mere objects. They know that they are not recognized as having the right to share in anything. They know that they have been excluded from the game the mighty play. They know that they had better be satisfied with leftovers. They are like the poor Lazarus languishing at the rich man's door.

Pope John Paul II did well to recognize, in this parable, the image of the world today, the mournful condition of today's humanity (RH 16).

(ii). A Christian Reading of the Structures of Domination. The Bible always presents humanity as polarized—divided between two antagonistic poles. The human race never appears as a homogeneous whole, or even as a synthesis of contraries, with each pole complementing the other in its diversity. The Old Testament builds its historiography on the antagonism between Israel and the empires or peoples who oppress it. On one side is oppressed Israel, and on the other, Egypt, Babylon, Assyria, and so on. In the view of the prophets, we find, in historical Israel, on one side the true prophets—the poor, the faithful remnant of Israel—and on the other, royalty, and the powerful—the false prophets, impious and unfaithful to God.

The New Testament shifts the terms of the opposition, but maintains the same bipolar structure. Humanity is composed of rich and poor. Rich and poor are antagonistic, and stand in a reciprocal relationship of causality: the rich are rich because they rob the poor and refuse to share with them. The opposition between rich and poor is extended: on one side, the side of the oppressors, are the Pharisees, the scribes, the chief priests, and the leaders of the people, who have everything; on the other side are sinners, the alienated, lepers, the sick, the blind, the deaf, the mute, the possessed, the poor, and the persecuted. In other words, on the one side are those who have all power, and on the other, those who have no power.

This bipolarization of human beings as such generates their bipolarization with respect to the Reign of God. The lot of the one pole is condemnation, the lot of the other, salvation. In this sense St. John's bipolarization is not unfaithful to the rest of the New Testament, but only represents a radical translation of what is found throughout all of the biblical writings.

Once more, however, we must not conclude that the two groups of persons alive today are one group of perfect persons and another of pure sinners. On the contrary, the biblical schema does not neglect the fact that each individual is part good and part evil. It is important, however, to grasp the basic structure of the biblical outlook. For the Bible, the basic structure of humanity is dualistic, and we must understand humanity's destiny from the viewpoint of this bipolarity. Without it, all Christian eschatology collapses.[1]

But there is no Manichaeism here. The Bible is different from Manichaeism. It does not say that all good is on one side and all evil on the other, or that there is anyone who belongs entirely to good or to evil. Biblical dualism is a structural division. An understanding of humanity from a point of departure in this dualistic structure is at once a challenge, a warning, and a promise. A wealthy person can become poor, and a poor person can grow rich. The New Testament speaks of structures alone, leaving a coefficient of insecurity as to the makeup of any individual.

What is the relationship between the poor of the Bible and the various social categories in Latin America today? Some deny that the *anawim,* the poor of the Bible, are "reducible" to the social classes of the present. Obviously, the poor of the Bible will not correspond either directly or exclusively to categories of the present. The Bible speaks of the poor of all times. But precisely because it speaks of the poor of all times, it speaks of the poor of Latin America today. We must identify those among us who, today, are the poor of whom the Bible speaks. After all, the Bible speaks of concrete human beings actually alive in history.

The Puebla Final Document has identified these poor very precisely. It has put its finger on the bipolarization of rich and poor in today's Latin American society (Puebla 28, 30, 47, 50). The Medellín document had been even more explicit (Peace 2–7). But even Puebla identified the structures of domination and subjugation by which some human groups oppress other human groups.

Domination is more than an incidental phenomenon of our existence. On the other hand, it is not reducible to an inevitable element of the human condition, to which it would be better to close our eyes. No, we cannot live on earth and escape the fact: domination is situational, but it determines the human condition. It is a challenge. Persons discover themselves as persons, and the human race embraces its destiny as the human race, in joining the struggle against domination and striving to build a society in which this domination will be no more.

(b) The People of the Poor and History

(i). Rise of the People of the Poor. Amidst a world of domination, where can we find the authentic human race, genuine human beings? Will human beings have fled, taken refuge, sought to flee the antagonisms that prevail between rich and poor? By no means. The true human race will be found in the midst of the struggle of the poor to overcome a world of domination. True human beings will be found in a state not of truce, but of combat. The human condition is delineated by struggle. From birth to death we are caught up in struggle, and this is what constitutes the substance of human dignity. A person who does not struggle can have no dignity.

Poverty is not human. It is inhuman. Of itself it begets nothing. It destroys. And still, from out of the midst of the poor, a new phenomenon arises. This new phenomenon is a testimonial to a genuine humanity, the sign of the coming of the new person who defeats and overcomes domination. This phenomenon is seen in the movements by which the poor join forces, organize, and constitute themselves a force in history.

The movements of the poor are manifold and varied. They spring out of the heart of a variety of dominations. They are the movements of native peoples coming to an awareness of their values and their human dignity, as they reject the contempt that has overwhelmed them and deprived them of all opportunity to live as a people. They are the movements of blacks rebelling against rejection and exploitation. They are the movements of peasants driven from their lands and stripped of all security. They are the worker movements, the movements of the barrios, the slum movements, all campaigns against want, misery, and exploitation.

In these movements of struggle for liberation, the people of the poor arise. This is what distinguishes the people from social institutions. The people are not the nation. The nation mounts an enormous effort of organization and ideologization to reduce and subjugate the people and integrate it within its goals. But the goals of the people are not the goals of the nation: the nation is filled with pride; it seeks power and greatness; the people seek to live, to have a better life. This cannot be done without power, but power is not the goal. Accordingly, the people will abide in a state of latent, at least, if not open, conflict with the nation, and especially with the state, and with the governing classes who claim to know the direction in which the nation ought to be moving. The people spring into being as a people when they begin to take cognizance of the difference between their own aspirations and those of their nation.[2] This applies first of all to native Americans, who cannot recognize themselves as a people in today's nations, and to blacks, who are coming to discover their African origins and are beginning to ask themselves about their true nation. But it is valid as well for all peoples who find the national conflicts of Latin America incomprehensible, and who would be happier in a *patria grande,* a great homeland.

Again, the people of the poor are not like the employees of a corporation, or a radio or television audience, or the groups of human beings joined by membership in social institutions. The people are made up of all who have no active social or political voice, all who are relegated to the margins of the dominant process. The people spring into being when all those human beings begin to join together in the project of a common social existence, when all those persons begin to strive to create an alternative to the existing situation. What makes the people a people is their common will to create a new social reality, a fabric woven of communion and participation. All those who are traveling through the desert, wayfarers in quest of a different society, are members of the people. Why do the dominant classes deny the existence of the people? Because they do not fit into their plans.

In Latin America the people are presently coming into being precisely as a people, and their appearance on the scene constitutes a theological event of the first magnitude. The people of God are materializing here on our continent. Again, some raise the objection that the biblical concept of the people of God is too broad to be "reduced" to an incarnation in the political and social activity of the Latin American people today. But are the people of God outside history? Are the people of God not composed of human beings? Are the people of God not a yeast and a ferment? Then they must be present somewhere.

Where? Precisely in those places, surely, where the poor gather together to act as a people.

The people manifest themselves by means of historical movements: unions, parties, local associations, liberation movements. Many historical factors enter into these movements: ideologies, schemas of organization, methods of action, psycho-social dynamics, and so on, none of which is a constituent of the people of God as such, but rather all are creations of human beings of every category. Indeed, the means by which the people of God are enabled to act are generally bestowed on them by members of the governing classes of established society. Beneath all these structural elements, however, is a basic movement: the faith of the people, their will to live, their goal of a new society. This is the substance and essence of the people. This is what makes the people of God a people. After all, the people of God, the new Israel, must be incarnate in history—in history's contingent, transitory, provisional forms. The people of God are not some immutable, impassible substance common to all centuries, abiding in perfect self-identity. The people of God are women and men, joined in a union that takes on successive historical shapes. This union cannot have all social contours at once. A current movement cannot be indicted for not bearing the characteristics of all similar movements in the course of the centuries. It need only be today's response to today's challenge. Today the activity of the people of God is transpiring in the area of the efforts exerted by the Latin American people for their social and political liberation (Puebla 1137).[3]

The people muster all categories of the oppressed and dominated and mold these categories into their project of a new society. These persons already exist as a people, if only in inchoate form. Indeed, they have always existed as a people. Whence does such a people proceed? Not from history alone, surely. History might explain why the Indians might wish to return to the condition in which they existed before the conquest. History could show why the blacks might wish to return to Africa, that workers should wish to take over the factories in place of the owners, and so on. But a return to the past is never enough to form a people. To create a people, it is not enough to topple empires, overthrow the power of capital, or recover the land from the plantation owners. This is why a new society of communion and popular participation cannot arise on the strength of mere historical factors. Neither the progress of the economy, nor the development of industrialization, nor social evolution, nor the dialectic of the internal struggle of social regimes will ever explain the creation of a people that cements all categories of the oppressed in the unity of a common project.

The people of the poor rise up at a call. The people spring into being as a people from a genuine collective vocation, out of a call to faith and a challenge to the accomplishment of a historical task. This call does not come from human beings alone. It comes from the Holy Spirit. It is the sign of the power of God at work. The Spirit rouses this collective faith precisely that a people may commence to act as a people. In this new people, the power of the Spirit becomes present in history.

A people is the locus of the maximal expression of freedom in history. Any freedom enjoyed by the governing classes of established society, by the state, by corporations, by cultural institutions, is heavily restricted by the need to keep society as it is. None of them can act for change. When they change, it is only because they have been pressured by the people.

All creative action is a struggle with the established structures. This is why freedom acquires its full expansion only in struggle. Men and women become fully free only when they actively assume the task of changing the world, changing a society of structures of domination and replacing it with a common life of partnership and communion. Freedom is not only the negation of that which is; freedom is above all the assertion of a new reality. Freedom is discovery, and positive creation.

The primary task of freedom is to discover an oppressed people's latent energies, awaken those energies, and weld them together in function of a single, goal-oriented activity. Freedom is social, collective; it tends to awaken the faith and courage of a whole people. A people takes up a task not of the promotion of the individual, but of the collective advancement of the people as such. A purely individual advancement inevitably relies on determinisms, on forces capable of guaranteeing a successful outcome. The people have no need of a guaranteed triumph. They never have such a guarantee. Those whose goal is primarily victory and success are condemned to accept the determinisms and conditionings of established society. The bourgeoisie have no access to freedom because they seek victory at any price.

In the people's struggle for their liberation from all forms of domination, we rightly sense the birth pangs of a creation. The world regards the self-manifestation of the daughters and sons of God with anxiety. This world is first and foremost the world of human society (Rom. 8:19–22). Why are the sufferings of this world so reminiscent of birth pangs? Because a real birth is occurring. A new creation is about to come to light, a new world is being born, and sure to be born. The novelty of this new world, this new creation, does not proceed from the evolution of blind historical forces. Our hope is not in economic development, or the dialectical interplay of social contrasts in the productive process, or the antagonisms of cultures, races, and sexes. Our hope is in the power of God, which makes all things new and prepares the rise of a new people out of the old ones. This is why the entire project of the people begins in the pains of birth. The sufferings of all who toil to arouse the people — all the persecutions, the disappointments, the tribulations, the weariness, all the perseverance in the struggle — are the pangs of a birth already occurring in our midst.

After all, the pangs of the new creation are not metaphorical. They are not the pain of actors on a stage. They are altogether real sufferings, the sufferings that flow from the struggles for liberation. In all of these struggles, something new is arising. While victory is not guaranteed, while the successes are always precarious and the failures many, the act of creation does not cease. A people seeks to be born, a force is at work. The new people continue to suffer their birth pangs. None of their efforts has flagged. It would be mistaken to attribute merely sociological meaning to the struggles of the people, as if the women and men who wage this combat were no more than the object of blind forces. In the midst of these forces God is working the mighty deed of the liberation of the oppressed, and restoring to those oppressed the human dignity of which they have been robbed.[4]

(ii). Builder of History: The People of the Poor. The most visible facet of history is the succession of empires. The Book of Daniel

is a good example. On the great stage of the world, the stars are the military, political, economic, and cultural powers. The mighty make history by forcing the great human masses to play their game. And as they make history, so do they record it. In Latin America even more than in other parts of the world, history has been made by the conquistadors and their heirs; and so history has been written only in praise of their heroic deeds. Someone once said that one of the sources of a sense of inferiority among blacks in Brazil is that no black has ever been said to have done anything great. History consists of the glorification of the non-black.[5]

Nevertheless, the Book of Daniel likewise shows that, amidst the poor, amidst the anonymous, oppressed masses, some will at last lift their heads. The disunited, disorganized poor have no history. They are pawns in the game of the powerful. However, the poor who unite, who organize, begin to exist. Beneath the history made by the powers of this world, another history is coming to light—the history of the rise of the people of the poor. And this history manifests the history of the Spirit of God in the world.

The new history is antihistory. It is opposition to the succession of empires. It is the permanency, in the ground and underground of history, of a new people, ever emerging, ever rejected, ever persevering.

Now eschatology can become history. History can now enter upon its eschatological stage. The empires of this world do not belong to the Reign of God. The Reign of God precisely succeeds them, replaces them. But as we know and believe, the Reign to come is at hand, already present, at least in seed and sign. The people of God are already present in the facet of history constituted by the rise and advent of the people of the poor. Wherever the hungry are fed, the weeping consoled, the poor exalted or the rich brought low, eschatology has already entered our world. Eschatology and history are not parallel dynamisms. The former enters into the latter, just as there are not two human races, but one.

The entry of the poor into history is uneven. Good and bad, favorable and unfavorable moments are always inextricably intertwined. There are moments in which an entire people join together to mount a public manifestation of their will to liberation. There are times of prolonged silence—times of the slow digestion of defeat and preparation for new battles. As the history of Israel testifies, the people have access to history only at special moments. The contemporary history of Latin America also furnishes examples of the collective self-assertion of an entire people, a people bonded together in the positive assertion of their existence as a free existence.

And yet the people of the poor only actually manage to work their lasting effect on history through the intermediary of historical movements. They draw their strength from the resources of established civilizations and empires. Hence the ambiguity of the movements holding themselves out as movements of popular liberation. All such movements are conditioned by the development of the economy and its needs, by national and international political relations, and by the limitations of culture, science, and technology. These can all make a popular movement into a launching pad for the ascent of new elite groups, such as we see so often in history—including the rise of the clergy in the era of the Christendoms. The needs of technology and the economy, of politics and security—needs partly real and partly ideological—very frequently result in the sacrifice of the cause of the poor.

It is altogether impossible for current history to embody all of the aspirations of the poor, which are the aspirations of the people of God, and constitute an aspiration to a new world. Still, some radical change is always possible. The limits of the possible are always drawn in more tightly by the activity of the elite, and expanded again by the poor. The people of the poor intervene in history to demonstrate the possibility of what all the scientists and scholars find quite impossible.

In these conditions, shall we say that there is no hope for humanity in our corps of scientists, technologists, economists, political scientists, artists, philosophers, literati, and orators? By no means; these too, of course, may hold hope for humanity. But the frame of reference of their activity must be the liberation of the poor. They are no exceptions to the universal rule: even the intelligentsia achieve their liberation by placing their abilities and talents at the service of the liberation of the poor and the promotion of the new humanity called for by the poor. After all, the basic framework of liberation is neither political power nor economic development, but the affirmation of a culture. Liberation transpires only in a context of the advent of the people of the poor. True, the poor can accomplish nothing of themselves. Their contribution, however, is precisely the all-important one: they supply the ultimate frame of reference for an authentic human existence.

To the eyes of Christianity, all empires established for their own glory are but pridefulness and idolatry. From Exodus to Revelation, the Bible is categorical in its judgment: all glory of empire is vanity, as fragile as the clay-footed statue in Nebuchadnezzar's dream (Dan. 2).

2. WAR AND THE WORD

What means of action are available in relationships among persons and groups? Only two alternatives exist: war or the word, violence or politics. Human history shows us every sort of war, every sort of politics, and every possible combination of the two. Today, just as at any other time in history, we face the challenge of having to choose.

(a) Illusions of War

(i). Seduction of War. We need not speak of the violence of disorder. Sheer violence has always existed as it exists today. The human body is always available as a tool for the exercise of violence against persons and institutions. The body itself is a weapon. And it is capable of inventing an infinitude of other weapons, to extend the aggressive capabilities of its members. This violence can be used without reason, without intent. It can proceed from affective, or "mental," imbalance, irrational impulse, from the desire to destroy or to wreak vengeance. This is pathological or quasipathological violence, and is more frequent in our times than any other kind: criminality, terrorism, lawlessness. This kind of violence is an individual or collective disease. It produces nothing. It can have no human value.

Irrational violence, however, is not the only kind of violence.

There is a violence that is rational, too. It is called war. War is the systematic, organized use of violence for the purpose of imposing our will on others. Rational violence seeks not destruction, ultimately, but the construction of a new order—one which, reasonably or unreasonably, suits ourselves.

War is a thing of great prestige—more in some cultures, less in others. Certain peoples, imperial peoples, have found their *only* glory in war: the Roman Empire, for example, and also, despite a superficial Christian culture, the heirs of the Roman Empire in Western society: the dominant class, the nobility devoted exclusively to war. In medieval Europe as in Rome, as in Sparta, as in the empires of the Mongols or Turks, war was the raison d'etre of the upper classes, and their sole activity.

Among almost all peoples, however, society places its highest glory in its wars and battles, however much it may devote itself to other activities as well. Latin America is no exception. Besides being a political and economic phenomenon, war is above all a cultural one: citizens feel themselves to be more human, more patriotic—more "citizens"—when at war. The prestige of war is so strong that governments find it the surest path to the restoration of national unity. This procedure is common to almost all nations. It is the recipe of politicians everywhere, and Latin America is no exception.

Of old it was the nobility who waged war, lest the peasantry have the experience of its grandeur and dignity. After all, the nobility were convinced that war was the source of dignity, and had imposed this ideology on the peasantry. A soldier feels more of a man, more worthy, than others. Why? Because he makes war. Male supremacy has always been based on the privilege of making war—hence men's opposition to the admittance of women to military service.

Latin America has now known twenty years of extreme militarism. The national security ideologies have exalted war to the status of be-all and end-all of history and of all the social activities of history. War has become the center of social life and the font of civil dignity. War has become total indeed, involving as it does the totality of citizens' activities (see Puebla 314). In Chile, the military has proclaimed the Chilean people to be superior to all the other peoples of Latin America on grounds of their descendancy from two particularly warlike ethnic groups, the Godos and the Mapuches. The most important fact here is not that militarism has been cultivated by the pride of professional militarists, but that it inspires such deep connivance in the citizenry itself. To this very day the prestige of the military in Chile paralyzes popular aspirations for liberation.

Many religions idealize war. Even the Bible is ambivalent here. In the Deuteronomic law and history, a holy war of implacable extermination is proclaimed by mandate of Yahweh.[6] Old Testament texts furnished abundant material for the crusades against alien peoples or against those internal enemies, the heretics.

The sacralization of war has profound roots in the human psyche. In many myths it is the supreme, most perfect relationship among human beings. War is almost the only source of popular heroes. Nor is its importance on the wane in the imagination of nations.

Whence this prestige of war, this perennial, ubiquitous idolatry? Why has war always been regarded as the ideal pattern for liberation? Why such frustration among peoples who have not had their wars of liberation? We may leave these questions to the sociologists and social psychologists. We need only point up one aspect of war: the sacrificial. Nowadays, in almost all traditional religions, the notion of sacrifice is disappearing, or at least it is in danger of doing so. One sacrifice alone has stood unshaken: the sacrifice of war. All automatically assume that soldiers fallen in battle have offered their lives in sacrifice. A combatant takes the risk of sacrifice. Exposure to the danger of death in war is conceived as an offering and a sacrifice. The aura of sacrifice also conceals another aspect of war: the death and destruction wrought by a soldier. The soldier's own spilled blood is exalted. The blood of others, spilled by that same soldier, is forgotten.

War is ambivalent. It is generosity, but it is homicide. It conceals its reality. It presents itself as heroism, whereas actually it is the supreme expression of pride: the imposition of one's own will on others. This is why it refuses to acknowledge itself for what it is. Finally, war has a bad conscience. All warriors insist that they are waging a defensive war. They never acknowledge their will to dominate. The extreme case was that of Rome, which managed to conquer sixty peoples without ever waging any but a defensive war. No one has ever admitted to waging an aggressive war. War will not see itself for what it is.

War is endemic. It does not prevail always and everywhere, but there is always war somewhere. There is no reason to think that we shall ever be without it. Its roots are too deep in our being. Still the voice of reason endorses the Christian message: war must be replaced by other means. War must be replaced by word. Politics is not reducible to war, nor is war its consummate expression.[7] Politics — the art of solving the problems of human relations — is constructed by way of word.

(ii). Desacralization of War. Jesus desacralizes war; he does not proclaim its suppression. On the contrary, Christianity preserves the apocalyptic discourse in which war is one of the inevitable events of the future. "You will hear of wars and rumors of wars" (Matt. 24:6). War will be waged against the people of God itself (Rev. 12:17). But Jesus does not have recourse to war to carry out his designs. Not only does he not use it, but he definitively rejects the use of arms.[8] Nor was he the first to do so. Social life would not have been possible in the history of humanity unless innumerable human groups had sought, in the course of the centuries, other means of resolving their conflicts. But Jesus confirms and ratifies, as well as adding force to, a tendency on the part of humanity which was precisely the tendency of the people of the poor.

The poor never have the means to wage war. War is the privilege of the powerful. The poor can win a war only if at least some of the powerful are on their side. This is why the poor have been the vessels of peace and of the policies of peace. The word springs up amidst the poor, who have no weapons. How could Jesus have taken up arms, if he was poor and of the poor? What is new with Jesus is his explicit rejection of the violence of war. He did not flee, he did not try to run away from the war being waged against him. He overcame his fear of death, and answered violence with other arms. He confronted the violence of weaponry with the power of the word. And in doing so he deprived war and violence of their prestige forever.

However, Jesus' message did not long desacralize war in the

mentality of his followers. Christians have made war like anyone else. This was normal enough, since they lived in history like everyone else. But they sought to sacralize war anew.

In our own century it was a Hindu, Mahatma Gandhi, who took up Jesus' message of the desacralization of war. He took his inspiration consciously and deliberately from the example of Jesus, at a moment when Christians were mercilessly slaughtering one another in the First World War. Slowly but surely, his message of nonviolent action for liberation spread. Today that message stands as a challenge to the traditional prestige of the violence of arms.

Latin American cultural legacy idealizes war and weaponry to the extreme. The Hispanic tradition has been reinforced by native traditions in various Latin American countries. The myth of insurrection is profoundly rooted in popular emotions. More than in any other culture, the nostalgia of liberation by force of arms has impregnated the imagination of Latin American people. What Latin American boy has never dreamed of taking up arms and setting his people free? As the scion of Spanish or Portuguese military heroes, he even daydreams of reconquering lands taken from Christendom by the Moors![9] In this kind of cultural context, the message of nonviolent action will not meet with a very enthusiastic welcome.

(b) Struggle for the Word

(i). Functional Value of Language. Even war has need of the mediation of the word. After all, the will of the victors must be proclaimed to the vanquished. Pure violence has no human meaning. But here the question arises: Would it be possible to solve all problems of human society, to defeat all domination, by word alone?

Many think not. Many regard war as a necessary means to liberation, at least in extreme cases, in which words have finally proved useless. Even Catholic moral theology has always permitted war as a last resort (see, for example, PP 31). Nevertheless, the Christian message insists that the power of the word be carried to the limit before this extreme solution is invoked. But to what word are we referring? What word could ever overcome domination? Is there really such a thing as a word of liberation?

At first sight, all human discourse would seem ultimately calculated to maintain and reinforce the status quo. But before we leap to this premature conclusion, let us briefly examine the functions of language.

The first function of human speech is to communicate an "affect." The affective function of communication is the first to manifest itself in us when we are infants, and it remains the most important function of communication throughout our lives. By gesture and body language, by written and verbal signs, by oral or written expression, language attempts to enter into emotive or quasi-emotive communication with others. This communication frequently fails. Much discourse fails to reach its interlocutor, and is actually addressed to the person uttering it. Still, some communication materializes. The ambiguity is not total. Persons and groups manage some visceral, existential understanding of one another.

Language functions first of all in the family, of course. But it also operates in business, in local or functional associations, in municipalities and other political entities, and finally, among nations and cultures, through the intermediary of enormous efforts of transmission and translation. The affective function of discourse naturally serves the purpose of social integration. It is the means par excellence of integration and unification. After all, our countless failures at communication, whence innumerable conflicts derive, are not the fault of the means, the words, but result from other factors. The only practicable ideal is the maintenance of as complete a communication as possible.

The unitive function of language furnishes a fairly well adapted instrument for human sociability. Human beings have a horror of being alone. They cannot live without human contact. Language always falls short of our desires for communion; but it does not, for all that, cease to be a fairly adequate instrument of this.

On a more complex level, words serve the organization of the work place. Work is an eminently cooperative, social activity. It cannot be performed without communication. Workers must reach some type of agreement about the matter upon which they intend to work. That is, they must share an empirical or scientific representation of the material world and its laws. A goodly slice of human dealings consists in an exchange of information about the world of matter, with a view to broader cooperation in the work of transformation of this same world.

The fabulous developments in the area of the communication of information over recent decades has tended to focus attention on this aspect of language. But there are other levels of language, of equal importance. We also speak in order to arrive at agreement concerning human relations themselves. Here the object of language is society itself, caught up in a constantly accelerating complexification. Here the object is politics in the broad sense of the word: politics in the family, in business, in trade, and at every stage of national and international organization. Clearly, then, the object of human speech, whether that speech bears upon work or upon society, is the harmony, integration, and orderly function of human relations.

Communication develops its own instrument. That instrument is language. Even the electronic media must ultimately refer to a human language. Every human group nowadays, every nation, tends to form one language, calculated to be its best means of integration. Thus, language constitutes the materialization of an entire network of communication in a society. Language is the repository of culture in all of its dimensions.

With the development of new tendencies in the linguistic sciences in the United States and Europe, some have gone to the extreme of proclaiming language to be the actual agent and cause of human thought. According to these scientists, we do not use language to think, rather language uses us to think. A person as such, we are told, is but the tool of a language. It is language, and not the person, that functions, performing the role of the maintenance and reinforcement of the integration of the cultural whole. It is an illusion to imagine that *we* think. Rather, we *are* thought by the language we use.

The systematic critique of ideologies takes the same tack. In this century, and especially since the work of the Frankfurt school, intellectual Marxism in Europe and the United States has devoted itself in large part to a systematic critique of ideologies, especially the ideologies that impregnate Western society, but, more recently, of the ideologies of the countries of "real socialism," as well. Latin America has not remained aloof from this movement. On the contrary, here as well, a goodly part of intellectual Marxism takes its inspiration in the critique of ideologies.[10]

Society's discourses spring overwhelmingly from the mind of the dominant classes, and thus reflect the interests of these classes. The basic interest of these classes is the preservation and extension of established society. Concretely, the Marxist critique of the dominant ideologies has come to conclusions similar to those of linguistics: the discourse emerging in a given society tends to preserve that society in its established structure. Its words are calculated to express that society's official "truth."

Actually, it has become so typical of contemporary Western culture across the board to criticize an ideology that we may scarcely any longer regard such criticism as a sure sign of Marxism. It has become impossible to enunciate a discourse in blissful ignorance of the ideological critique of which that discourse will at once become the object. Certain religious groups and agencies have not yet assimilated this cultural orientation, familiar as the latter has become to the rest of the intellectual community, and continue to pronounce their discourse with the habitual naiveté of those who regard themselves as above criticism. Indeed, we often find that many of the objections to, or denunciations of, so-called Marxism at the hands of contemporary theologies proceed from a cultural backwardness in the form of a resentment of this criticism. These theologies do not yet realize that any and every discourse is now open to an ideological critique.

Will not even the human sciences escape indictment for the crime of ideology? No, not even they. The nineteenth century saw the rise of a self-styled scientific historiography. History had never before been regarded as an object of science. But in the new heyday of rationalism there were those who thought that history could be elevated to as scientific a status as physics. Then it was sociology's turn: it, too, could be purely scientific; now there could be a genuine science of society. So thought positivism, and then, in short order, Marxism, deceived by Engels who had in turn been seduced by the promises of a positivism that, to our day, has never been expunged from the official doctrine of the Soviet Union. After sociology came psychology. Then sociology merged with psychology, and the linguistic sciences were born—the last to entertain delusions of pure scientific objectivity.

Actually the humane sciences are no more immune from indictment for ideology than is popular knowledge. No human science is exempt from ideology. There is no purely objective, purely scientific sociology, or history, or psychology, or linguistics. All sciences are practiced amidst social interests. Either they express the interests of the powers that be, or they express the convictions and interests of the classes aspiring to power. Power is the bosom friend of science, for science confers power on society. All scientific work is socially situated.

Ideologization does not exclude all approach to truth. All sciences and all systems express something of the truth. They ideologize more by what they do not say than by what they say, and by their manner of saying what they say, by the choice they make of themes and words, and their choice of connections between themes and words. Indeed, although they all express something of the truth, they are all engaged in these subtle forms of ideologization and are open to be criticized as such, even when the critique itself is ideological.

Furthermore, none of the levels of discourse just listed are completely closed in upon themselves. Neither are the societies of which they are the expression. All discourse is capable of adopting a new outlook and a new scope through penetration by another form of language, another type of word. And it is to this type of word that we are about to turn our attention.

Language reduced to its social function represents a theoretical, asymptotic limit. That language can never exist in reality. At stake is an immense quantity of uttered material that receives its soul and spirit from new words that seek their path through its midst.

(ii). The Power of the Word. Words can have yet another import and intent. This is the case with the word that can be designated by its biblical name: the "cry" of the poor and oppressed. This cry is the proper act of the people of the poor. In the Bible it is the privilege of the people of God, who are not always the people of Israel. Indeed, they can actually be

foreigners oppressed by Israel. The cry of the poor is heard by God because it ultimately originates with God. The cry of the poor is taken up by Jesus on the cross. The cry of the poor is the voice of Christians. In the power of the Spirit, Christians take up the cry of the oppressed. The cry of the poor is heard by God. It is effective. It receives a response.

The cry of the poor was present in humanity before Jesus' coming. It had already resounded in all cultures, although it was not recognized, identified, attended to, in the same way as it was once the Bible gathered it up and openly propagated it throughout the world, promoting it to the status of the voice of humanity par excellence.

If the cry of the poor is addressed to God, by this very fact it is directed to all women and men as well. God is present in humanity, and responds to the appeals of human beings by means of human beings. The cry of the oppressed constitutes a new discourse, foreign to all of the discourses by which societies defend and consolidate themselves.

The cry itself is the first act of the liberation of the poor. By means of their very cry, the oppressed begin to conquer their fear, assert their worth, and claim the right to act in history as subjects, as agents, and not as passive objects at the mercy of their dominators. The cry is both a call and an assertion of confidence that that call will be answered. It is both a call for liberation and an affirmation of the inevitability of that liberation.

The cry of the poor interrupts the endless repetition of one and the same ideological discourse of established society. It breaks a terrible silence: the silence that blankets the dark side of the world. In this sense, the cry of the oppressed brings the truth to light.

First, the cry denounces all that exists. It denounces history, which is the history of the conquerors. It proclaims that history erroneous and incorrect. There is an official social doctrine in this world, consisting in the proclamation that the governance of the world belongs to the most developed, to the mightiest. In time of crisis, more than ever, governance falls to the strong. The cost of the crisis falls on the shoulders of the poor. The poor finance the rich, lest the latter suffer want and hardship.

The cry of the poor reveals this otherwise hidden reality.

Second, the cry destroys the false solutions concocted by the powerful, who invoke rigid laws that supposedly keep society a prisoner of insuperable determinisms. That which, according to official teaching, has been impossible, becomes possible when the people lift their voices at last. The cry of the poor restores flexibility to the world. The world becomes human once more. It loses its mechanical rigidity.

Finally, the cry of the poor is an assertion of confidence in a new world. It is an act of faith in the future. It refuses to accept the future being prepared by the mighty. It proclaims another future. And this protest becomes the seedbed of an unforeseen, unforeseeable society, a different society from the one envisioned in the official projects. This future is not yet total liberation. But it is a step in that direction. Every step toward liberation is a sign and promise of final liberation, while, at the same time, furnishing Christian eschatology with its historical content.

To the ears of the mighty, the cry of the poor is the irruption of irrationality into history. Actually it represents a higher rationality: it manifests a reality that is more real, more human and more humane, more dense in human content, than the established, whitewashed society of the dominators.

The cry of the poor is a biblical and theological category. But it is also incarnate in concrete historical realizations. In none of these incarnations is the content of the biblical concept exhausted, it is true, but that content would have no value were it not to be enfleshed in concrete realizations.

The irruption of the poor into Latin American history in the twentieth century is a paradigm of the cry of the poor.[11] This is not the place to rehearse the history of the popular struggles — the history of the word of the people — in Latin America in this century. Suffice it to recall just a few of the events of that history.

After the installation of the national security regimes, a popular movement gradually formed in protest, first requesting, then demanding, more freedom. In the current decade of the eighties, that movement has broadened into the massive popular manifestations that have undermined the foundations of our military regimes. They destroy an enforced consent based on the fear maintained among the people by the regimes of oppression. The historical power of the cry of the poor is thus being manifested.

These immense popular protests against Latin American dictatorial regimes are to the twentieth century what the great labor strikes were to the nineteenth century in Europe and the United States: the heroic struggle of unarmed peoples confronting harsh, armed repression. The popular masses are transformed into an organized, disciplined people, and confront arms, death, imprisonment, all the tyrannies of irrational power, with the sole resource of the word: the cry of the poor in a pure state. The Latin American poor cannot even threaten to withhold their services as laborers. That labor is worth less and less to the oppressor. They have only their human existence, their pure cry for respect for their dignity.

In Latin America, the cry of the poor, which has been heard for twenty years now, is growing in volume and intensity. The object of its demands is a respect for human rights, in the face of the violation of those rights by the state terrorism of military governments. But this cry has been raised first and foremost on behalf of the radical transformation of a society that systematically ignores the poor.

Some movements have arisen with the explicit intent of encouraging nonviolent political action.[12] In some countries these movements actually have considerable influence, as in Argentina. The power of the word in general is capable of an infinitely broader expression than that of specific movements. The voice of the people has been raised by unions and popular parties—legal ones, or, often enough, clandestine ones—by local or national associations, by public marches and protests. All of the various kinds of gatherings that have defied the violence of the armed forces in recent years at the very heart of our massive urban centers have been more than a symbol. They have been signs of the maturation of the popular masses, who are more and more capable of joint, disciplined, organized action. The masses represent humanity precisely in its human reality.

Can the poor raise their cry if there is no one to stir them to life? Experience shows that peoples react to the stimulus of prophets. Prophecy is a Judeo-Christian category, but a prophet is not necessarily a formally religious person. Prophets have always been active in all areas of human life. They have always been an active presence in politics and society. Their existence and function are not limited to the Christian world. They have their analogues in all societies, since the Holy Spirit acts in all societies. Further, there are those corresponding to prophets in the political and social world. Not that they exhaust the charism of prophecy. But the charism of prophecy would have no reality were it not to be enfleshed in concrete persons at work in contemporary society.

Prophets have arisen in recent times: certain bishops, certain priests, certain members of religious orders, and thousands upon thousands of lay leaders of popular movements. Often their names are unknown, or known only where they have performed their activity. But they are no less prophets for their anonymity. How many names do we know of prophets of the primitive church? But they were no less prophets for not having their names recorded in history.

Prophets receive a mighty word, one capable of awakening sleeping peoples, a word with the power to conquer fear, fatalism, and resignation in the masses of oppressed.

The choice between the violent power of arms and the pacific power of the word is at the heart of Christianity as it is at the heart of the drama of human society. The confrontation between Jesus and Pilate in the Fourth Gospel makes the choices abundantly clear. Pilate alludes to the power of his physical might (John 19:10). Jesus does not deny that Pilate has this power, but he pits against it the power of witness (John 18:37).

In societal life, the cry of the poor becomes a cry of testimony. It has the value of witness. We do not find the oppressed speaking at scientific conferences or writing in the learned journals. They would be lost there. And they would fall victim to the ideologies that accompany the sciences. Neither do we find them using a high literary style, rhetoric, or figures of speech. Their culture cannot compete with the subtleties of discourse employed by the leaders of our society. The discourse of the poor is testimony because it enunciates a truth. That truth denounces the lie in which society is enveloped, and which would make that society the locus of the privileges of a minority while denying the majorities the right to exist. The discourse of the poor does not demonstrate truth; it only points to it. But the truth is that the world must change, and that it will change by making room for everyone and constituting a society of communion and partnership. The truth of witness does not dwell on details, or analyses of reality. It simply enunciates forgotten or distorted reality.

Despite closed systems and supposedly scientific laws, the truth is that history will change by the will and might of the poor. Again, this concrete truth does not exhaust all truth.[13] But it states a great deal of it. What would the truth of the gospel be were it not to be present in concrete, everyday truths, were it not present in life, were it not actively exposing the social and historical realities hidden by the lie of established, routine discourse? The truth of Jesus is certainly more than the revelation of the reality of the social world. But it includes this revelation.

Witness contains its own truth. It has no need of argumentation. Jesus' witness is his person. The poor and oppressed, too, are witness, are testimony. They need only show what they are, in order for the truth to appear to those who wish to see.

For a world closed in upon itself, like the world of Pilate, truth is meaningless. " 'Truth!' said Pilate. 'What does that mean?' " (John 18:38). For the established world, the sole reality is the functioning of society. Truth is irrelevant — an empty concept. Or rather, truth is a beautiful word with which to adorn ideological discourse. It is simply precious for its emotional value. What is important is the degree of acceptance it can summon forth.

Finally, though, human beings have a capacity for truth. Now, where is this truth to be found? It is in the liberation of the poor. The liberation of the poor is occurring at this very moment, and the occurrence of that liberation has the value of truth. Other history is superficial, and without deep human value. We do not deny the limited truth of the human sciences, of the political art of leading human society, of the conduct of business, of arts and offices, of professions, or of literature. It is only that the truth of these cognitions comes from their position with reference to the central axis of the liberation of the poor. If they are subordinate instead to the maintenance of the established order, they lose their profound truth-value.

Our understanding of Catholic dogma today presents a somewhat similar case. The various dogmas cannot be understood and appreciated in separation from one another; they owe their truth to the whole of which they are a part. Each dogma, by virtue of its insertion into the basic truth of the totality of the Christian mystery, represents a partial aspect of the truth. Now, what is the total truth of Christian revelation? The total truth of Christian revelation is the truth of the mystery of liberation from the sin in which humanity has been held captive—in other, more up-to-date, words, the liberation of the people of the poor.

Truth is not immediately apparent. On the contrary, it is very much hidden. It subsists only beneath a visible, recorded history. The successful quest for truth requires a genuine conversion. This conversion will be more than a reflexive, internal attitude. It will consist in a radical change in one's social situation. To be converted to the truth is to enter within the deep, hidden history of the liberation of the poor.

The word of the oppressed itself offers no positive alternative, no concrete focus of conversion. It is neither science nor art, and replaces none of the cognitions or abilities that can organize societies. It is simply a call to conversion. Of itself it is the most frail of human forces. Ultimately, however, it is the mightiest, since it has the capacity to enlist other forces in its cause. It inspires to sacrifice and dedication. In sum, it generates dialogue. However, we must know what is meant by the word "dialogue."

(iii). Dialogue. The word "dialogue" achieved common currency in Christian language with the Second Vatican Council, and especially with Pope Paul VI's inaugural encyclical, *Ecclesiam Suam.* It has also entered political discourse. Like all expressions adopted in political discourse, it was immediately abused. The dominant classes of society have now adopted the word to denote the repetition by inferiors of the discourse addressed to them by their superiors. To the dominators, dialogue consists in a homogeneity between discourse of call, which is always their own, and discourse of response, whose content is defined in advance by discourse of call. Dialogue, then, means tautology. Dialogue is a new form of ideologization.

This was not the meaning of "dialogue" when it came to be

used in Christian discourse. The prelude to authentic dialogue transpires in a situation of inequality. The stronger speak first. After all, the oppressed are still asleep. But once the dominator has spoken, the oppressed take the floor. Their first utterance is "No!" The liberating word of the oppressed is "No!" This is an extremely difficult syllable for the oppressed to pronounce. But this negation shatters established discourse, depriving it of its specious value. Despite its apparent truth, official discourse comes to be seen as idle chatter, devoid of all substance.

Then dialogue begins. Now the dominators are obliged to come down from their pedestal and expose themselves to the fire of the everlastingly excluded. Without this authentic condescension there can be no dialogue. Leaders cannot expect the poor to answer with arguments on a level with their own. The poor understand neither political science nor economics, and they are equally ignorant of the rhetorical and logical artifices available to the professional community. When they speak, they simply tell the truth. It is up to the experts to develop an acceptable alternative to the status quo, which comes under fire in dialogue. An acceptable alternative is one that will accommodate the claims of the poor.

The history of Christianity is one of the progressive growth, amidst success and failure, of such a dialogue. The poor learn to speak, to deny (not to refute), and to demand. They constitute a force that can "make its words count."

Is there such a thing as pure dialogue? A dialogue will seem to be going along satisfactorily, when suddenly repression will have recourse to violence. In extreme cases the poor see no chance for their survival apart from armed insurrection. Latin American history is replete with the rebellions of natives, black slaves, and peasants driven from their lands. What is occurring in Central America today is the prolongation of a five-hundred-year-old history. The repression has become extreme, and so has the reaction. This reaction does not belie an underlying openness to dialogue, which can recommence the moment the repression abates.

The power of the word existed before Christianity. But only with the practice of Jesus was the word uttered in complete confidence. Then it began to spread to the world outside. Today more than ever before, we have the experience of authentic dialogue.

3. CONCLUSION

Men and women are more than workers. We are political animals, as well, to use Aristotle's formula. Actually, the two activities are closely intertwined. Politics seeks a path midway between war and dialogue. The choice is always there. Medellín shook its finger at the ever present temptation to go to war (Peace 15–16), and Dom Hélder Câmara denounced the escalating "spiral of violence."[14] But despite the idealization of the warrior in the culture of nearly all peoples, the human solution lies in dialogue. Dialogue rests on the power of the word. I am not referring to the routine palaver published by the dominant classes in order to justify the maintenance of the status quo. Dialogue commences with the cry of the poor. This cry is always present in latent form. But the call of prophets is necessary if the oppressed masses are actually to voice an organized, disciplined cry. Only then can the poor bear witness to the truth. Truth is stirred up in the women and men who are weakest and most deprived of human resources. But then that truth protests the whole existing order of things. It obliges us to invent a new order, ever a precarious one, but all the same another step in our onward march toward a new creation, toward a humanity of communion and peace.

CHAPTER VI

Individual Liberation

Ultimately, human beings are their individual bodies. The human body is not merely a link in the succession of the generations, as with other animal species. Human individuals are more than mere specimens of their species. In the other animal species, individuals are all equivalent; all are representatives of their species, nothing more. No individual member of the species changes anything in the species. With human individuals, something genuinely new appears. Every individual has the capacity to modify the species. Each individual has a specific destiny and a unique value.

We must not say, however, that individuals acquire value from the human history that they help to construct. It is not history that confers value on the individual, but the individual who confers value on history. As John Paul II, in particular, has indicated, it is not work that bestows value on human beings, but human beings that bestow value on work. In work, and consequently in the history built by work, it is the worker who has priority, and not the product the worker constructs (LE 7–9).

Ultimately the human being is the human body. But the human body is born alone, dies alone, and takes up its destiny alone. If it melts into a collectivity, to become a mere number, it abdicates the properly human. The properly human is what is unique, original, and incommunicable in each individual. No body can communicate to another body its life, its strength, its thought, its destiny, or its responsibility. No individual is interchangeable with another.

Humanity, then, is the multitude of individuals who have lived, who live, or who are to live in the course of history. Humanity is neither the human species, nor history, nor the last generation produced by evolution out of the totality of earlier generations. The meaning of human existence is not found ultimately in the perpetuation of the species, or in the construction of history, or in the preparation of coming generations. Every individual human being is his or her own end, value, and raison d'être.

No other religion or philosophy has emphasized the unique, radical value of every human person as has Christianity. A certain formula dear to traditional Catholic piety was a particularly fine expression of the radical priority of the individual in Christianity: "I have only one soul to save." To save one's soul is precisely to take on the unique, individual, and nontransferable responsibility that falls to each human person.

I am not denying that humanity is moved by biological and social forces. Of course it is. These forces often move individuals without their being aware of it. Still, what is most specifically human, what genuinely humanizes humanity, proceeds from the conscious action of persons. Human liberation, in particular, does not proceed from anonymous biological or social forces, although persons have need of these, too. Human liberation cannot be experienced by persons unaware that they are being liberated, or persons moved from without by anonymous social forces. Ultimately the liberation of humanity proceeds from the free activity of free persons, and consists of the harmonization of the free actions of individually free individuals. No one liberates another; each individual must liberate herself or himself personally, and yet in solidarity with others. The act of liberation is effected by concrete persons, and transpires first and foremost within concrete persons. Just as alienation is concretely verified, embodied, only in the alienated condition of individual bodies, so liberation is really present only in the living, experiential disposition of these same bodies, which move themselves, and are not simply moved by internal or external pressures.

1. INDIVIDUAL LIBERATION

The process of the liberation of the individual is the object of St. Paul's anthropology. The Pauline anthropology must be complemented, however, by the more sapiential approach of St. Matthew's Gospel. Indeed, all historical currents of Christian "spirituality" actually illustrate both of these biblical anthropologies. The available material is inexhaustible. Given the limits of this brief study, I can only allude to the most fundamental themes of individual liberation: this first section examines the principal aspects of "liberation from"; the next studies "liberation to." Liberation consists in emerging *from* a condition of slavery *to* a condition of freedom.

Individual liberation must overcome various levels of alienation. It makes use of means gradually recognized and perfected by a long spiritual tradition and now renewed in terms of the challenges of the twentieth century—challenges so different from, and in various respects more difficult than, those of earlier centuries.

(a) Aspects of Individual Liberation

(i). Liberation from Established Structures. St. Paul speaks of liberation from the world, from sin, from the flesh, and from death. He views humanity as the prisoner of a vitiated world, even though humanity is itself a part of that world. Paul himself feels a solidarity with the world that oppresses him and keeps him in a state of alienation (Rom. 7:16–23). The "world," for Paul, is that set of corrupt and deviant human forces and realities that go to make up society. The world is society in terms of its sinful realities. Sin is the vice, the disorder, the corruption affecting all of the concrete realities which fall under Paul's observation. Death is more than the final destiny of current human realities. Death is more than the end of sin and the end of the flesh. Death affects human reality in all its aspects. People seek death, through their tendency to destroy the human in themselves and in others.

The description of the human condition presented by St. Paul is not mythical. It is a perfect description of the Latin American experience of the human condition. The situation in Latin America, from the conquest to our own day, is correctly interpreted within the framework of the Pauline themes. Called to an awakening by the gospel, each and every human being is summoned to deliverance from this human condition—the condition so well defined by the structures of Latin American society.

Another traditional theme of Christian anthropology is that of the passions. The passions are the chains that bind a person to the concrete world. By the passions, individuals are bound to their surroundings and ruled by them. To yield to passion is to allow oneself to be manipulated by one's surroundings rather than managing them.

The passions are dangerous. They are a manifestation of forces that move us internally. There was an old ascetical tradition in Christianity—far older than Christianity, actually—that attempted to counter the tyranny of the passions by subduing and taming those passions. This tradition molded a rigid, austere, "impassible" person, without emotion, vivacity, or spontaneity. This model has been totally rejected by the modern world since the Renaissance. Liberation will never come by way of some interior stunting. Liberation demands genuine wisdom, from which, to be sure, the modern world is very far indeed.

What is the contemporary equivalent of the traditional theme of the passions? We might indicate two areas of human psychology. The first area that coincides with that part of human life that used to be defined as the passions is the area of the unconscious. We are beginning to take account today of the enormous extent and intensity of the activity of the unconscious, by which the entire past history of the human species and civilization becomes present and active in the individual without the individual's being in a position to perceive its activity. And yet that activity prompts the individual to a great many feelings, thoughts, and deeds. In the vast unconscious part of the psyche, not only the past, but the entire present bursts surreptitiously over our body, shaping its desires, aspirations, and movements. A part of all this world, interiorized in the brain, in the nervous system generally, and in the complex of systems of communication extending throughout the human body, reaches the level of consciousness in the form of emotions, affects, representations, or desires. And these conscious products of the unconscious constitute the second area covered by the old concept of the passions.

Through the passions, individuals tend to reflect the models presented by their surroundings, present and past. Through the passions, we become not a self, but the empty expression of the world around us. This is why the passions strike such a solid alliance with the sin of the world, and the death of the world. It is not by the unconscious, or by affectivity, or by the emotions, that a person is liberated.

A person discovers the road to liberation by saying "No." The rejection of the world as we find it, its forces and solicitations, a conscious rejection of all unconscious or semiconscious irrational tendencies, is the beginning of liberation.[1] Inevitably, in individual liberation there is a moment of rejection and retraction in which persons as it were recollect themselves, gather themselves back up into themselves, and separate themselves from all else beside. In individual liberation there is a moment of silence, an act of suspension of all desires and perceptions — a moment of "retreat," as the traditional language of spirituality had it.

Among all the passions, we must single out the one that is the root of all other forms of interior alienation: fear. Jesus achieved freedom by conquering fear (see Mark 14:33–36; Heb. 2:14–15; 5:7–10). A slave mentality lives under the domination of fear. Its supreme value is security. Once we succumb to the fear of losing our security, we shall simply submit to all of the demands of the established order.[2] Significantly, it has been the most oppressive regimes in the history of Latin America that have appealed to national security as the supreme human value (see Puebla 49, 314, 547, 549, 1262). To the quest for security, the wisdom of the Gospel according to Matthew opposes precisely the duty of insecurity. In fact, this is the substance of the Sermon on the Mount (see Matt. 6:25–34).

(ii). Liberation from Law. Paul places special emphasis on liberation from law. Exegetes now agree that the law denounced by Paul is not only the legislation of the scribes and Pharisees,

which went beyond its biblical inspiration, nor even the law of
Moses, but any kind of law—moral, religious, civil, or any other
kind of organization or discipline, every form of subjugation of
the human being to something external.³ The law of which Paul
speaks is not only unjust law, but even just and good law.

That the individual must be delivered from the unjust laws
that structure today's Latin American society goes without saying. But let us take law in its highest acceptation: for example,
the organization and discipline of the liberation movements. The
individual must be delivered from this law, as well, in order to
be free. Law, St. Paul acknowledges, is a good thing. The Pauline
exaltation of freedom from law does not mean that law is not
good (see Rom. 7:7–12; Gal. 3:19–22). However, unless a person
maintains freedom vis-à-vis law, law becomes a new agent of
domination and subjugation. Contemporary history is replete
with liberation movements that have degenerated into implacable dictatorships. These movements have refused to acknowledge the autonomy of its members, and the latter have accepted
total subordination and subjugation. The right to criticize is a
duty as well as a right. We must retain our autonomy vis-à-vis
even the most praiseworthy movements and the noblest organizations. No organization is of itself capable of achieving the
freedom of the individual. The ultimate basis of freedom vis-à-
vis any law or system is the individual's right to say "No," the
right of the individual to criticize the status quo. In scholastic
theology, the autonomy of the human being is ultimately enunciated in the form of the subjective obligation to follow one's
conscience even when that conscience is in the wrong.⁴

(iii). Liberation from the "Powers." Scripture scholars have not
yet come up with a clear interpretation of the Pauline doctrine
of the powers. However, there are certain elements of our society today that are scarcely likely to fall outside the compass of
the concept.

When we have recourse to strong and powerful means of
liberation, we run the risk of subjugation to the very means to
which we have had recourse. Examples of these strong, powerful
means would be great political power, the great economic
resources of a highly developed technology, or powerful means
of mass communication such as television networks or newspa-

per chains. It is difficult to maintain freedom of thought or action in collaboration with such forces. They all have their internal needs, their will to power, precisely, and they are in and of themselves indifferent to all that is not to their own enhancement.

Here we can appeal to the experience of the church. This experience is of universal value, and can shed light on a good many events occurring in the course of history. Whenever the church has sought to rely on the support of powerful states or mighty economic alliances, it has used the resources that it has received to set up a bureaucracy on the pattern of those of its allies, and in doing so has forgotten the poor, who had furnished the original pretext of its megalomania. The Medellín document, Poverty of the Church, expresses a universal human value: service to the liberation of the poor must rely primarily on poor means, lest it be taken prisoner by more powerful means.

(b) Avenues of Individual Liberation

(i). Asceticism. Beginning with the monastic movement, which arose in the third and fourth centuries, mainly in Egypt, Syria, and Palestine, a very rich ascetical tradition developed in the Christian church, molded by monks and nuns, and lived mainly by them, but always having many imitators among the laity, either as individuals or in religious associations. Consecrated religious held no monopoly over the ascetical methods they practiced. Nor are these methods specifically Christian. They have long been practiced in other religions, and even outside the orbit of religion by philosophers and sages hoping to attain a higher human equilibrium. Asceticism has universal human value. It is part of all human upbringing. For the health of the body, for a balance of the emotions, for harmony of mind and thought, for efficiency of action, asceticism — the systematic practice of individual self-control — will always be an indispensable tool.

Many of us have been reared to the practice of an ascetic, controlled, disciplined life to the extent that we do not know we are practicing asceticism. It has become a habit, and is henceforth part and parcel of the practitioner's personality. Others have practiced asceticism systematically, as nuns, or monks, or

as members of secular associations who are discovering today
the age-old value of traditional bodies of wisdom such as those
of the East.

With the abrupt entry of the Catholic Church into the modern
age in the aftermath of the Second Vatican Council, many religious rejected all forms of the asceticism that had been practiced
by Christians for so many centuries. Many of these methods had
indeed fallen into routine. Some were practiced without conviction, others had lost all relevance to real life. In many instances
the ascetic life was more a matter of a formalism and tradition
than of true pedagogy. We must also remember that, in the past,
and especially in literature that rehearsed the exploits of the
ancient monks for the supposed edification of contemporaries,
there were a great many excesses, and an enthusiasm that was
not far removed from downright psychological imbalance. Suddenly the ascetic life was in disrepute. We had thrown out the
baby with the bath water.

Simultaneously, the West was permeated with "new" educational methods, and total permissiveness was now regarded as
the foundation of moral training. Authority and discipline in
pedagogy had fallen into disrepute. This contributed mightily to
the exclusion of asceticism from the outlook of the new generations.

At the time of writing, a reaction has set in, although it does
not yet dare publicly identify itself as asceticism, but does openly
call for a return to earlier ("Victorian") values.

Asceticism is the practice of self-control. Self-control of
course has intrinsic limitations, although far less narrow ones
than those with which it has been saddled by pseudoscientific
systems seeking to represent the individual as the product solely
of psychological and sociological forces. The experience of the
Far East demonstrates that our capacity for self-control is far
greater than most Westerners would ever have suspected.

This is not the place to set forth the variety of ascetic methods
that have been practiced throughout all of Christianity's various
traditions. Suffice it to say that the end proposed is still perfectly
valid. It is a matter of acquiring what the Greeks called *apatheia,*
and the Latins, "indifference." "Holy indifference" is the state
of those who refuse to allow themselves to be moved by interior

or exterior forces that never come to the conscious surface of our minds. These persons then also employ other avenues of expression, to complement this exercise of their will power.

(ii). Modern Scientific Critiques. Modern scientific critiques strive to expose the unconscious motivations that move persons to think and act. They demystify the rationalizations inspired in the conscious part of the psyche by the unconscious mind in its endeavor to conceal the forces governing it. To this purpose, the sciences mount a critique of behaviors and ideologies alike. A sociological or psychological analysis of behavior, as of the representation given that behavior, will of course be of help to all who take it seriously. Marx and Freud are the pioneers here, although the lines of critical approach they initiated have been extensively developed and diversified. Up to a certain point, they actually help persons acquire control of their unconscious psyche: or at least they expose certain aspects of this unconscious and suggest appropriate means of intervention.

(iii). Option for the Poor. Asceticism, then, like introspection or objective cognition, is necessary for liberation from oneself. However, another mediation is equally necessary: an active solidarity with the poor. Nothing can replace direct contact, direct participation, and the activity of a life in common, if we are to achieve interior freedom.

As the actual experience of a great many Christians shows, the basic step in the process of liberation from oneself has always been the shock of collision with material reality. We are aghast at the sight of the poverty and subhuman living conditions of so many of our fellow human beings. More important, however, is the discovery of the human wealth hidden even in such depths of misery. More important, without doubt, is the discovery of the human race in the struggles by which certain oppressed human beings are reborn. Horrendously abused and mistreated, they rise up out of their misery and live.

This contact with an awakening, regenerated humanity becomes a personal challenge. Now the individual feels a call to become free to serve, and to take an active part in, the processes of liberation. Has not a physical, material encounter of this kind almost invariably been at the origin of vocations to the service of humanity?

In one way or another, the new person proclaimed by the gospel cannot be the fruit of a purely collective history, or of a history conceived as a collective flux. It is true that structures (like persons) must be converted, but the transformation of structures does not automatically engender the liberation of persons. That is, the liberation of the individual does not depend on the collective liberation of humanity. The example of Jesus shows that the reverse is the case: corporate liberation begins with a single individual. Liberation passes from individual persons to the whole of humanity in all its dimensions.

2. INDIVIDUAL FREEDOM

In a certain sense, the freedom of the human individual is Christianity's most specific contribution to an understanding of the human being.[5] It lies very near the heart of the Christian message. It is certainly at the center of Pauline anthropology. At the same time, individual freedom is also the hue and cry of Western society today, or of the so-called free world as contradistinguished from the so-called communist world. Manifold historical connections obtain between Christian freedom and the freedom of the Western world, which, in part, is still the offspring of ancient Western Christendom. There are radical differences, however, between Christian freedom and freedom in the Western sense (not in the popular Western sense, but in the sense of the political constitutions of Western nations—in the meaning of "liberty" in the Declaration of Independence of the United States, or of the Declaration of the Rights of Man and the Citizen of the French Revolution, as well as in the civil codes of these nations).

The prevailing concept of freedom in the Western world can be expressed in the saying, "Freedom favors the strong, law defends the weak." And indeed the liberty or freedom promulgated by the nations of the West is essentially the freedom of the strong. Freedom is the right to use all available resources precisely as one pleases, and the right to reserve exclusively to oneself the greatest possible part of these resources. Whoever is capable of appropriating a social force may use this social force entirely in accordance with his or her own convenience.

Freedom is the self-assertion of the individual, in exclusivity, independently of anyone else, in isolation in one's own domain. Freedom is free competition. But in free competition the strong grow stronger and dominate the weak. Thus the weak never learn what freedom is except through the frustration of their own.

Now let us identify the meaning of personal freedom in Christianity. We shall have need of a clear picture of the similarities and differences between Christian freedom and Western, or "liberal," freedom. In First World countries, it may be appropriate to underscore the analogies between Christianity and liberalism, be it only to transcend the age-old antagonism between "Catholic conservatism" and anti-Catholic liberalism. In the Third World, however, liberalism has sown only oppression and death. By favoring small minorities exclusively, liberalism sets the stage for the oppression of the great majorities.

(a) "The Truth Will Set You Free" (John 8:32)

The first model of the free person offered by Christianity is the martyr. The martyr is the slave of truth who surrenders life itself in the service of truth. Here, freedom and radical obedience come to be identified. To be free is to obey truth. Christian freedom, then, is not primarily the self-assertion of the individual as such, in his or her particularity as individual. Christian freedom is the assertion of the truth of which a person is the vehicle (John 8:32–40).

The value of the human person resides not in the objective status a person may occupy in the world, but in the truth of which that person is the vessel. We contain a truth. In asserting ourselves, we assert that truth. The truth of the slave, of one who is oppressed, is the implicit assertion, in the very existence of the one oppressed, that oppression is unjust, and must no longer be permitted to exist—that the oppressed one, too, is a human being, is a person, and ought to have access to all the values of the world of human beings. The oppressed are not being self-seeking when they defend their rights. They are obeying a truth screaming within them. They are lending their voice to truth so that truth may speak through them.

Freedom begins with faith. We have all been reared on a theology—really rather shallowly rooted in Christian tradition—that ties faith to enunciations of a "supernatural" doctrine. In this old, nontraditional theology there could seem to be no connection between faith and the rest of human life. It used to be said that reason belongs to the human nature it directs, and faith to supernatural elevation—as if there were no reason in Christianity, or any faith in the "natural" life. Christian faith, however, is actually only the last phase of the faith that lies at the basis of all human life—and especially, at the basis of freedom.

Freedom in the Christian sense is born, grows, and lives in conditions of opposition and struggle. We know no freedom but freedom in the midst of oppression. From the heart of oppression and domination, the opposite of these arises. The free are those delivered from the bonds of the world, of society, of sin, of the flesh, of law, of the powers, and above all, from the bonds by which they had delivered themselves as prisoners to these dominators. A message, a cry, of liberation resounds within persons themselves. These persons hearken to that cry, and begin to have faith. To have faith, then, is to believe in the impossible, in the never-seen (see Heb. 11:1–31), the utterly new. To have faith is to believe in the face of all the evidence of the established world that appears to be truth and is not.

To have faith is to believe in something mightier than the established world. To have faith is to believe in a force that has not yet overcome. To have faith is to believe that the world is about to change despite the fact that nothing has changed yet. But faith is itself the first fruits of victory, and that victory's guarantee. Victory is won the moment a person has the faith to rise up against the established order. The first victory over the world is faith (see John 16:33; 1 John 5:4–5).

Jesus manifested the fullness of freedom when he overcame his fear and lived the fullness of his faith before his people, who, on the whole, did not believe. This is an image of freedom capable of revealing to anyone whomsoever the meaning of freedom (see John 12:31–32; Heb. 12:1–4).

Those who have overcome fear, have overcome death. Freedom is mightier than death, for it is the affirmation of life's victory over death (see John 12:31–32; 1 John 2:14).

(b) Freedom and Service

After reminding the Galatians that their calling is a call to freedom, St. Paul anticipated misinterpretations of his thesis and stated his response. He knew what freedom meant to many people in the Greek. For many, freedom meant the absence of rules. Freedom meant anarchy, caprice. Liberty was libertinism. Freedom meant the freedom to do just anything at all, the freedom to yield to the whims of the moment. In our own day, as well, this interpretation of freedom has its patrons and devotees. For example, in the civil codes of the West the right of ownership is understood as the freedom to use and abuse certain goods. In other words, in these political systems freedom consists in the exclusion of all reference to other persons.

In its Christian meaning, freedom is precisely the contrary of all this. Freedom is service to others. Genuinely free persons are those who assert, and put in practice, their right and ability to serve the liberation of others. Freedom exists for service, and has neither meaning nor foundation apart from service (Gal. 5:13–14).

But service does not consist in being anyone's slave. Service does not consist in having to do the arbitrary will of another. This would be the "service" of slavery, which is the opposite of freedom. But there exists in our neighbor, even in our oppressive neighbor, another, unspoken will, and that will is the will to be free — a will that proceeds not from caprice, but from the human calling. Deep within the oppressor is a will to be a genuine human being, the will to realize the vocation of a human being. Freedom is to be at the service of this vocation of our neighbor.

Here a new question arises. Could it not happen that people would attempt to impose on others a mode of being and acting that these others simply do not wish to maintain, and do so in the name of liberation? What if our neighbor will have nothing to do with the so-called liberation that we claim to be promoting?

One can be liberated only by oneself. A liberation from without would be a self-contradiction. Consequently, service to our neighbor must be accompanied by a persevering dialogue, in which neither the liberators nor the liberated force their will on the others. Both must seek the deeper will that associates them in a common enterprise: the will to liberate all that is human.

Service is very patient, then, and calls for the embodiment of all of the adjectives with which St. Paul describes Christian *agapē* in his Letter to the Corinthians (1 Cor. 13). The freedom of service does not exclude law. Obviously it cannot exclude laws regulating the social organization of service itself! But neither does it exclude law that forces and represses those who do not wish to serve, those who seek only to have their particular interest prevail. Law does not beget liberty, but it protects it. It sees to its extension to all members of the human community.

(c) *Freedom in Public and Private Life*

Both truth and service propel the human person into public life. This is where freedom is born and bred. However, this is also the source of two major problems with the meaning of freedom, especially in modern life. The first bears on private life, the second on the political aspect of public life, that is, on the relationship between freedom and political power.

(i). Public and Private Life. With certain rare exceptions, human beings are incapable of acting in the theater of public life moment after moment, without respite, lifelong. Public life is role-playing, dramatization; it is struggle, tension, and constant vigilance. Human beings—ultimately, human bodies, let us recall—cannot abide in a state of unremitting tension. Hence the compartmentalization of life into a public life and a private one. The time and space of life are divided into a sector reserved for private life, and a sector devoted to public life.

The distinction has not always been as radical as it is today. Even today it is not nearly as much in evidence in the last refuges of traditional neolithic civilization. But in cultures of urbanization and industrialization, the separation of public from private life is a matter of increasing urgency.

In order to continue to live as a person, the individual must find isolation and refuge, far from the theaters of public activity, far from work and toil, far from political parties and struggles. Hence the phenomenon of "city living" with its family intimacy, its groups of friends, its weekends, its relaxation, its leisure, its clubs, the beach, the mountains.

Further: activity in a complexified society calls for more and more preparation: years of schooling for the young, training courses, refresher courses, psychological preparation, sociological preparation, maturation.

Finally, the human body is not a Cartesian robot. It has an intrinsic psychological need for affectivity, emotion, and human relationships.

All this and more besides constitute the area of private life. Private life is unwilling to be absorbed into public life. It will not accept the same rules or the same discipline. But very often nowadays persons subjectively live their public activity (their work, their social and political struggles) out of a kind of necessity, as a kind of slavery or alienation. For such persons, the refuge of freedom is private life. Consequently, to strive for freedom is to strive for a broadening of the area reserved to private life. Increasingly, this is the meaning of freedom for the impoverished masses of capitalist society, and many observers suspect that the situation is the same for the socialist masses as well.

For many men and women, to be free is to be able to devote more time to liberal pursuits, such as play, sport, or art. To be free is to be able to give more time to affectivity, not to have to obey a strict program, to be able to relax more. This is what these persons think, and therefore it merits our attention. Human freedom attains to genuine maturity only when a person's life becomes public. But such freedom is not attained at one fell swoop. It presupposes a long, constant labor of preparation. It calls for a maturation of the personality. Respect for the necessities of private life also forms part of concrete liberation, especially in countries, regions, or cities traumatized by the lifestyles of modernity.

(ii). Freedom and Politics. Since the days of the Greek city-states, Westerners have been extremely wary of and sensitive to the phenomenon of tyranny. In the history of nations and empires, dictatorship has been the rule, democracy the excep-

tion. A person can remain basically free in a dictatorship. The experience of recent years proves this. Still, the price of this freedom is terrible, and few are willing to pay it.

This is not the place for a discussion of the nature of democracy. Most theories purporting to explain democracy are generated by competing ideological systems. Here we need take account only of what peoples have most sought, for centuries, in a democracy. All know very well that peoples alone, peoples as such, have never governed societies and never will govern them. Nevertheless, they aspire to a share in the selection of their rulers and the major decisions of government. They wish to be able to supervise the acts of their governors, and punish any abuses. They wish to be protected against the tyranny of their governors and the caprices of the mighty, through individual and community safeguards and rights.

Democracy is far from providing an adequate vehicle for the entire content of freedom and liberty. Nevertheless, humanity attributes an exceptional value to this particular political system and philosophy. It is in the name of democracy that human beings claim the right to disagree with those who govern them, and to manifest their opposition without fear of retribution. Many go so far as to define freedom as the right of free self-expression. In Latin America, experience shows that the majority of persons ascribe more value to this freedom than to any other good — more than to economic goods, surely, and more, it may be, than to their own lives.

For centuries, the clergy refused to listen to this democratic aspiration of the Christian peoples. Even today democracy is not accepted in the church itself. But the official church today does accept democracy in civil society. Beginning with the Second Vatican Council, the hierarchy has officially supported democratic claims; although in practice the complacency, indeed the coziness, of so many of the clergy with Latin American military dictatorships shows that the conversion is not yet complete.

Many generations must pass before the rulers of nations will ever accept the limitations of power imposed on them by democracy. They appeal to the argument from efficiency. A democracy must be protected by a dictatorship, otherwise it may go too far! Even the leaders of liberation movements or liberation govern-

ments fall victim to this particular anxiety, which seems so con-
natural to power. They are caught in the clutches of a fixed idea:
that of the greater efficiency of unquestioned power. In practice,
the recent political and economic disasters known as national
security regimes belie the thesis of dictatorial efficiency. Human
liberation cannot be detached from citizens' long, deep aspirations to what they call democracy. No solution will be found in
the attempt to replace the perceived content of democracy with
other content. The solution will lie only in a forthright endorse-
ment of the aspirations to freedom that we see to be so strong
and persevering in our times.

(d) Freedom and the Future

Everything that I have said about liberation, in the foregoing
chapters or in the present one, refers to the future. To be free
is to be able to act upon the future. But the question is: How
can a human being act on the future? This question brings us
to a basic theme in Christian anthropology: prayer. Prayer is not
the monopoly of the "religious life," or of the "Christian life"
understood in a narrow sense. Prayer belongs to all. Prayer is
of the very essence of the authentic Christian life.

A human being who could program and build the entire
future would be a superhuman being indeed. This superperson
would be a kind of engineer, who would regard the human race
as a branch of industry; this person would have a kind of blueprint in mind, a basis to be used to construct a future built
entirely by human striving.

But such a superperson would not be human. There is no
science of the future. Nor could there ever be an instrument or
tool for controlling the future. No human force can impose upon
the future a project conceived by human beings. Whenever such
an insane idea has manifested itself in history, real, existing men
and women have resisted it and destroyed it.

True, one individual can serve as the stage for the world
drama of liberation in its entirety. One human being can experience, in his or her own heart, all of the misery and all of the
hopes of all peoples of all times. Our capacity to perceive and
feel is without limits. We can gather up the world's cry and

express it in our language. That is, we can express it in symbols. But we are incapable of adequately responding to that cry. There is no proportion between our ability to know and our ability to act. Knowing is potentially infinite. Acting is miniscule. What any of us can do in the course of our individual lives is infinitesimal. Nor would it basically alter this state of affairs to group the abilities of thousands or millions of individuals. These abilities will always be infinitesimal as contrasted with the infinitude of tasks to be performed.

It is in the abyss of this incommensurability that prayer occurs. In our inner experience of the drama of the world, we abide in hope: the liberation of the world is in process. It always has been, since the dawn of humanity. We are not in control of it. We are only called to intervene in it. But where? When? How? These are the great questions. Prayer is hope. We stand before the spectacle of the world and call out for some response, some sign. We want to know where we belong in all this. History punishes mistaken interpretations. History will brook no rationalizations, whether of idleness or of precipitancy. Before acting, all human beings must pray, whether or not they know what they are asking, and regardless of the name they give their prayer. True, this means accepting a dependency on far greater forces than ours. But this is only freedom being human.

3. CONCLUSION

It used to be said that the only human problem is how to be a saint. This old saw, and others like it, of which there were many in the past, were dangerous. The real saints certainly knew what holiness consisted of. However, Western modernity abounds with an enthusiasm for interiority that overflows into individualism. It loves to wrap the individual in sheer individuality. Individualism almost always underlies all modish human ideals. It has deep roots in Western pedagogy. This "holiness" is open to interpretation as an exaltation of the ego. It recommends a certain moral or "supernatural" individualism whose first concern is with self-improvement; as for the world, it is here only to provide an opportunity for individual perfection. We see this especially in bourgeois religion.[6] Christians are not immune to infiltration by religious narcissism.[7]

The liberation of the individual simply cannot be undertaken apart from the struggle for the liberation of all humanity. At the same time, humanity does not exist apart from concrete individuals, these unique bodies of ours so crisply delimited by a place in space and time. There can be no liberation of humanity apart from the liberation of these individual, concrete men and women, always so unexpected and surprising, always so different from the abstract, universal models of being human that claim to embody the whole of humanity.

CHAPTER VII

Humanity in the Sight of God

All creatures exist in dependence on God. But only in the case of human beings can it be said that God is part and parcel of a creature's life. Human beings are the only religious beings. Humanity has been religious since its first beginnings. God is part of its life, and it cannot live without including God in that life. Of course, it is the reality that is important, not the name. There are atheists, including many Marxists, who are far more religious than many of our self-styled defenders of the faith.

Human life receives its most fundamental value from religion. Humanity lives in the sight and presence of God. It has need of a spectator before whom to present its life. Goodness, justice, and truth seek an absolute reference. Evil, injustice, and oppression, far from being mere accidents of history, are experienced as "sin"—as absolute evil somehow. But oppression would not be this absolute evil were there no God to stand as its condemnation.

Once more the manifestation of God in Jesus Christ has repercussions on our understanding of human beings and human existence. Behind all that I have said of humanity in this book lies the figure and person of the human being Jesus, the central reference in Christian anthropology.

Finally, the revelation of the Spirit of God has been so hidden from so many Christian generations, and the very concept of the

Spirit is open to so many false interpretations, that we must not omit at least some brief reference to the meaning of the Holy Spirit in the conceptualization of "humanity." A companion volume of this series deals more extensively with the Holy Spirit,[1] but some of its themes need to be repeated here in that they shed light on the Christian view of what it means to be a human being.

1. LIVING IN THE PRESENCE OF GOD

Humanity's relationship with God is essential to that humanity, both collectively and in its separate individuals. Human beings have need of a God to be the foundation of the value of their existence. What we see in human behavior considered empirically or scientifically, is confirmed and enlightened by the Christian message. That message explicitates our negative relationship with God as sin, especially so-called original sin, as well as our positive relationship with God, whose names vary throughout history: image of God, sanctifying grace, divinization, and so forth. Hence the three subdivisions of this section.

(a) Human Life in Reference to God

History and prehistory alike show us the truly pervasive presence of religion in the existence of humanity. No people has ever been found that did not have some form of religion.[2] Certain moderns — Feuerbach, for example — concluded, in the spirit of eighteenth-century Enlightenment, that religion is our total alienation: we attribute to an alien, infinitely distant being, whom we call God, what is rightfully our own. But this is only to transfer the content of divinity. In order to dispense with the presence of God, these thinkers find it necessary to attribute to human beings what is God's, thereby precisely confirming, not disproving, the universal need for God. Most of the modern atheists fall victim to this fallacy. Others, following Freud, reduce religion to a neurosis. But then they have to confess that this neurosis is crucial for living. Once "freed" from this neurosis, men and women no longer know what to do with their lives. The traditional language of the Christendoms is in crisis, no doubt. But the crisis is far from signaling the demise, or even the decadence, of religion.

Ancient and medieval Christian theology expressed the relationship between God and human life in terms of the image of God. The theme is a biblical one (Gen. 1:26; 5:1, 3; 9:6; Ps. 8:5, 6; Ecclus. 17:3–4; Wisd. of Sol. 2:23; and in the Pauline texts).[3] It is a favorite theme of the Church Fathers of East, especially, and West. It is a central topic in medieval theology and spirituality. It was lost to modern times, replaced by a theology of "grace." But it has returned in the twentieth century, in the wake of the biblical and patristic renewal. The "image of God" can be explained in many ways, and every theology gives it a particular nuance.[4] In this brief study we need only single out certain aspects of special importance for the actual life of the faithful of our local churches.

(i). "Image of God." With the intent of asserting their self-worth, their basic equality with other persons, the poor frequently say: "I, too, am a child of God." In laying claim to this title, Christian persons proclaim their conviction that their value is somehow absolute, that they have a value in themselves. Simultaneously, they proclaim their demand that this value be recognized. Why is a human being something more than a specimen of a species, after the fashion of the other animals — a brief moment in an endless evolution, a transitory modification on the surface of the earth, like a leaf on a tree?

Some philosophers and sages have sought refuge from the traumas of life in a stoical resignation to nonvalue. They persuade themselves that they are next to nothing. But they persuade no one but themselves. We human beings claim a relationship with God. In other words, we claim to be bound to the source of all value and meaning. We are unwilling to be a fragment of a whole. We are determined to be related to the ultimate reality, the foundation of all. We are unwilling to be confounded with the totality of things, lost within the creaturely "all." We are driven to emerge from this amorphous totality, thereupon to contemplate the totality of things from above, as it were. We insist on being at the side of the creator and judge of the universe. The promise made to the apostles that they would judge the universe is the figurative representation of the boundless intrinsic meaning of every human existence.

We human beings are incurable thespians. We play out our lives as if we were actors on a stage. We make a spectacle of ourselves. We cannot bear to act out our lives alone. We must have someone watching. None of us simply lives. We play a human role. Other human creatures will not do for our audience. We need a "big audience," one that "won't miss" anything, a wise, profound, impartial, comprehending audience. And whether that audience be called God, the gods, spirits, history, humanity, the people, our nation, or what you will, is ultimately immaterial to us.

Men and women attribute a transcendent value to this performance of theirs, this playing-out of their lives. They accept no basic rule or immanent reference. They will not submit to the judgment of their peers. They will not submit to the verdict of the effects their activity may produce in the material world, even in society. They appeal to a transcendent judgment. They feel responsible before God. If they do not believe in the word "God," they appeal to the "future," to the "people," or to "history," always in the sense of some transcendent reality never adequately identifiable in the concrete. In other words, they live in the presence of God as their judge. The place occupied by the judgment of God in the Bible is writ large on the heart of human action. Implicitly, we all desire this judgment. No one is resigned to meaninglessness.

As we know only too well, recorded history always absolves and consecrates the victors, the winners. The vanquished, however, the losers, the oppressed, do not accept this criterion. They appeal to another history. They appeal to God.

At the same time, human beings attribute enormous importance to the role they play in this world. They understand it as a mission. They have an implicit need to believe that someone has sent them to accomplish all these things at which they strive with such sacrifice and perseverance. They act upon reality in the capacity of delegates of God, and this is what makes what they do so important. This is why parents take the upbringing of their children so seriously; this is why workers work so conscientiously; this is why political leaders seek to govern their people responsibly. Parents (see Puebla 586, 589), workers (see

LE 25), and politicians (see Puebla 1238) have a divine com-
mission, and when they are remiss or corrupt, we are filled with
indignation.

Human beings, then, whether singly or in community, live in
many different relations with God. These objective relations
ought to be experienced and lived subjectively, as well. Religion
is the subjective expression of our objective relationship with
God, our existence in God. Hence our need for the conscious
relationship with God called prayer. Prayer is the culmination
of human existence. The fullness of our self-awareness is
attained in the various forms of prayer. All aspects of human
life, and all acts of human life, achieve their plenitude only when
they are lived in a state of prayer, in the experience of prayer.
It is this that creates personal and community balance, the harmony of the various components of human life, and the ultimate
projection of human life upon its true center.

Christians did not invent prayer. Far from it. There have
always been peoples who have prayed more than we do. In this,
too, we are unfaithful to our calling. Jesus, however, and the
history of the people of God, have always tended to discern in
the life of prayer of the human race the positive amidst the
negatives, the truth amidst the illusions. The proper Christian
balance would be a balance of prayer and activity, as in St.
Benedict's celebrated program, "Ora et labora": pray and work.

(ii). The Soul. The word "soul" in today's popular usage does
not have the meaning it had in the Bible, or even in an authentic
Christian tradition, and this is a source of constant confusion.

The common meaning of the word "soul" today reflects the
legacy of a popular philosophy handed down in the West since
the time of the ancient Greeks. This philosophy understands the
human being to be composed of two distinct elements, a material
body and a spiritual soul. Of the two, the soul is the more excellent. The proper characteristic of the human being, we are told,
is the spiritual element. The body, then, is a mere instrument
of the soul. But none of this has its origin in Christianity. True,
in the common Christian mentality this is the human being. But
the authentic Christian message has always resisted the incli-
nation to divide a person in two, into a soul and a body. Christian
tradition has always emphasized the oneness of the human per-

son, and all of the texts of the magisterium that deal with the subject are concerned precisely to inculcate a unity rather than a dualism in the human composition.

In order to recover the authentic Christian meaning of the word "soul," we must return to the Bible. The Bible never divides a person into parts. The names it uses for the various aspects of the human being, like "soul," denote aspects, not parts. In the Bible, we do not *have* a body, a soul, a spirit, or a heart; we *are* a body, a soul, a spirit, and a heart.[5]

Soul and body, then, are not parts of a person. Rather, the soul is precisely the life of the body. The soul is what makes the body a living "I," the subject of responsible acts. As life, the soul proceeds from God, the source of life. The human soul is "life more so" than the life of the other animals. It is more closely united to God. It can resist death. The body dies, but only incompletely. Its vital center, its soul, abides. The life of the body remains after the death of the body. The "I" that this body has been does not disappear. This is what the church means when it asserts the immortality of the soul.[6] And the church teaches not only that this "I" is immortal, but that human reason can discover that immortality without reference to Christian revelation.[7]

Without the Christian message of the resurrection of the flesh, however, the destiny of the immortal soul remains very obscure. Not surprisingly, then, human religions have devised the most widely varying explanations. Often these explanations seem irrational—spiritism, for example, or reincarnation. After all, what could the soul be without the body? Before the coming of Christian revelation, religions hesitated between the conviction that not everything dies in human death, and the difficulty of understanding the life of a human being without a body.

(iii). The Heart. In the biblical sense of the word "heart," once again, the human being does not *have* a heart, the human being *is* heart. The heart is interiority, sensitivity, affectivity, emotion, thought, reflection, meditation, attention to reality and to other persons. By our heart, we know God. Through our heart, and in our heart, God acts in us. Our heart is the place of communication with God.[8]

(b) Sin

(i). Evil and Sin. Established societies and their governors have
always claimed that oppression and injustice pertain to certain
inevitable processes. Black slavery, for example, the forced labor
of native Americans, the privileges of the powerful, the per-
quisites of the large landowners, any economic inequalities,
underdevelopment, the scourges of drought, famine, epidemic,
malnutrition, and so on, are natural catastrophes, we are told.
And they are necessary: either they are part and parcel of a
process of development, or they belong to a provisional, temporary situation. Today we only hear these "explanations" more
and more frequently. They are offered in the hope of persuading
us that the evil in question is really "not all that bad." After all,
it is merely an aspect of good-in-process! Be patient. Behold
even now the light at the end of the tunnel. Whose fault? No
one's. Sin? Oh no, there's no sin here. And indeed, the very
concept of sin is difficult to integrate into these everlasting
explanations.

Oppressed, exploited peoples, reduced to death, reply: Someone is responsible. The evils of the world are not all mere accidents of historical development. They are not due to necessity
alone. The human will intervenes.

Nor are the humiliation and death of the oppressed a necessity of history to be redeemed by that history in triumph. Human
acts are limited. They have boundaries. But there is a life that
cannot be destroyed because it has a transcendent value. Those
who in any way destroy human life lay violent hands on a transcendent value: something we call God. The traditional formula
continues to be true, then: sin is an offense against God. If you
oppress someone, you are rebelling against an absolute reference. You are committing sin.

The countless human rights violations denounced by the
church in Latin America, especially by Puebla, are sins. They
constitute an assault upon God, the author of life (Puebla 40,
319, 320). God is the inspiration and ultimate foundation of the
denunciation of these sins. Denunciation is more than a protest
calculated to be understandable to the victim. It is the expression of a transcendent voice, the voice of God.

(ii). Universality of Sin. Personal sins do not occur in isolation. They do not proceed merely from individual wills. Quite the contrary, personal sins also proceed from social and cultural contexts. No one is forced to sin; but cultural and social conditions are such that sin becomes, as it were, normal and easy. While someone is personally responsible for individual sins, these sins are also bound up with situations of sin — tied to social, structural sin (Puebla 28, 287, 328, 452, 487).

The subjugation of our neighbor and the destruction of that neighbor's life proceed from established structures. They are the natural product of established societal contexts. Thus, all the members of a society, by the very fact that they participate in that society, collaborate in its structural evil and injustice. Without intending to do so, indeed while intending just the opposite, members of an unjust society nevertheless lend their support to this particular society, and hence to its particular injustice. For example, in the slave society of the past, all were guilty: the owners, the slave-traders, the civil authorities, those who could have spoken out and did not do so — even the slaves, who resigned themselves to their condition. In the current Latin American situation, again, all are guilty, since all somehow accept the situation as it is. Even the opposition neglects its opportunities. The victims sin by cowardice, laziness, and indifference. The masses sin by their silence. Sin is not only in structures; it is in all persons who assimilate those structures. Persons neither live nor define their actions independently of the society in which they live; they may wish to change that society, but even the most revolutionary among them still adopt, in their action, a great part of the prevailing societal structure. There is no such thing as total revolution. Even the most glorious of revolutions retains and maintains an enormous component of the old order.

A sinful situation proceeds not only from such and such a social regime, or from such and such a culture. It is not only the culture of the white world, or capitalism as a flawed historical regime, that generates sin. The sinful element in these cultures or regimes does not disappear by simple virtue of the rejection of the culture or a change of economic or political regime. For unexplainable reasons, situations of sin are constantly renewed.

No society has ever been exempt from structural sin; nor, Christian eschatology is convinced, will there ever be such a society on this earth. The roots of sin in the human species reach mysteriously so deep, that sin is sure to reappear in all cultures and societies, thereupon to constitute a new challenge. Sin is bound up with humanity's very origins. Therefore it is called original sin.[9]

(iii). Original Sin. Inspired by St. Augustine of Hippo, Western theology has promoted original sin to the status of its central theme. It develops the message of redemption from a point of departure in original sin. However, the Western version of original sin has very little connection with collective human history. St. Augustine identified it as part of the individual life, giving it close ties to sexuality, and making it most emphatically a matter of interiority.

Scholastic theology suppressed even these connections with concrete human reality. Original sin wafted above history. We all sat in the audience of a drama of sin and redemption being played out on a stage beyond our reach.

Western theology has placed a great deal of emphasis on the origins of original sin. Enormous importance has been attributed to the account of Genesis 3, as if the Bible were here reporting history's all-decisive event. The same exaggerated importance has been conferred on Romans 5:12, which is thereupon taken out of context and made the basis of a "Pauline anthropology."[10] The debates with Pelagianism and Protestantism also served to exaggerate the consideration accorded original sin, especially the so-called sin of Adam. To the sin of Adam was attributed a value almost equal, although of course opposite, to that of the redemptive deed of Christ. Spin-offs from the doctrine of the original sin of Adam were the scholastic inventions of the state of pure nature, the distinction between the natural and the supernatural, the preternatural condition of Adam, and so forth—a whole hypothetical history, replacing real history. It was this hypothetical history, and not real history, then, that was submitted to the lens of a theological reading. It is time we returned to reality. Reality is a situation of sin that is deeper and more radical than the various cultural and historical regimes, to be sure; but it exists only as incarnate in those regimes. There, original sin is visible in everyday experience, whether or not that experience be regarded under the formality of sin—that is, as a reference to God. And only there, in everyday experience, is original sin to be found.

As for the "origin" of original sin, the role of theology will be to pare away at the many texts of our Western past until we reach their valid kernel. The Bible is particularly sober on the subject. The New Testament attributes no importance to original sin at all. The importance of Romans 5 has been vastly overblown.

(c) Grace or Divinization?

The vocabulary is extensive and confusing: grace of God, elevation to the supernatural order, friendship with God, the new covenant, sanctification and justification (the state of justice and holiness in the biblical sense), divinization (as used in the Christian East and West), participation in the divine life. . . .

For our present purposes, then, we need to consider the potential ambiguity of certain vocabulary, but we also need to examine certain tendencies of a theology born in a Hellenistic context. Those theological tendencies shaped or colored the understanding of concepts such as "divinization" or the "supernatural order" and a great many expressions or figures of speech employed by the Fathers of the church, as also by ancient and medieval theology—expressions such as "God became man that man might become God," or "that we might share in the divine nature."

Language of that kind would seem to suggest that the great human difficulty is the limitation of human nature, and that the salvation of the human race will consist in its emergence from the human condition and promotion to another level of being, a suprahuman one.

Ideas like these actually penetrated Christian theology from two sources: Platonic—and especially neo-Platonic—philosophy, and a more or less heterodox monastic ideology, once upon a time called Origenist, which often influenced monastic literature.[11] Hence the prevalence in this spurious Christian tradition of notions and practices like flight from the world, the condem-

nation of the body or sexuality, the "angelic life," spirituality as
spiritualization, extreme privation, a life completely divorced
from the normal human condition, and so forth.

The Bible never uses any such disincarnate language. Nor
does it ever suggest that the problem with human nature is that
human beings are limited in their nature. The problem with
humanity is not that we are too human, but that we are not
human enough. The Christian message of freedom does not
proclaim a condition superior to the human—a "divine" or
"angelic" mode of being. All of these expressions must be corrected if they are to express the authentic teaching of the Bible
and the actual life of the Christian people.

The divinization of which the Greek Fathers spoke is actually
a humanization. What Jesus offers us is the opportunity to
become utterly humanized beings. The gospel promise is
couched in human terms: earth, the city of Jerusalem, abun-
dance, a banquet, food and drink, wealth, the absence of sorrow,
sickness, and fear—in a word, life (Matt. 5:3–6; 22:1–14; 25:1–
13; Rev. 21:9–22).

For Christians, the ultimate end of the human being is not a
suprahuman state wafting above the earth, but, on the contrary,
complete human perfection—the satisfaction of all of the
dimensions of the human. Surely the life of Jesus and the promise of the resurrection of the flesh confirm this so abundantly
and irrefutably that all speculations and lucubrations of philosophers or monks who had not yet received the message of the
Son of God are simply confounded.

2. JESUS: *ECCE HOMO*

In a sense, the whole contribution of Christianity to a compre-
hension of the human condition consists of a single datum: Jesus
Christ. All is contained in the person of Jesus—God become
human. All that I have said in this book is inspired directly or
indirectly in the contemplation and discipleship of Jesus.

"Look at the man!" Pilate said (John 19:5). Behold the
human being. In the Christian perception, through the mouth
of Pilate the Roman Empire had been forced to acknowledge
that the destiny of all humanity was completely summed up in

this Jesus of Nazareth. The secret of a Christian anthropology, then, is a christology, so let us consider, in succession, Jesus raised, Jesus crucified, and Jesus in his historical life.

In a traditional formula borrowed from the theology of St. Thomas Aquinas, the openness of human beings to God is often expressed as a "natural desire for the vision of God." In an ancient Greek philosophical perspective, this desire to see God is thought of as human beings' inner thrust to fly their bodily, limited human condition. The natural desire for the vision of God would be a self-transcending movement on the part of human beings.

But for the Jesus of the Gospels, we need not emerge from the human condition in order to see God. God has taken the initiative of becoming visible to us. God has become a human being, has taken on human form, in order to be visible to human eyes (see John 1:18; 3:11; 12:45; 14:9). If you see Jesus, you see God. And in turn, to see Jesus, you need not have been with him in the Palestine of two millennia ago: Christians see Jesus in their neighbor. To see God, we need not elude the human condition. We need only be fully human in the sense that Jesus explains (see John 14:19; 16:16). God does not withdraw us from what is human. On the contrary, God thrusts us more deeply into what is human than the anthropocentric philosophies themselves could ever manage.

(a) Humanity in Jesus Raised

Jesus raised from the dead epitomizes and demonstrates the destiny of humanity. That destiny is life, and life's definitive victory over death. Our certitude that we die only to live is so great that it justifies the sacrifice of our present life. Jesus' resurrection is the guarantee of humanity's resurrection (John 15:11–22; Rom. 8:11). It has always been the mainstay of the martyrs, who have borne witness to it in the very shedding of their blood for the truth of their proclamation.

Jesus' resurrection also shows the nature of the relationship prevailing between God and us. That relationship is a relationship of life. God's will for humanity is life, and life in every human being (see John 5:24; 10:10, 28; 11:25–26).

The resurrection is personal, and individual. It constitutes the definitive foundation of the value of each and every human person. Every individual has a particular eternal destiny. No one may be reduced to the status of a means to another's end.

Finally, Jesus raised from the dead reveals the oneness of the human race. In the risen Christ is embodied all humanity of all times and places. The destiny of humanity is unity—not by the fusion of persons into a superior being, but by a universal reconciliation of opposites, and in the solidarity of an everlasting covenant (see John 17:21–22; Eph. 1:10; 2:14–18; Col. 1:20, 22).

(b) Humanity in Jesus Crucified

The cross of Jesus is the demonstration of what it means to become fully human. For God, to become genuinely a human being means to enter into solidarity with the cry of the oppressed. The human condition is such that, choosing between sharing in the condition of the oppressors or oppressed, God chose to share in the destiny of the oppressed. Jesus enters into the condition of the victims not out of any masochism, or predilection for suffering, but because in this world the lot of those who defend the truth is persecution. There is no other way to be genuinely human. Jesus' cross shows that, in order to be human, we must confront persecution and death to their face. Jesus suffers not out of sympathy or compassion, but out of dignity and worth—out of faithfulness to his human calling, lest he degrade the human element within himself. Fidelity to the human condition obliges him to accept an abasement so low that he, even he, has to raise the cry raised by the people of God since the days of the Exodus.[12]

The cross of Christ likewise shows the dignity—that is, the moral value—of the poor. Jesus is humiliated, he is oppressed, but he is not destroyed. He does not quail; he does not capitulate to his persecutors. Christian heroes are not extraordinary persons—the doers of mighty deeds, adventurers, conquistadors, or persons endowed with extraordinary powers. They are not stars or champions. They are simply the poor, who, day after day, must face the struggle of humiliation and persecution. But the poor know how to conquer fear and shame: by standing firm in the strength of their faith. Their cry is their protest of their dignity, a dignity unwilling to be subjugated and trampled under foot (see Matt. 27:46–50).

The cross of Jesus teaches the priority of the salvation of humanity over individual salvation. Life is given to be given in turn for others. In appearance, life is lost; in actuality, it is won (see Matt. 10:39; 16:25; Mark 8:34–35; Luke 9:23–24; 17:33; John 12:25).

Finally, Jesus crucified teaches faith in the victory of truth and life even in the sorest adversity. The cry of the oppressed is also a cry of victory, sounded at the very moment death seems to triumph. Jesus shows that the faith of the poor is more powerful than all the weapons of the mighty.

The cross is the center of the gospel. The cross was not just an accident Jesus suffered in the course of his life. The cross is the gospel itself. Consequently, the deepest level of human value is reached the moment human beings begin to share in that same mystery of the cross. The experience of the Christian people has given us countless examples of the truth of this gospel. What the written word of the Bible expresses, becomes concrete experience. Humanity's most exalted moments occur precisely in those periods of its history when it has plunged to the depths. We all know the dates, places, and circumstances of such moments, together with the names of the persons involved, and can recount many a true tale of the exaltation of humanity precisely at the low points of its course. Here is precisely the human element in humanity. The cross is no obstacle to the victory of resurrection. Cross and resurrection are experienced simultaneously. Never again will the cross be pure humiliation. It will always be a sign of triumph. At the same time, we shall never have the experience of the fullness of resurrection in this life. There is no victory without the limits of the cross. Human life is struggle, and it contains all the aspects of struggle: defeat and victory, victory in defeat and defeat in victory, until the final fulfillment. On earth, victory is never as beautiful as the struggle that prepares the way.

(c) Humanity in Jesus' Historical Life

From the moment the Gospels were restored to the Christian people, the earthly life of Jesus has been an inexhaustible source of practical applications. Here Christians find a guide for their own lives.

Jesus teaches service to life. He teaches concern for the weakest, the most abandoned, the neediest. To elucidate this we need not here explore the specific events and details of Jesus' life; we need not launch into a full-blown christology. What interests us for the moment is the fact that everything Jesus teaches bears on our relationship with other persons. Jesus teaches us neither the interior life, nor a relationship with God in prayer, nor our intellectual or cultural formation. Everything has to do with our neighbor. Never does Jesus withdraw human beings from one another. Never does he envisage an individual in his or her inner isolation. Jesus is the individual who lives wholly for the sake of his people, like a shepherd in search of an entire lost flock.

The life of Jesus is also a model for an interpretation of the situations of each successive age. The situations of Jesus' life reappear constantly in history. Jesus' life develops among archetypal conflicts. Indeed, Jesus' life was pure conflict. The Gospels show us that all of Jesus' deeds and words acquire their meaning from the conflict in which they appear—conflict with the priests, the doctors of the Law, the Pharisees, the leaders of the people, the Roman or Herodian political system, and so on. It is in Jesus' conflicts that Christians learn to recognize the structures of their own struggles. For that matter, not only the life of Jesus, but the totality of the ancient history of Israel that laid the groundwork for that life, furnish principles for an interpretation of the struggles in which Christians are caught up, and for the solutions to be found for these struggles. Jesus defines himself by the positions he takes in actual, concrete combat. He is not a professor, inculcating abstract, fleshless principles. He teaches by doing, by taking sides. And this is what Christians try to do as good disciples of Jesus.

Finally, Jesus was not a philosopher propounding his opinions for the consideration of his fellow human beings. Jesus came to challenge human beings, to force them to take sides. Jesus demands a concrete definition of what being human means. The Gospel calls for such a definition. Being human is more than the raw material for intellectual speculation. Being human is the material of a commitment. It is impossible to speak of human beings indifferently or disinterestedly. This is the way one speaks of a scientific object. An utterance concerning human beings is justified only if it constitutes an act of emancipation, an act of commitment to the liberation of humiliated and oppressed human beings. Jesus teaches us to speak of human beings in an altogether special, radically challenging manner.

As we see, then, the Gospels contain no developed teaching on humanity. They shed a light that obliges us to review any such teaching in depth, and pay it far more serious heed than thinkers customarily do.

3. HUMANITY UNDER THE IMPULSE OF THE SPIRIT

The word "spirit" is hopelessly tainted by our legacy of Greek thought. In the common usage of Western languages, we have no word by which to express the meaning of the Hebrew *ruach*. We say it means "spirit." But unfortunately, "spirit" means for us today not what *ruach* meant for the ancient Hebrews, but what *pneuma* meant for the ancient Greeks. For want of a better word, the Jews who wrote the Greek translation of the Old Testament known as the Septuagint, like the writers of the New Testament, settled for the Greek word *pneuma*, leaving us awash in a sea of confusion.

In the tradition that comes down to us from ancient Greece, spirit is the antithesis of matter. Despite all the old philosophers who exalted spirit at the expense of matter, however, the common woman and man have always known that matter is of more worth than spirit—that spirit is a lower, almost degenerate form of reality, rather like the irreality of a phantasm, in eerie contrast with the dense, solid reality of matter. True, the bourgeois exalted "spiritual things." But this was because the bourgeois already had material things, and therefore saw little point in calling attention to them, especially in view of the suspect manner of their acquisition.

Before I speak of spirit, then, I am obliged to remind the reader that, in authentic Christian language, spirit is not opposed to body or matter. The opposite of spirit is called not matter, but sin (destruction and death), flesh (weakness, the fragility of one who is doomed to die), and law (obligation, fear, and punishment). Consequently, spirit is life, construction, action, strength, and freedom. If we had a single word to express all of this, it would adequately translate the biblical concept we render with our halting translation, "spirit."

God is Spirit, in all of the senses of spirit that I have just named. Jesus lived, died, and was raised by the power of the Holy Spirit. The same Holy Spirit is poured forth in our hearts (Rom. 5:5; see Rom. 8:11, 14, 16, 26).

That the Spirit has come to us means that we already live in the world of the resurrection. It means that women and men who accept and receive that Spirit can in some sense celebrate their final victory here and now. Something of their existence is already living the final triumph. In the very midst of our present struggles, the Spirit grants us the strength and joy of final victory. In other words, the Reign of God is present here and now. It is here in the presence and action of the Spirit. The risen life, the life that triumphs over death, is already being lived, in some sort, in the Spirit.

And what is the action of the Spirit? The action of the Spirit consists in our being strengthened. The action of the Spirit vivifies, enlivens, bestows life on humanity, individual and collective — humanity with its cultures, its peoples, all its diversity. The Spirit has no other manifestation, no other outlet, no other reason for being here, but the greater vitality of humanity.[13]

The effect wrought by the Holy Spirit is not "religious," then. The effect of the Holy Spirit is an increase of human life, and the resurrection of downtrodden, abased human creatures.

A long tradition in our Western languages associates "spirituality" and "spirit" with interiority — the interior life, recollection, the intimacy of our own personhood. To be sure, the intervention of the Spirit in the area of interiority is not to be excluded. However, the Bible shows us that the action of the Spirit is first and foremost expression and exteriorization. There is absolutely nothing in the Bible to support the prioritization of interiority in the area of the spiritual. Traditions that tend in this direction depend far more on pagan philosophical or monastic sources than they do on Christian ones. Interiority has its place; but the Spirit is primarily expression. The Spirit moves to speech, to utterance; for the Spirit, the word is more important than silence. The authentic deed of the Spirit consists in bringing the words of the silent to utterance. The biblical gifts of the Spirit all are forms of expression.

Expression has a value in itself. It is not a pure means to an end. The case is somewhat the same as with what the social teaching of the church says of work: it is not a means, but an end. In expression—words, art, festival, liturgy, and so on— humanity exists as it will exist in the resurrection. It asserts its life. In this, true religion consists.

(a) The Spirit and Freedom

We are not born free. We are only born with a calling to freedom. Freedom is precisely the work of the Spirit (see 2 Cor. 3:17; Puebla 204). This is not the place for a rehearsal of the debates on freedom and the Spirit—debates between Catholics and Protestants, Christians and moderns, revolutionaries and reformists, atheists and theists. What I wish to stress here is that the message announcing the coming of the Holy Spirit places extraordinary emphasis on freedom as the human calling, and hence makes freedom superior to any other consideration.

If we are witnesses in Latin America to an awakening of freedom in all areas in which we are called to act, this is a sign of the presence of the Spirit. But our freedom is incomplete. It falls into many a trap, and wanders down many a blind alley. Obviously, the Spirit does not yet reign in fullness.

How often we have all heard that Christianity is encumbrance, and diminishment of vitality. God and Christ are obstacles to freedom, we are told, as if we could not be human where God is. The message of the Holy Spirit, however, belies this fatuous claim. After all, we can reach God only through Christ. And we can know and attain Jesus Christ only through the Holy Spirit. And the Spirit makes us to exist, and makes the human in us, and in our neighbor, to exist. In and by the Spirit, therefore, the Father and the Son are revealed so that the human in us may at last appear on the surface of our existence instead of being concealed in its depths.

Human beings, too, are spirit. Through the spirit that is ourselves, we are receptive to the divine Spirit. We are not programmed beings, as the brutes are. We are open to novelty, creativity, invention, self-domination. We are endowed with the ability ever to transcend the present, to transcend ourselves. We are open to the calls of freedom. We can discover ourselves and discover the world. We can discover our slavery, dream freedom, and gain that freedom. The human spirit is the echo of the Spirit of God. Through it, Christ is born anew in human beings, and the Father reigns.

(b) The Spirit and Community

The Christian community is more than a sociological phenomenon, and more than simply the consequence of determinate historical circumstances, although these circumstances surely have their repercussions on its modalities. Today we have the base church communities. We have long had religious orders in the church. In the beginning were the Pauline communities, and the other Christian communities. There have been an infinitude of like phenomena throughout the course of our history.

Community pertains to the very essence of human beings. It is part and parcel of our destiny. It proceeds from the Holy Spirit, who confers upon it an exceptional status among the phenomena of creation. Community life is as important as individual freedom. Indeed, it is but another aspect of human freedom: to be free is voluntarily to serve in community.

Community exists for mutual service. It springs not from law, but from the will of persons held apart for lack of community. It is born of the reciprocity of human relations; it is where the Holy Spirit dwells (see Puebla 638).

The base community is an end in itself. It is not a mere means to an end. It is, as it were, an anticipation of the eschatological banquet, of the community of all those raised to new life in Christ. It embodies the calling to be and being human: we are called to realize ourselves not in our aloneness, but in community.

The diversity of base communities likewise proceeds from the Spirit, who creates unity without uniformity. The strength of the Spirit is manifested in a Christian community that gathers to itself the ostracized, the outcast, the rejected. It rebuilds the lives of these afflicted, by reintegrating them into a life of exchange and reciprocity. The poor do not come back to life singly; they come back to life in community. It is in community that they learn to be active, to serve.

(c) The Spirit and the People

The Spirit who is at the origin of community is the same Spirit who is at the origin of the people. In the Third World, a people are in gestation. The multitudes presently live in disconnection, manipulated and exploited by tiny elite groups tied to great world powers. They live their lives without any awareness of their number, their human potential, their virtual power, their collective calling, or their future.

The human ideal of a people is expressed for the first time in the Bible. The word *laos* in Greek, denoting the city-state, still referred to an elite living by the toil of their slaves. But the biblical people are composed precisely of emancipated slaves. Here at last is a people: the people of the poor.

The journey of the Spirit through history (see Puebla 199, 200, 201) consists in the reunification, into a single, living, organized body, of a people scattered across the surface of the earth (see Eph. 1:13–14; 2:18). True, this people has its manifestation in the church, but it extends far beyond the church; the church is but the sign of a people *in via*, a people of wayfarers. Baptism, which recalls the passage of the people through the waters of the Red Sea, and the eucharist, which is our paschal repast, are signs of the coming to be of a free people. So the meaning of the church is not limited to itself. The people assert themselves in the area of economics, politics, and the unification of the entire earth. They are the principal agent, the motive force, of unification, until the day they appear in resurrection, in full reconciliation, completely a people, the new Jerusalem (Rev. 21:9–22). The message of the Spirit sets in relief the final objective of all human labors: a free people, alive forever now, where all persons may find their fullness, a human group in which freedom and service at last form a single human reality.

4. CONCLUSION

Modernity has done battle with God in the name of human emancipation. Many today, among conservatives and Marxists alike, are still the heirs of a modernity that functions as ideology, and hence remain convinced of the existence of an insurmountable opposition between God and freedom. There has, however, been a visible evolution. More and more often the question arises: But who could this god be, who would stand in the way of human freedom? And more and more frequently the answer comes thundering back: Certainly not the God of Jesus Christ and Christians. Perhaps the god of certain philosophers. It may even be that certain Christians have adopted a god of the philosophers, mistaking this god for the God of Christians. But the Christian God is the recompense of the poor, defender of the human, champion of the oppressed. The Christian God does not defend the abstract idea of humanity. The Christian God defends humiliated, demeaned humanity itself.

A sign of this divine defense has been the opposition mounted by representatives of the church against the conquerors of America and the oppressors of the Indians. It was for religious reasons that Pope Paul II proclaimed that Indians are human beings, endowed with all human rights.[14] It was for religious reasons that missionaries took up the defense of the freedom and life of the Indians.[15] God has always been the deciding factor in the battle for liberation.

Summary

1. Christianity has brought to the human race a new human being, not primarily as the object of a doctrine, but in concrete reality: in the base Christian communities, in the missionaries, and in the practice of evangelization.

2. This new person has entered into the old humanity in such a way that human history has become first and foremost the drama of the birth of a new humanity from the womb of the old one, the birth of life from death, justice from sin, and freedom from slavery.

3. The pilgrimage of the new person begins among the poor, who are the special vehicles of liberation from the old, former person.

4. While the poor must be the ones to guide the process of liberation in order for that process to be authentic, they cannot renew humanity by their own efforts. They must employ available historical forces, among which they must choose through the exercise of discernment.

5. The concept of the human person, with the dignity and rights of the same, is a product of this century, and has emerged by way of reaction to both totalitarianism and liberal individualism. But the authentic person exists only in community. In actual reality, the rights of the human person take on their full meaning only in the struggle for the rights of the oppressed.

6. Christianity rejects all dualism in human beings, whether that dualism has its roots in ancient Greece or the modern bourgeois. It defends the oneness of the human being, who is the human body, and primarily the brain. The soul is simply the life of the body, and therefore not really distinct from that body, since it is the soul that makes the difference between a living body and a dead one.

233

7. The real body is not the object observed and reconstituted by the sciences. Rather, the real body is "my" body, which renders it unique and irreplaceable.

8. The body is the foundation of community, inasmuch as the body is the human being in self-expression, and communication with others, in community. The sexuality of the body is the first stage of sociability.

9. The body is not annihilated at death, since the life it has contained, which has made it a person, is not extinguished, but lives on in anticipation of the resurrection.

10. The human body exists only in space, on earth, in a geography which conditions it, in a particular country, and in a culture surrounded by other cultures. Thus it is bound to a place, but it is free, as well, "having no lasting country," and striking root in cities or smaller communities.

11. Human life is brief, and situated at a precise point on a timeline of immense extent. It passes from childhood to old age as part of a link in a chain of generations, each generation having its limited, specific task.

12. Human beings are fashioned in such a way as to act on the matter of the entire universe, which they can do only through the intermediary of the sciences and technologies. These, however, instead of serving as tools of the human communities, can come to dominate those communities, erecting their own growth into the be-all and end-all of human activity.

13. Workers, who are the principal end and purpose of work, can become its primary alienation, as well. Accordingly, the liberation of workers is the fulcrum of all authentic human liberation.

14. Some human beings oppress other human beings. Therefore humanity suffers violence, and is subject to forces of death. The transformation of human society is the deed of the poor, who are the victims of oppression.

15. Domination springs from war and violence. Liberation cannot reject out of hand all recourse to war; but liberation is basically accomplished by the force of the word, since it is in self-assertion through its word that the human race attains to the authentic human condition.

16. The human race cannot be liberated without a labor of

liberation on the part of the individual, who is called to over-come fear and resist the temptation to submit to any resistance or pressure, internal or external: after all, only the individual can be emancipated. No external structure can dispense the individual from this personal responsibility.

17. Individual freedom consists not in the isolation of the individual, as for example in private ownership, but in free serv-ice to the other members of the community, although each of us has need of some protection for our private life and rights against the tyranny of any authority.

18. Every human being lives in the presence of God, in virtue of both a sense of responsibility for a mission received, and a sense of reference to the final judgment of this deity, by what-ever name it may be called. Thus the human being is the image of God, and cannot live without reflecting the being of God. This objective relationship of the entire human being to God ought to be lived subjectively in constant prayer.

19. The new person is Christ raised, crucified, and living his historical life. Christ contains all of the human value of all times and places.

20. The mission of the Holy Spirit does not consist in raising human beings above humanity in a divinization that would with-draw them from the limits of their corporeal condition. On the contrary, the Spirit gives life to the body for the sake of life eternal, moving persons in such wise that each and all may attain to the fullness of human existence, in all diversity and freedom. Thus there is more than one model — indeed there are millions — of the imitation of Jesus.

Glossary

ALIENATION—the condition of a human being commanded by or working for others, without thought, initiative, goal, or personal enhancement, empty of self, the plaything of external forces.

BODY—Unlike the bodies of the other animals, the human body is reflexively conscious, free, and responsible. It is "my" body, and therefore unique. This body is one with me, in that it is part of my "I," in such wise that I shall be raised from death with it and no other. Body is not opposed to spirit. On the contrary, the body will be ultimately spiritualized: body and spirit will be one and the same.

DISCERNMENT—The act or habit of taking all data, facts, and events into account, understanding their meaning, and creating a new response to a new, unique problem. It is not a matter of choosing from among two or more already existing channels of activity: the road is always open, and unique.

DUALISM—One form of dualism is the teaching that soul and body are two adequately distinct principles, each leading a life independent of the other, although joined to that other and sharing a common destiny with it. Another form of dualism is the teaching that human history is the theater of a profound, constant struggle on the part of two primordial and principal forces, one good and one evil.

EVANGELIZATION—is used in its proper sense in this book: to evangelize is to proclaim something new that constitutes "good news" for human beings.

FLESH—In St. Paul, flesh is the weakness of the body. It manifests itself in death, sickness, weariness, and vulnerability to assaults from without. Flesh in this sense has nothing to do with sex.

HISTORY—in this book is not the mere sequence of events, but all things produced by any human being, along with all of the facts and events that have influenced human beings in the production of these things.

MANICHAEISM—the teaching, attributed to an ancient heretic, that the body, and hence the properly human element in our makeup, ought to be the object of contempt, and ought to be despised, as if human beings were authentically spirit alone, not body.

PERSON—I, you. That which permits me to say that this act is mine, that I am responsible for it, and that I am prepared to answer for it.

PROPHET—A prophet is not merely someone who teaches, but one who speaks in order to denounce the prevailing lie, and to proclaim the truth, cost what it may. God's word is always painful. The prophet strikes hard, but shows us the way to our salvation.

SOUL—the life that moves the human body. The soul is not a part of the human being, distinct from the body; the soul is precisely the life of the body. In some inexplicable fashion, the soul does not die, but awaits the resurrection of the body. Thus the life of the body does not totally die. Most Christians conceptualize the human being as formed of two really distinct substances, soul and body; but this is not the teaching of the church.

Notes

I. THE NEW PERSON

1. See Gustavo Gutiérrez, *The Power of the Poor in History: Selected Writings* (Maryknoll, N.Y., 1983).
2. See José Comblin, *O tempo da ação* (Petrópolis, 1982), pp. 352–89.

II. PERSON AND BODY

1. Numerous documents on the defense of human rights have been compiled in collections published by Ediciones CEP, of Lima. See especially *Signos de liberación* (1973), *Signos de lucha y esperanza* (1978), and *Signos de vida y fidelidad* (1983).
2. Vatican Council II opened the doors for the modern church's conception of freedom; it did this through being very optimistic as to the scope of modernity and democracy, but without yielding to the mirages of Western individualism. See GS 17, 30, 73.
3. The decisive sign was recognition of religious freedom, the last bulwark of resistance of those who opposed a so-called democratic society. On freedom, see Puebla 321–29. In his radio address of December 25, 1944, under pressure from the victorious Allies, Pius XII spoke of the requisite conditions for a genuine democracy. It was the first time a pope had spoken approvingly of democracy. It was not, however, a full acknowledgment of the legitimacy of the basic inspiration of democracy. The pope showed that the church could adapt to democracy, but his pronouncement fell short of the full recognition of human rights that we have with Vatican II.
4. See C. Schütz and Rupert Sarach, "O homem como pessoa," in *Mysterium Salutis,* vol. 2/3 (Petrópolis, 1972), pp. 74–77.
5. Some Jewish personalists: F. Rosenzweig, F. Ebner, Martin Buber, Emmanuel Levinas, A. Heschel. Some Christian personalists:

Romano Guardini, P. Wust, T. Haecker, Gabriel Marcel, Emmanuel Mounier.

6. Enrique Dussel, *Introducción general a la historia de la Iglesia en América Latina* (Salamanca, 1983), pp. 258–80.

7. See CELAM, *Os grupos afro-americanos* (São Paulo, 1982), pp. 30–34.

8. See Jon Sobrino, *Monseñor Oscar Arnulfo Romero, mártir de la liberación* (Cuernavaca, 1980). For an English translation see *Archbishop Romero* (Maryknoll, N.Y., 1990). On Monseñor Angelelli, see *Paz y Justicia* (Buenos Aires), no. 84 (August–October 1982).

9. On conflict, see Jon Sobrino, *The True Church and the Poor* (Maryknoll, N.Y., 1984).

10. Bartolomé de las Casas, *Del único modo de atraer a todos los pueblos a la verdadera religión* (Mexico City, 1942), p. 7.

III. HUMAN BEINGS IN THE WORLD

1. Enrique Dussel, *Introducción general a la historia de la Iglesia en América Latina* (Salamanca, 1983), pp. 537–60.

2. On the Jesuit effort, see Regina Maria A. F. Gadelha, *As Missões Jesuíticas do Itatim* (Rio de Janeiro, 1980). On the instructions from Propaganda Fides, see Dussel, *Historia de la Iglesia,* pp. 348–55.

3. See J. Ellul, *Apocalipse* (São Paulo, 1980), pp. 156–86. Eng.: *Apocalypse: The Book of Revelation* (New York, 1977).

4. See José Comblin, *O Provisorio e o definitivo* (São Paulo, 1968).

5. See Hans Walter Wolff, *Antropologia do Antigo Testamento* (São Paulo, 1975), pp. 117–210. Eng.: *Anthropology of the Old Testament* (Philadelphia, 1974).

6. See Ernst Käsemann, *Perspectivas paulinas* (São Paulo, 1980), pp. 43–71. Eng.: *Perspectives on Paul* (Philadelphia, 1971).

IV. HUMAN BEINGS AND THE CHALLENGE OF MATTER

1. See J. David, "A Força criadora do homem," in *Mysterium Salutis,* vol. 2/3 (Petrópolis, 1972), pp. 212–14.

2. See Eduardo Novoa Monreal, *El derecho de propiedad privada* (Bogotá, 1979), pp. 5–7.

3. See ibid., pp. 71–95.

V. HUMANITY AND THE HISTORY OF ITS LIBERATION

1. Both the Pauline and Johannine theologies are built on a series of bipolarities: death and life, heaven and hell, condemnation and jus-

tification, Spirit and flesh, Spirit and law, slavery and freedom, non-people and people, darkness and light, descent and ascent, annihilation and exaltation, and so on. The entire New Testament is rooted in apocalypticism, which is bipolar. Greek philosophy could not accept this outlook. The Hellenization of Christianity reached the point that, for example, some of the Greek Fathers denied the eternity of hell. They could not accept the ultimate frustration of the cosmic tendency to a universal unity.

2. Medellín denounced nationalism in its Document on Peace, no. 12. Puebla had to face the extreme nationalism of the national security regimes, in which the most legitimate aspirations of peoples are radically subordinated to the "national interest" (see Puebla 314, 547–49, 1247, 1262).

3. See also the National Conference of Brazilian Bishops, *Exigências cristãs de uma orden política,* nos. 24–32; idem, *Comunidades de base no Brasil,* Estudos da CNBB, no. 23 (São Paulo, 1979), pp. 67–75.

4. "A like solidarity is called to make its presence felt where the social humiliation of the human subject of work, the exploitation of workers, and broadening regions of impoverishment, indeed of hunger, so require. The Church finds itself vitally committed to this cause, which it regards as its mission, its service, and a confirmation of its fidelity to Christ, if it is to be genuinely the 'Church of the poor' " (LE 8).

5. See Leonardo Boff, *Teologia do cativeiro e da libertação,* 2nd ed. (Petrópolis, 1980), pp. 103–16.

6. The military powers in Latin America at the height of the success of the national security doctrines did not neglect to cite this biblical material. See José Comblin, "Las fuerzas armadas y el cristianismo en algunos países de América Latina," *Mensaje* (Santiago, Chile), no. 259 (June 1977), pp. 267–73.

7. The national security doctrine has inverted Clausewitz's classic teaching and made all politics a form of war.

8. The activity of the Zealots was in keeping with an ancient tradition in Judaism, reaching at least as far back as the Maccabees. But Jesus remained completely aloof from their cause.

9. See Enrique Dussel, *Introducción general a la historia de la Iglesia en América Latina* (Salamanca, 1983), p. 194; Dominique Barbé, *Grace and Power* (Maryknoll, N.Y., 1987).

10. See Otto Maduro, *Religion and Social Conflicts* (Maryknoll, N.Y., 1982); Hugo Assmann, *Practical Theology of Liberation* (London, 1975).

11. See Gustavo Gutiérrez, *A Theology of Liberation: History, Politics and Salvation,* rev. ed. (Maryknoll, N.Y., 1988).

12. For example, the Peace and Justice movement, founded and

promoted by Nobel laureate Adolfo Pérez Esquivel. See also Barbé, *Grace and Power.*

13. Here again, as in the following pages, we encounter the tension between history and eschatology. The principles governing the relationship of the two were enunciated, from a starting point in the parallel tension between evangelization and liberation, by Pope Paul VI in *Evangelii Nuntiandi,* nos. 30–36, and in the Puebla Final Document, nos. 480–90. See some comments in José Comblin, "Evangelização e libertação," *Revista Eclesiástica Brasileira* 37 (1977), pp. 569–97.

14. Hélder Câmara, *Spiral of Violence* (Denville, N.J., 1971).

VI. INDIVIDUAL LIBERATION

1. This is the "No!" of the prophets and apocalyptics, like the "We will not serve your god" of Shadrach, Meshach, and Abednego (Dan. 3:18).

2. See the evangelical dialectic between preserving one's life and losing one's life (Mark 8:34–35; cf. Matt. 10:39; Luke 9:23–24; 17:33).

3. See Stanislas Lyonnet, *Libertad y ley nueva* (Salamanca, 1967).

4. See Bernard Häring, *Livres e fiéis em Cristo,* vol. 1 (São Paulo, 1979), pp. 224–27. Eng.: *Free and Faithful in Christ: Moral Theology for Clergy and Laity* (New York, 1978).

5. See ibid., pp. 5–11.

6. See Johannes B. Metz, *Para além de uma religiã burguesa* (São Paulo, 1984).

7. See the articles by Jarl Dyrud, Jack Dominian, and Brian Mahan in *The Challenge of Psychology to Faith, Concilium* 156, no. 6 (1982).

VII. HUMANITY IN THE SIGHT OF GOD

1. José Comblin, *O Espírito Santo e a libertação* (Petrópolis, 1987). Eng.: *The Holy Spirit and Liberation* (Maryknoll, N.Y., and Tunbridge Wells, 1989).

2. See Annemarie de Wael, "Introducción a la antropología religiosa," in *Verbo Divino* (Estella, 1975).

3. The Pauline texts are cited in John L. Mackenzie, "Imagem de Deus," in *Dicionário bíblico* (São Paulo, 1984).

4. See Wolfgang Seibel, "O homem como imagem de Deus," in *Mysterium Salutis,* vol. 2/3 (Petrópolis, 1972), pp. 230–40; B. Mondin, *Antropologia teológica,* 2nd ed. (São Paulo, 1984), pp. 91–140.

5. See K. H. Schelkle, *Teologia do Novo Testamento,* vol. 1 (São

Paulo, 1978), pp. 84–86. Eng.: *Theology of the New Testament* (Collegeville, Md., 1971).

6. E.g., at Lateran Council V, held from 1512 to 1517: text in Denzinger-Schönmetzer, *Enchiridion Symbolorum* (Freiburg im B.), no. 1440.

7. See the condemnations of L. Bautain in 1844 (ibid., no. 2776) and Bonnetty in 1855 (ibid., no. 2812).

8. See T. Sorg, "Corazón," in *Diccionario teológico del Nuevo Testamento,* vol. 1 (Salamanca, 1980), pp. 339–41.

9. See Piet Schoonenberg, "O homem no pecado," in *Mysterium Salutis,* vol. 2/3, pp. 265–354.

10. See ibid., pp. 317–21.

11. See Leonardo Boff, *A graça libertadora no mundo,* 2nd ed. (Petrópolis, 1977), pp. 209–19. Eng.: *Liberating Grace* (Maryknoll, N.Y., 1979).

12. See José Comblin, *Cry of the Oppressed, Cry of Jesus* (Maryknoll, N.Y., 1988).

13. See José Comblin, *O Espírito no Mundo* (Petrópolis, 1978); idem, *O tempo da ação* (Petrópolis, 1982), pp. 35–39.

14. Paul III, *Pastorale Officium,* brief to Cardinal João de Tavera, Archbishop of Toledo, May 29, 1537 (Denzinger-Schönmetzer, no. 1495): "Inasmuch as they are human beings and consequently capable of faith and salvation. ... "

15. See Juan Villegas, "Providencialismo y denuncia en la 'Historia de las Indias' de Fray Bartolomé de las Casas," in CEHILA, *Bartolomé de las Casas e historia de la Iglesia en América Latina* (Barcelona, 1976), pp. 19–44.

Bibliography

I: THE NEW PERSON

The New Person in the Bible

Comblin, José. "A mensagem da Epístola de S. Paulo a Filemon." *Revista Eclesiástica Brasileira* 44 (1984), Estudos Bíblicos supplement 2, pp. 50–70.
———. *Cry of the Oppressed, Cry of Jesus.* Maryknoll, N.Y.: Orbis, 1988.
Käsemann, Ernst. *Perspectives on Paul.* Philadelphia: Fortress, 1971.
Murphy O'Connor, Jerome. *A vida do homem novo.* São Paulo: Paulinas, 1975.
Schelkle, Karl Hermann. *Theology of the New Testament.* Collegeville, Md.: Liturgical, 1971.

The Community

Boff, Leonardo. *Ecclesiogenesis.* Maryknoll, N.Y.: Orbis, 1986.
Sobrino, Jon. *The True Church and the Poor.* Maryknoll, N.Y.: Orbis, 1984.

The Missionary

Comblin, José. "O novo ministério de missionário na América Latina." *Revista Eclesiástica Brasileira* 40 (1980), pp. 626–55.
Theissen, Gerd. *Sociology of Early Palestinian Christianity.* Philadelphia: Fortress, 1978.

Evangelization

Comblin, José. "Evangelização e libertação." *Revista Eclesiástica Brasileira* 37 (1977), pp. 569–97.

Dussel, Enrique. *Introducción general a la historia de la Iglesia en Amér-ica Latina.* Salamanca: Sígueme, 1983, pp. 281–365.

The New Person and History

Boff, Clodovis. *Sinais dos tempos.* São Paulo: Loyola, 1979.
Comblin, José. *O tempo da ação: Ensaio sobre o Espírito e a história.* Petrópolis: Vozes, 1982.
Gutiérrez, Gustavo. *The Power of the Poor in History: Selected Writings.* Maryknoll, N.Y.: Orbis, 1983.

Church Documents

Latin American Bishops Conference. Medellín Final Documents. In vol. 2 of *The Church in the Present-day Transformation of Latin America.* Washington, D.C.: USCC, 1970.
———. Puebla Final Document. In *Puebla and Beyond.* Ed. John Eagle-son and Philip Scharper. Maryknoll, N.Y.: Orbis, 1979, pp. 122–285.
Vatican Council II. *Gaudium et Spes: Pastoral Constitution on the Church in the Modern World,* part 1, chap. 3: "Man's Activity throughout the World." In *The Gospel of Peace and Justice.* Ed. Joseph Gremillion. Maryknoll, N.Y.: Orbis, 1976, pp. 269–99.

II: PERSON AND BODY

The Human Person

Arns, Paulo Evaristo, et al. *Direitos humanos: um desafio à comunica-ção.* São Paulo: Paulinas, 1983.
Concilium. No. 124 (April 1979): *The Church and the Rights of Man.*
Dussel, Enrique. *El episcopado latino-americano y la liberación de los pobres — 1564–1620.* Mexico City, 1979.
Dussel, Enrique, and Daniel E. Guillot. *Liberación latinoamericana y Emmanuel Levinas.* Buenos Aires: Bonum, 1975.
Gutiérrez, Gustavo. "Bartolomé de las Casas, Libertad y liberación." In *Profecía y evangelización. Páginas* 2. Lima: CEP, 1978, pp. 26–45.
Montealegre, Hernán. *La seguridad del estado y los derechos humanos.* Santiago, Chile: Academia de Humanismo Cristiano, 1979.
Schütz, C., and Rupert Sarach. "O homem como pessoa." In *Mysterium Salutis,* vol. 2/3. Petrópolis: Vozes, 1972, pp. 73–89.

The Body

Boff, Leonardo. *A Ressurreição de Cristo: A nossa ressurreição na morte.* Petrópolis: Vozes, 1972.

Dussel, Enrique. *El dualismo en la antropología de la cristiandad.* Buenos Aires: Guadalupe, 1974.

Fiorenza, Francis P., and Johannes B. Metz. "O homem como união de corpo e alma." In *Mysterium Salutis,* vol. 2/3. Petrópolis: Vozes, 1972, pp. 27–72.

Flick, Mauritio, and Zoltan Alszeghy. *Los comienzos de la salvación.* Salamanca: Sígueme, 1965, pp. 205–68.

Gevaert, Joseph. *El problema del hombre: Introducción a la antropología filosófica.* Salamanca: Sígueme, 1981.

Kosik, Karel. *Dialética do concreto.* Rio de Janeiro: Paz e Terra, 1969.

Snoek, Jaime. *Ética sexual e matrimonial.* Petrópolis: Vozes, 1976.

III: HUMAN BEINGS IN THE WORLD

Space

Barros Souza, Marcelo de. *A Bíblia e a luta pela terra.* Petrópolis: Vozes, 1983.

Centro de Estudos Migratórios. *Migrantes: Éxodo forçado.* São Paulo: Paulinas, 1980.

CNBB (National Conference of Brazilian Bishops). *Igreja e problemas da terra.* Documentos da CNBB. São Paulo: Paulinas, 1980.

————. *Pastoral da terra I.* Estudos da CNBB. São Paulo: Paulinas, 1977.

————. *Pastoral da terra II.* Estudos da CNBB. São Paulo: Paulinas, 1977.

————. *Pistas para uma pastoral urbana.* Estudos da CNBB. São Paulo: Paulinas, 1979.

————. *Solo urbano e ação pastoral.* Documentos da CNBB. São Paulo: Paulinas, 1982.

Hoornaert, Eduardo, et al., eds. *Das Reduções latino-americanas às lutas indígenas atuais.* São Paulo: Paulinas, 1982.

Ianni, Octavio. *A luta pela terra.* 3rd ed. Petrópolis: Vozes, 1981.

Santos, Milton. *A urbanização desigual: A especificade do fenômeno urbano em países subdesenvolvidos.* Petrópolis: Vozes, 1980.

————. *Espaço e sociedade.* Petrópolis: Vozes, 1981.

Various authors. *Pastoral urbana.* São Paulo: Paulinas, 1980.

Time

Boff, Clodovis. *Sinais dos tempos.* São Paulo: Loyola, 1979.

Braudel, Fernand. *La historia y las ciencias sociales.* 4th ed. Madrid: Alianza Editorial, 1979.

Comblin, José. *O tempo da ação.* Petrópolis: Vozes, 1982.

Dussel, Enrique. *Introducción general a la historia de la Iglesia en América Latina.* Salamanca: Sígueme, 1983, pp. 103–204.

Noemi Callejas, Juan Alejandro. *Interpretación teológica del presente.* Santiago, Chile: Universidad Católica de Chile, 1976.

Teilhard de Chardin, Pierre. *The Phenomenon of Man.* Rev. ed. New York: Harper and Row, 1965.

IV: HUMAN BEINGS AND THE CHALLENGE OF MATTER

Science and Technology

Ferreira Alves, Ephraim. *A fé do cientista e a fé do crente.* Petrópolis: Vozes, 1982.

Ladrière, Jean. *Os desafios da racionalidade.* Petrópolis: Vozes, 1979.

Leite Lopes, J. *Ciência e libertação.* Rio de Janeiro: Paz e Terra, 1969.

Work

ACO (Ação Católica Operária). *História da classe operária no Brasil.* 3 vols. Lins, Brazil: Todos Irmãos, 1976–78.

Astrada, Carlos. *Trabalho e alienação.* Rio de Janeiro: Paz e Terra, 1968.

Braverman, Harry. *Labor and Monopoly Capital.* New York: Monthly Review, 1976.

Castoriadis, Cornelius. *La experiencia del movimiento obrero.* 2 vols. Barcelona: Tusquet, 1979.

Dias, Everardo. *História das lutas sociais no Brasil.* São Paulo: Alfa-Ômega, 1977.

Friedmann, G., and P. Naville. *Tratado de sociologia do trabalho.* São Paulo: Cultrix-Edsup, 1973.

Gutiérrez, Gustavo, et al. *Sobre el trabajo humano: Comentario a la encíclica "Laborem exercens."* Lima: CEP, 1982.

Kosik, Karel. *Dialética do concreto.* Rio de Janeiro: Paz e Terra, 1969.

Leuridan, J., and G. Múgica. *Por que a Igreja critica os ricos?* São Paulo: Paulinas, 1983.

Novoa Monreal, Eduardo. *El derecho de propiedad privada.* Bogotá: Temis, 1979.

Richta, Radovan. *Economia socialista e revolução tecnológica.* Rio de Janeiro: Paz e Terra, 1972.

Singer, Paul I. Força de trabalho e emprego no Brasil, 1920–1969. Cadernos CEBRAP, no. 3. São Paulo: Cebrap, 1971.

Weil, Simone. *A condição operária e outros estudos sobre a opressão.* Rio de Janeiro: Paz e Terra, 1979.

Church Documents

John Paul II. *Laborem Exercens,* encyclical letter of September 14, 1981.

Vatican Council II. *Gaudium et Spes: Pastoral Constitution on the Church in the Modern World,* part 1, chap. 3: "Man's Activity throughout the World." In *The Gospel of Peace and Justice.* Ed. Joseph Gremillion. Maryknoll, N.Y.: Orbis, 1976, pp. 269–99.

V: HUMANITY AND THE HISTORY OF ITS LIBERATION

Historicity of Human Beings

Boff, Leonardo. *O destino do homem e do mundo.* Petrópolis: Vozes, 1974.

———. *Teologia do cativeiro e da libertação.* 2nd ed. Petrópolis: Vozes, 1980.

Gevaert, Joseph. *El problema del hombre: Introducción a la antropología filosófica.* Salamanca: Sígueme, 1981, pp. 231–62.

Gutiérrez, Gustavo. *The Power of the Poor in History: Selected Writings.* Maryknoll, N.Y.: Orbis, 1983.

———. *A Theology of Liberation: History, Politics and Salvation.* Rev. ed. Maryknoll, N.Y.: Orbis, 1988.

Holzherr, Georg. "O homem e as comunidades." In *Mysterium Salutis,* vol. 2/3. Petrópolis: Vozes, 1972, pp. 180–211.

Míguez Bonino, José. *Ama y haz lo que quieras.* Buenos Aires: América 2000, 1972.

The Word

Comblin, José. *Cry of the Oppressed, Cry of Jesus.* Maryknoll, N.Y.: Orbis, 1988.

Gevaert, Joseph. *El problema del hombre: Introducción a la antropología filosófica*. Salamanca: Sígueme, 1981, pp. 153–86.

La no-violencia evangélica, fuerza de liberación: Encuentro de obispos de América Latina. Barcelona: Fontanella, 1978.

Sobrino, Jon. *The True Church and the Poor.* Maryknoll, N.Y.: Orbis, 1984.

Ulrich, Ferdinand. *O homem e a palavra.* In *Mysterium Salutis,* vol. 2/3. Petrópolis: Vozes, 1972, pp. 90–141.

Church Documents

John Paul II. *Laborem Exercens,* encyclical letter of September 14, 1981.

———. *Redemptor Hominis,* encyclical letter of March 4, 1979.

Latin American Bishops Conference. Medellín Document on Peace. In vol. 2 of *The Church in the Present-day Transformation of Latin America.* Washington, D.C.: USCC, 1970.

———. Puebla Final Document. In *Puebla and Beyond.* Ed. John Eagleson and Philip Scharper. Maryknoll, N.Y.: Orbis, 1979. pp. 122–285.

Vatican Council II. *Gaudium et Spes: Pastoral Constitution on the Church in the Modern World,* part 2. In *The Gospel of Peace and Justice.* Ed. Joseph Gremillion. Maryknoll, N.Y.: Orbis, 1976, pp. 282–326.

VI: INDIVIDUAL LIBERATION

Colombás, García M. *El monacato primitivo.* Vol. 2: *La espiritualidad.* Madrid: BAC, 1975.

Gevaert, Joseph. *El problema del hombre: Introducción a la antropología filosófica.* Salamanca: Sígueme, 1981.

Häring, Bernard. *Free and Faithful in Christ: Moral Theology for Clergy and Laity.* New York: Crossroad, 1978.

Käsemann, Ernst. *La llamada de la libertad.* Salamanca: Sígueme, 1974.

Pastor, F. A. *Existência e Evangelho.* São Paulo: Loyola, 1973.

Vergés, Salvador. *Dimensión trascendente de la persona.* Barcelona: Herder, 1978.

Vidal, Marciano. *Moral de atitudes.* Vol. 2: *Ética da pessoa.* São Paulo: Santuario and Aparecida, 1979. Trans. of: *Moral de Actitudes.* Vol 2: *Etica de la persona.* 4th ed. Madrid, 1977.

VII: HUMANITY IN THE SIGHT OF GOD

"Antropologia teológica." In *Mysterium Salutis,* vol. 2/3. Petrópolis: Vozes, 1972, pp. 230–354.

Boff, Leonardo. *Liberating Grace.* Maryknoll, N.Y.: Orbis, 1979.

Flick, Mauritio, and Zoltan Alszeghy. *Los comienzos de la salvación.* Salamanca: Sígueme, 1965, pp. 205–542.

Gutiérrez, Gustavo. *We Drink from Our Own Wells.* Maryknoll, N.Y.: Orbis, 1984.

Küng, Hans. *On Being a Christian.* New York: Doubleday, 1976.

Mondin, B. *Antropologia teológica.* 2nd ed. São Paulo: Paulinas, 1984.

Rahner, Karl. *O homem e a graça.* São Paulo: Paulinas, 1970.

———. *Theology, Anthropology, and Christology,* vol. 13 of *Theological Investigations.* New York: Crossroads, 1977.

Rey, B. *A nova criação.* São Paulo: Paulinas, 1974.

Schillebeeckx, Edward. *God and Man.* New York: Sheed and Ward, 1969.

Church Documents

Arns, Paulo Evaristo. "O pecado contra a comunhão do povo." *Vida Pastoral,* no. 116 (May-June 1984), pp. 11–12.

John Paul II. *Dives in Misericordia,* encyclical letter of November 30, 1980.

———. *Laborem Exercens,* encyclical letter of September 14, 1981.

———. *Redemptor Hominis,* encyclical letter of March 4, 1979.

Latin American Bishops Conference. Puebla Final Document, nos. 304–39: "The Truth about Human Beings: Human Dignity." In *Puebla and Beyond.* Ed. John Eagleson and Philip Scharper. Maryknoll, N.Y.: Orbis, 1979, pp. 164–71.

Synod of 1983. Final Message.

Vatican Council II. *Gaudium et Spes: Pastoral Constitution on the Church in the Modern World,* part 1, chaps. 1–3. In *The Gospel of Peace and Justice.* Ed. Joseph Gremillion. Maryknoll, N.Y.: Orbis, 1976, pp. 252–74.

Index

Books in the "Liberation & Theology" series

Volume 1
Introducing Liberation Theology
Leonardo and Clodovis Boff

"This book is compact, clear, devastating, readable and highly controversial! You should read it."

Methodist Recorder

Volume 2
Trinity and Society
Leonardo Boff

"No one reading this passionate book is likely to echo Kant's dictum that 'the doctrine of the Trinity provides nothing, absolutely nothing of practical value, even if one claims to understand it.'"

Church Times

Volume 3
Ethics and Community
Enrique Dussell

"A comprehensive, introductory approach to what liberation theology has to say about ethics and morals."

Church Times

Volume 4
The Holy Spirit and Liberation
Jose Comblin

"This is one of the most remarkable books to come from Latin America; a serious yet accessible theological study."

Renew

Volume 5

The Memory of the Christian People
Eduardo Hoornaert

"I commend this book to all students at theological colleges and anyone who has to study the Early Church—or indeed anyone who just has to practise and preach basic Christianity. It is a gem of beautiful stories, provocative models and great encouragement for all."

Methodist Recorder

Volume 6

The Bible, the Church and the Poor
Jorge Pixley and Clodovis Boff

Looks "... not just at Church history and the situation today, but also at the liberative practises of the poor themselves and at practical aspects of the option for the poor..."

Doctrine & Life

Volume 7

Mary, Mother of God, Mother of the Poor
Ivone Gebara and Maria Clara Bingemer

"From the prospective of feminist liberation theology, Mary is seen again as mother of the poor and oppressed. Marian dogmas are critically assessed for their relevance in today's social, economic and political climate..."

Catholic Herald

Books of general Christian interest as well as books on theology, scripture, spirituality and mysticism are published by Burns and Oates and Search Press Limited. A free catalogue will be sent on request:
BURNS AND OATES Dept A,
Wellwood, North Farm Road, Tunbridge Wells, Kent TN2 3DR
Tel. (0892) 510850